FLORIDA STATE
UNIVERSITY LIBRARIES

MAY 15 2000

TALLAHASSEE, FLORIDA

The Skeptic's Oakeshott

Steven Anthony Gerencser

St. Martin's Press
New York

JC
257
.0244
G47
2000

THE SKEPTIC'S OAKESHOTT

Copyright © Steven A. Gerencser, 2000. All rights reserved. Printed in the United States of America. No part of this book may be used or reproduced in any manner whatsoever without written permission except in the case of brief quotations embodied in critical articles or reviews. Form information, address St. Martin's press. 175 Fifth Avenue, New York, N.Y. 10010.
ISBN 0–312–22303–X

Library of Congress Cataloging-in-Publication Data

Gerencser, Steven Anthony, 1963–
    The Skeptic's Oakeshott / by Steven Anthony Gerencser
        p.   cm.
    Includes bibliographical references and index.
    ISBN 0–312–22303–X
    1. Oakeshott, Michael Joseph—Contributions in political science.   I. Title.
JC257.0244 G47 2000
320.52'092—dc21
99-042076

First published: March 2000

10   9   8   7   6   5   4   3   2   1

For Elaine Ruth Case

Contents

Acknowledgments

At a show on the Beat writers, I saw the typewriter that Jack Kerouac used when writing *On the Road*. What was next to it impressed me more: a roll of butcher paper which contained the original draft of the novel. Kerouac had fed in one end and typed continuously over a few days until he finished the classic. Like Kerouac himself, this style of writing is attractive and romantic—and unbelievable. The book I have written could not have been produced in a manner more different from Kerouac's scroll, but it does share one small thing with his novel: during much of the writing of this book I have been "on the road." I wasn't burning up the blue highways with Dean Moriarity, but schlepping from one short term academic appointment to another until Indiana University South Bend offered me something much more stable. Maybe the completion and publication of *The Skeptic's Oakeshott* can offer some small hope to those many involuntary scholar gypsies who find themselves academically on the road.

I would like to acknowledge the kindness and support of some of those places where I stopped along the way: Hamline University, Allegheny College, and especially Saint Olaf College. I would also like to thank Indiana University South Bend for its support of my writing with a Summer Faculty Fellowship (1998), and especially the department of political science at IUSB for its welcoming good cheer, which makes writing so much easier. The list of persons who have given help, sustenance, and support during this writing project is long and I fear I cannot acknowledge all on it and their acts of kindness. However, some do deserve at least to be mentioned for all they have done. First and foremost I thank Lisa Jane Disch; from her model of discipline in writing to her love of thinking through politics (even while scrambling over the Theodosian walls), from her material support (including many helpings of pasta, sauce, and Big House Red) to her patience during the itinerant writing, Lisa has made this book both a reality and a pleasure. There have been many helpful and critical readers of this work in various stages who deserve mention, even if I have not always heeded their advice well; especially worthy of note are Jeffery Isaac, David Mapel, Martyn Thomas, and most importantly Mary G. Dietz, an advisor who has always been a careful and enthusiastic reader of my work. Thankfully, I also have had helpful conversations with many fellow scholars and friends who have challenged me to think more clearly about different aspects of the manuscript, including Susan Bickford, Dana Chabot, Samuel Chambers, Andrew Davison, Greg McAvoy, Ted Miller, Andrew Seligsohn, Michael Stanley-Jones, Ron Steiner, and Mark Yellin.

Some people have worked to provide the circumstances, recent and past, to help me to write this book, and so my thanks also go to Charles Umbanhower and John Lewis, the chairs of the departments of political science at Saint Olaf College and Indiana University South Bend for treating me with the civility and respect that other young academics often struggle without. I would also like to acknowledge the importance of two teachers, Ronald Pape, formerly of Michigan Lutheran High School, and Calvin Katter (PhD) of North Park College, who early on taught me to value the study of texts. Of course, I must thank my family: my sisters JoAnn Klug and Elaine Case, my brother John Gerencser, and their families, my mother Mickey Gerencser, father William Gerencser and grandmother Camille Streit, all of whom have dependably encouraged me, even when not entirely sure what I was up to. Ed and Elaine Disch also deserve (and hopefully accept) my gratitude for providing important treats and goodies to keep me going. This book is dedicated to Elaine Case, whose perseverance in life dwarfed mine in writing. This work is one small thing I have to give to her for all she gave me.

I would also like to thank the *Journal of Politics* for allowing me to include portions of "Voices in Conversation: Philosophy and Politics in the Work of Michael Oakeshott, (August 1995, Vol. 57, No. 3: pp 724–42) and *Political Research Quarterly* for allowing me to include portions of "A Democratic Oakeshott?" (December 1999, Vol. 52 No. 4): pp. 834–869, which I first published in those journals.

S.A.G.
Saint Joseph, Michigan, October 18, 1999

Introduction

The Skeptic's Oakeshott

I

About nine months after Michael Oakeshott's death on December 19, 1990, the journal *Political Theory* introduced its August 1991 edition with three short essays dedicated to his memory. In the same edition, grouped under the title "The Faces of Conservatism," the journal published three essays on Edmund Burke. Here, *Political Theory* brought together consideration of two of the best-known voices of British conservatism. Yet, regardless of all he wrote about tradition, Oakeshott explicitly separated himself from the heritage of Burke; for example, in "On Being Conservative" Oakeshott asserted "there is more to be learnt about this [conservative] disposition from Montaigne, Pascal, Hobbes and Hume, than from Burke or Bentham."[1] Still, one of the *Political Theory* essays on Burke does reveal an interesting similarity between Burke and Oakeshott: the manifold nature of their legacy. In "The Skeptic's Burke," Michael Mosher observes that while it is common to think of Burke as the defender of prescription and natural law, some conservatives like Leo Strauss have rejected him for the very same reason that some nonconservatives have been attracted to him: Burke's belief that "the foundations of political order lie in nothing stronger than the memory and habits of its adherents."[2] Mosher shows how we might begin with the traditional conservative Burke, advocate of prescription and natural law, but we then have Strauss's fallen conservative Burke, and now we find what Mosher calls "a 'deconstructionist' Burke," developed by those attracted to the very sentiments that distressed Strauss.[3]

A fortune similar to Burke's has befallen Oakeshott. He never took up with the idea of natural law or the idea of politics as the pursuit of the Good, and while his conception of politics as the "pursuit of intimations" may be characterized as conservative, it has none of the force of the politics of prescription.[4] Yet Oakeshott understood himself as a political conservative—and so have his detractors, such as Perry Anderson, who considers Oakeshott to be a member of the "Intransigent Right at the end of the Century."[5] Accordingly, Robert Devigne has traced out the political restructuring of British conservatism in terms of what he calls Oakeshott's "Response to Postmodernism."[6] In an attempt to wrench him from debates within and about conservatism, Paul Franco seeks to re-anchor Oakeshott's work as philosophy, and to interpret his political philosophy as a "restatement of liberalism" that can provide a palliative to the debate between liberals and their communitarian critics.[7] To a more radical debate about liberalism and its foundations still others have attempted to draw Oakeshott. Thus, surprising some has been the attempt by so-called postmodern theorists and advocates of radical democracy, such as Richard Rorty and Chantal Mouffe, to claim association with Oakeshott as a theorist of contingency and pluralism.[8] Like Mosher's Burke, then, we have a variegated Oakeshott: the conservative Oakeshott, the liberal Oakeshott, the Oakeshott who responds to postmodernism and the Oakeshott who is hailed by postmoderns and radical democrats. Oakeshott's work is varied enough to allow support for each the interpretations above and perhaps more. Like Mosher's argument for a "skeptic's Burke," a skeptic's Oakeshott can account not only for the varied and changing face of Oakeshott's work but also for the variety of responses to it. In this work I take up the task of presenting an Oakeshott who is primarily a skeptic, both in philosophy and politics, and whose political theory offers something to contemporary skeptics. Although most other interpreters of Oakeshott's work have noted his skepticism in some way, few have placed it close to the center of his political philosophy.

In arguing for a "skeptic's Oakeshott," I begin from a position similar to that developed by Jeremy Rayner in "The Legend of Oakeshott's Conservatism: Sceptical Philosophy and Limited Politics."[9] However, Rayner's argument needs to be supplemented in significant ways. First, to account for Oakeshott's skepticism, one must engage with his early association with philosophical idealism. Careful interpreters such as Paul Franco have not only considered the importance of idealism in Oakeshott's early thought and but have gone on to argue that his political philosophy must be seen as a reflection of his attachment to Hegel and idealism. In an alternative interpretation, I trace the formation of skepticism in Oakeshott's thought from his earliest writings as he moved away from British idealism. The signal work that clearly reveals this change is Oakeshott's "The Voice of Poetry in the Conversation of Mankind"; this essay shows Oakeshott to have abandoned many of the commitments of philosophical idealism by the mid-fifties.[10] The effect of this change upon Oakeshott's thoughts on political philosophy is illustrated in Oakeshott's writings on Hobbes, the philosopher about whom Oakeshott wrote considerably more than he did of Hegel. Oakeshott's writings on Hobbes are worthy of study, not only for what they reveal about that seventeenth-century English skeptic, but to see how Oakeshott's own skepticism is intimated through his interpretation of Hobbes's political philosophy. A supplementary benefit accompanies an examination Oakeshott's growing skepticism: it provides a new understanding of the relationship of theory and practice in his work. He holds a skeptical view that is too cautious either to recommend an absolute separation of theory from practice or the reduction of one to the other. Oakeshott recognizes the limits of both philosophy and politics and holds open the possibility of a relationship between the two that is contingent: an interaction that neither entails nor proscribes anything by necessity but that may act as a spur to action or reflection.

Rayner's argument needs to be supplemented in a second way, by considering the relationship between Oakeshott's skepticism and the work of some contemporary skeptics who have expressed interest in him. While there has been some interest in Oakeshott by those of a skeptical, non- or antifoundational inclination, Oakeshott scholars have generally either ignored or dismissed these overtures; Franco, for instance, rejects out of hand of Rorty's claims about Oakeshott. However, as I have discussed in another work, viewing Oakeshott from the perspective of his skepticism allows considerably more latitude in the particular issue for which Franco dismisses Rorty: the pragmatist's relation of theory to practice.[11] From the perspective of the changes I discuss in Chapter 2, the overture that Rorty makes to Oakeshott in *Philosophy and the Mirror of Nature* seems quite intriguing. After those changes, it becomes apt for Rorty to claim, "Philosophy is not a name for a discipline which confronts permanent issues, and unfortunately keeps misstating them, or attacking them with clumsy dialectical instruments. Rather it is a cultural genre, a 'voice in the conversation' (to use Michael Oakeshott's phrase), which centers on one topic rather than another at a given time not by dialectical necessity but as a result of various things happening elsewhere in the conversation."[12] The irony of Rorty's allusion to Oakeshott here is that it is the former's antifoundationalism that has caused some like Jürgen Habermas and Cornell West to cast him as something of a conservative. The latter suggests, for instance, that "For Rorty we are Emersonian sailors, rebegetting creatures, adrift on Neurath's boat—forever inventing and creating new self-images, vocabularies, techniques and instruments in light of a useful backdrop of mortal beliefs and values which have no philosophical foundation or transhistorical justification. . . . In this sense, Rorty's neo-pragmatism is a form of ethnocentric posthumanism."[13] If Rorty has a primarily philosophical (or antiphilosophical) interest in Oakeshott, there also have been those interested in the political implications of Oakeshott's skepticism from democratic, even radically democratic, positions. In this work, I take up the question of whether Oakeshott's ideas concerning civil association, based on a conception of authority, can sustain his own skepticism and possibly offer anything to contemporary (or any other) theorists of democracy.

To consider any potential in Oakeshott's work for democracy means taking seriously his writing on authority—a concept not always dear to the democrat's heart. Authority is among the political terms Oakeshott examined in his earliest writings; later, after his study of Hobbes, authority, authorization and authenticity return as central concepts in Oakeshott's political thought. What distinguishes Oakeshott's use of these terms from that of Hobbes is his claim that authority is not created by contract or compact. Oakeshott takes these terms to imply a substantive agreement among citizens about the purposes of the state; in turn, he argues that a requirement for consensus erases—perhaps destroys—plural human identity and purpose. In Oakeshott's understanding, authority does not require consensus about purposes, only recognition. Authority so conceived protects the capacity for human freedom because citizens need not align their purposes to those of the state or each other.

Oakeshott's arguments concerning authority reveal both promise and limitation. They disappoint because even though Oakeshott rejects the idea of common purpose or consensus as a basis of authority, he implicitly reintroduces this through his requirement for a common recognition of authority. The need for consensus is quietly shifted from that of belief about ends or purposes to that of recognition of authority. Here Oakeshott's skepticism reaches its limits. Nonetheless, Oakeshott's thoughts on authority do open questions about the exercise of power by a state that claims authority, and his reflections can be extended to question the myths and mechanisms that create and maintain authority. Just as Oakeshott rejected the idea of consensus regarding the end or purpose of action, his skepticism can be turned back on his own central concept of authority. Skepticism can serve as a reminder that what is seen as an authoritative exercise of power by some citizens may appear as mere coercion to others. This focus on questions of authority opens another locus for democratic questioning and action. A skeptical democratic citizen neither rejects the idea of state authority nor attempts to judge if this particular state or state action accords with a universal principle of what might sanction or grant authority. A skeptical democratic citizen asks whose beliefs the state recognizes in its claims to authority and, just as importantly, asks who regards state action as simply an imposition of power.

Skepticism can result in certainty reborn, as for Descartes, or in a call to accept the absence of universal truth. It may reveal a pure human nature shorn of the accoutrement of society, or it may reveal that humans always (and only) create themselves through conventions such as language, custom, and habit. Mosher points out that, in Burke's time, skepticism "leads to two oddly opposed political understandings. Burke's opponents [defenders of the French revolution] believe that skepticism helps them see through tradition. Burke believes that the skeptics will see new reason to cling to tradition."[14] Skepticism may denigrate political action by rejecting universal markers for liberation and judgment, or it may invigorate action through criticism of politically oppressive practices and regimes that claim to incorporate universal principles. This work is not a reflection upon all these questions of skepticism and politics, yet it places Oakeshott in the midst of them. It is the discussion that previously unpublished works of Oakeshott, such as the posthumously published monograph *Morality and Politics in Modern Europe* and the essay "Political Philosophy'" reveal him to have positioned himself.[15] This reading also aligns Oakeshott with a more radical skepticism than the liberal skepticism that Franco attributes to him, and traces the philosophical underpinnings of Oakeshott's ambivalence about politics. Finally, it reveals the limitations and opportunities of Oakeshott's skeptical theorizing for democratic politics.

II

Michael Oakeshott was a political philosopher better known for his conservative politics than his philosophy. Although he published only one real book of philosophy, he wrote many political essays and book reviews; these and his editorship of *The Cambridge Journal* and the collection of essays *Rationalism in Politics* established his voice in discussions about British politics after the Second World War. A famed and self-proclaimed conservative, Oakeshott was a critic of what he called rationalism, which variously meant being an opponent of the welfare state, ideological politics, and technical

approaches to politics. Yet Oakeshott did not only purvey political opinions. He was a philosopher, and it is his political philosophy that generates
much interest in him now, although Oakeshott's understanding of the relationship of philosophy to politics is contested. Of those who have examined the philosophical foundations of his ideas, Paul Franco, the most
thorough to date, has developed the connection of Oakeshott to Hegel, and
has argued that Oakeshott refused philosophy a relationship to politics.
Although I recognize the importance of Hegel for Oakeshott, this study
will emphasize the importance of the skeptical character of Oakeshott's
thought and his connections to Hobbes. In the interpretation I develop, I
contend that attention to Oakeshott's philosophical skepticism provides an
understanding of the subtle connections between his philosophy and his
politics, and, in turn, makes it possible to bring his skepticism to bear on
issues of democratic practice.

Whether Hegel or Hobbes is more important in the end, it is with
Oakeshott as a philosopher that we must first contend, so I begin this study
by examining Oakeshott's earliest philosophical works, arguing in Chapter
One that the roots of his later skepticism can be found there. Focusing
upon Oakeshott's first major work, *Experience and Its Modes,* and locating
his early work at the end of the tradition of British idealism, I contend that
while his thought at this time was steeped in an English style of Hegelian-
ism, it also evinces a type of skepticism.[16] Oakeshott's examination of the
"modes" of "experience" reveals a concern that no experience can claim
final certainty or uphold a universal claim to truth. No experience, that is,
except for philosophical experience can make such a claim. It is because of
this latter contention that Oakeshott's early philosophy cannot be considered fully skeptical; his early contention that philosophy alone can integrate
a unified world of coherent ideas prevents a thorough skepticism. However,
in his examination of the modes and their relationship, Oakeshott begins
the exploration of the issues that become familiar in his later works, such
as his famous concern that politics not only be safe from philosophy but
also from the impress of scientific rationality, that the claims of practical
experience not disrupt the work of the historian, and that poetry not be
overwhelmed by either science or practice.

This stage, however, as important as it is for understanding the beginnings of Oakeshott's skepticism, is one he leaves behind, and in Chapter
Two, I trace Oakeshott's changing views of philosophy. In particular, I argue
that Oakeshott can rightly be considered a philosophical skeptic once he
abandons the understanding that philosophy is the quest for an absolutely
unified system of coherent ideas. Such an alteration can be found fully

developed in Oakeshott's essay "The Voice of Poetry in the Conversation of Mankind." I suggest that the use of the metaphor of "conversation" is both a symbol of and substantively constitutes this change. I examine the invocation of the metaphor and the place of philosophy in the "conversation" to illustrate Oakeshott's reconstituted conception of philosophy, which, I suggest, is also evident in *On Human Conduct*.[17] Against most but not all of Oakeshott's interpreters, I argue that in this later work Oakeshott does not return to his earlier conception of philosophy, but continues to develop his skepticism. An issue that highlights the changes in Oakeshott's thought is the relationship of theory to practice. It is common to assume that Oakeshott called for a strict separation of theory and practice, in particular of philosophy and politics.[18] This view, however, is reflective only of Oakeshott's early, absolute idealism, and once again, with the use of the metaphor of conversation, he opens the possibility for a contingent relation of theory and practice.

These changes in Oakeshott's conception of philosophy are interesting, however, not only for their own sake, but for the affects they have on his political thought. To emphasize the importance of the shift in Oakeshott's philosophy from idealism to skepticism, in Chapter Three I return to his expressions of political philosophy in the early idealist period. Among his earliest concerns was to explore the notion of authority and to argue for a separation of political philosophy from the practice of politics. Yet as Oakeshott left behind the strict idealism in his philosophy, he did so as well in his political philosophy. Authority, however, remains a central concept, not because it is expressive of the idealist notion of the social whole, but because it is a limited human creation that serves to condition contingent human relationships. I first focus upon the thoroughly Hegelian notion of the state found in Oakeshott's early "The Authority of the State."[19] After this work, Oakeshott retreats from consideration of politics to philosophy more generally, but he does have a few remarks about political philosophy in *Experience and Its Modes*. There, from the absolute idealist perspective of concrete experience, he disparages even the notion of political philosophy as "pseudo-philosophy."[20] Yet, Oakeshott does return one last time to consider a philosophy of politics on a wholly idealist base. I examine two previously unpublished essays that reveal the changing basis of his political thought from idealism to a more cautious skepticism. In the course of this discussion, I challenge the dating of one of these essays, "The Concept of a Philosophy of Politics." I argue that Oakeshott must have written this piece in the thirties, not in the late forties, as suggested by the editor, Timothy Fuller; as such, it is an example of his earlier idealist concerns in political thought.[21] The other essay, "Political Philosophy," I argue, reveals a transitional stage in which much of the previous idealism is gone, although the concerns from the earlier period remain.[22]

To track the career of Oakeshott's philosophy and political philosophy in a different way, in Chapter Four, I attend to his interpretation of Thomas Hobbes.[23] From the late thirties and into the forties, Hobbes fills the gap that is left by Oakeshott's abandonment of Hegel and idealism; in turn, Oakeshott's increasing skepticism is reflected in his presentation of Hobbes. One need not work too hard to create a Hobbes who is a skeptic, but Oakeshott does so in an unusual way. By emphasizing Hobbes's nominalism and his connection to the tradition of scholasticism, and by rejecting the conception of Hobbes as a materialist, Oakeshott produces a Hobbes whose philosophical concerns reflect his own increasing skepticism and even the residue of idealism. In Oakeshott's interpretation, Hobbes—like Oakeshott himself—rejects the assumption that humans have a capacity for certain knowledge of an objective reality. For both theorists truth and meaning are based upon human convention. Having finished with Hobbes's philosophy, Oakeshott returns to the question of authority, but now in a distinctly Hobbesian fashion.

The importance of Oakeshott's stressing Hobbes's skepticism and nominalism can be seen when he claims "Hobbes's theory of law and government has, indeed, no ethical foundation, in the ordinary sense; . . . [it] begins in a theory of language."[24] As in Oakeshott's interpretation of Hobbes's theory of language, law and government are understood to be merely human creations with no absolute sanction. I argue in Chapter Five that this manner of interpreting Hobbes's political philosophy also reveals Oakeshott's adoption of much of Hobbes's political philosophy—at least as he interpreted it. To put this differently, Oakeshott expresses his own political thought in a manner that replicates much of his interpretation of Hobbes's political thought. There is, for instance, no significant difference between his explication of Hobbes's understanding of civil association, a term Oakeshott imputes to Hobbes, and Oakeshott's own understanding. I do not argue that Oakeshott's political thought is merely warmed-over Hobbes. Instead, his interpretation of Hobbes reflects an evolving political vocabulary and set of interests that he shares with Hobbes, or at least his idea of Hobbes. By this recognition, I draw out the basis of Oakeshott's distinctly skeptical position.

In the penultimate chapter, I suggest that focusing upon skepticism as the basis for Oakeshott's thought provides a fresh insight into the fundamental distinction of his political thought, that between enterprise and civil association, and this also illuminates his preference for the latter. This preference began in a theoretical claim by Oakeshott that few have pursued in his thought: the state is a coercive and comprehensive institution. Since citizens seldom, if ever, choose their state, the question for Oakeshott becomes: can the state exercise power and still recognize plurality and human freedom? His answer is: yes, so long as the state not only has power, but also authority. Oakeshott rejects any basis for the authority of the state that would require citizens to adopt or approve a common good or agree to a universal standard of the right. Any of these would destroy what Oakeshott calls "the link between belief and conduct which constitutes moral agency."[25] Oakeshott claims that authority is based solely on recognition and acknowledgment, not approval.

In the concluding chapter, I consider the possibilities and limitations of Oakeshott's skeptical understanding of civil association. Oakeshott considers authority based on acknowledgment to protect freedom because it does not require citizens to change their conception of the good to match that of the state; rather, as civil association, the state asks only that citizens recognize its authority to regulate their self-chosen actions. I argue that Oakeshott stops short of his own skepticism by not extending it to authority itself. Doing so would involve examining the plurality of beliefs about authority, asking whose beliefs get recognized by the state, and exploring how the state acts to generate authoritative beliefs and reproduce them. It is to these questions, central to contemporary democratic theory, that Oakeshott's skepticism speaks in a provocative way. To conclude, I trace out in a brief fashion what the democratic politics that incorporates such questioning might entail.

Chapter One

The Idealist's Oakeshott

I

To return to the commencement of Michael Oakeshott's intellectual career ironically requires examining the waning moments of a philosophical trend. Oakeshott studied at Cambridge with the last of the renowned British idealists from 1919 through the early twenties, attending lectures in philosophy by John Ellis McTaggert.[1] Oakeshott's early philosophical writings, and in particular his first major work, *Experience and Its Modes,* reveal the strong impress of his exposure to idealist philosophy. It may appear surprising or merely irrelevant that Oakeshott early on dabbled in a philosophy that many considered arcane to begin with and whose intellectual energy was dissipated at the time Oakeshott wrote. Instead, it is Oakeshott the eloquent essayist and conservative political philosopher that interests them. Hannah Fenichel Pitkin, for example, implies that *Experience and Its Modes* and the philosophical positions developed therein do not significantly contribute to an understanding of Oakeshott's conservatism or his political philosophy. In a close examination of Oakeshott's conservatism and its relationship to other forms of conservatism, Pitkin simply claims "An earlier work on epistemology, *Experience and Its Modes,* cannot be discussed within the confines of the essay."[2] At least she acknowledges this strategy. Many others simply write as if Oakeshott wrote nothing prior to the essays collected in *Rationalism in Politics.* I argue below, however, that Oakeshott's skepticism, which is the grounding for his conservative disposition and the resulting political philosophy, can first be glimpsed during this early period, and so this stage should be understood as more than mere juvenilia.

There are, of course, interpreters who do not disregard this early stage of Oakeshott's work, those who see all his political philosophy as an expression of idealism. W. H. Greenleaf, for instance, laments "that most commentators have simply had a too limited acquaintance with what Oakeshott has written."[3] Greenleaf goes even further, suggesting that "Oakeshott's political ideas are . . . very definitely the reflection of a philosophical standpoint . . . [which] has remained constant throughout."[4] For Greenleaf, one must have a broad "acquaintance" with Oakeshott's writings, because it is through the idealism he worked out explicitly in earlier works such as *Experience and Its Modes* that his later political philosophy is conceived.

Given these two options, ignoring Oakeshott's early work or seeing it as a key to all, I pursue a *via media*. While a broad acquaintance with Oakeshott's work is important for a full understanding of his philosophical ideas, this is not because Oakeshott's later political philosophy is simply a subsequent expression of his earlier idealism; instead, such a study is important for understanding the concerns that remain consistent, those he alters, and those he abandons. Oakeshott's early association with idealism revealed itself in his thought in two forms that took different directions in his works. There is an element of Oakeshott's early philosophical idealism that posits philosophy's capacity for experience of the Absolute, of complete and fully coherent experience. I label this aspect of his early thought absolute idealism. However, Oakeshott also reveals in this early idealist period a form of skepticism, which I argue establishes the evolving framework for his later political thought. It is a skepticism that in the early stage is dependent upon the idealist perspective, and so I label this Oakeshott's skeptical idealism. In Chapter Two, I will argue that Oakeshott abandons the absolute idealism, while the skeptical idealism he recasts throughout his work. So, in a way, I agree with Greenleaf that it is important to understand Oakeshott's early, explicitly idealist work to have a richer insight into his political philosophy. However, it is necessary, as well, to have greater precision in understanding the forms of idealism in his early thought in order to grasp the different courses they take in his later writing.

To follow the trajectory of Oakeshott's thought, then, involves a difficult initial task: to explore some of the important elements of the state of philosophical idealism in which Oakeshott began his intellectual career and how they feature in his early work. In this chapter I will briefly lay out the central tenets of the British idealist tradition with which Oakeshott associates himself, and then discuss Oakeshott's absolute idealism and the understanding of philosophy and experience it entails. This will help to illustrate what I take to be Oakeshott's skeptical idealism and his early concern for the necessary limits of different modes of experience and their relationships to each other; from this perspective it will be possible to view more familiar aspects of Oakeshott's later thought. I will conclude with some observations about the tension of absolute and skeptical idealism for earlier idealists and for Oakeshott.

II

In the introduction to his first book, *Experience and Its Modes,* Oakeshott himself takes up the mantle of idealism. He claims, "I ought perhaps to say that [mine] is a view which derives all that is valuable in it from its affinity to what is known by the somewhat ambiguous name of Idealism, and the works from which I am conscious of having learnt most are Hegel's *Phänomenologie des Geistes* and Bradley's *Appearance and Reality.*"[5] Oakeshott evinces a curious candor in this admission, since for almost three decades idealism in Britain had been subject to increasingly greater criticism and dismissal. Further, its proponents, with few exceptions, had little institutional presence in 1933 when Oakeshott brought out *Experience and Its Modes.* Rudolf Metz, whose *A Hundred Years of British Philosophy* was published a mere five years after *Experience and its Modes,* contended in 1938,

> After its long decline the idealistic movement has almost come to an end within the last ten years or so. Obviously worn out and having no fresh reserve of creative energy, it has tended more and more to withdraw from encounters with its opponents, to abandon construction along its own lines, and to find its feet in other ways of thinking. . . . There are few survivors of the day of greatness; the movement has now almost entirely receded into history.[6]

While more recently A. M. Quinton suggests, "[British idealism] exercised its full intellectual authority between 1874 and 1903. . . . For the two decades after 1903 it remained the best entrenched movement institutionally. . . . But after the deaths of Bradley and McTaggert, in 1924 and 1925, and [G. E.] Moore's appointment to a chair in Cambridge in the latter year, no new idealist work of any significance appeared in Britain except those of Collingwood."[7] Noticeably lacking here, of course, is any mention of Oakeshott and *Experience and Its Modes,* but the primary point is that in Britain when Oakeshott wrote his first book, idealism was at an ebb tide, both intellectually and institutionally. Oakeshott himself wryly observes that "the abuse which was formerly the lot of philosophy in general is now reserved for philosophical Idealism, which (it is the common opinion) is decadent if not already dead."[8] Oakeshott, however, seems willing to engage in some philosophical necromancy, and perhaps his book can be considered a fresh attempt to define and defend idealism—one clearly ignored by Metz and Quinton. Paul Franco, for instance, sees *Experience and Its Modes* as the text where Oakeshott is engaged to "answer the question of the task of philosophy in this age of science in a different way from that implied in the notions of philosophy as the [positivistic] 'synthesis of the sciences' or the [neo-Kantian] *scientia scientarum*."[9] Combining both enthusiasm and caution, Oakeshott himself suggests that "what seems to be required is not an apology for Idealism as a restatement of its first principles, and so far as my view is Idealistic (and how far it is, I do not myself know), this is what I have attempted."[10]

Situating Oakeshott in this theoretical context of idealism is problematic, because it is a varied tradition that could conceivably contain a wide range of philosophers from Plato to Berkeley as well as Hegel and Bradley. To understand Oakeshott's place in this tradition and the concerns he shares with it I will work within the limits he sets and attend exclusively to the philosophical movement of British idealism as it existed in the second half of the nineteenth century through the time in which Oakeshott wrote. I concentrate on Oakeshott's British forebears since it was through them that Hegel was mediated into England and Oakeshott's work in part can be seen as an attempted continuance of that movement.

The beginning of the distinctly British idealist movement has been located variously from 1865, when James Sterling published *The Secret of Hegel,* to 1874, the year in which T. H. Green and T. H. Goose brought out an edition of Hume's *Treatise of Human Nature* with a severely critical introduction.[11] Regardless of exactly when it began, historians of thought agree that the idealists were responding both to social conditions and philosophical trends as they had developed through the nineteenth century in Britain. There are, however, various opinions as to the specific conditions that allowed idealism to develop and to which it responded. Metz, in his comprehensive study *A Hundred Years in British Philosophy,* suggested that in Britain "the mental atmosphere was prepared for the reception of an idealistic view of the world by means of poetry and literature generally."[12] It was from the Romantic poets, and especially Samuel Taylor Coleridge, who explicitly relied upon German idealist sources, "that a new attitude to life grew up [in England] which superseded the antiquated forms of the enlightenment."[13] Yet while Coleridge and the other Romantics prepared the way and introduced German idealism to England, Metz suggested that two other factors were the immediate catalysts in the growth of British ide-alism. The first was a crisis in religious faith precipitated by Darwinism, nat-uralism and materialism; thus a turn to idealism was "prompted . . . by the desire to confirm orthodox theology and revivify the imperiled faith, against Agnosticism, Naturalism, religious indifference, and open unbe-lief."[14] This crisis coincided with a second and quite independent develop-ment: the rejuvenation of the study of classical Greek philosophy in England, especially under the influence of Benjamin Jowett. "The affinity of Greek and German Idealism was patent, and in Oxford more than any-where else the younger generation of scholars [under Jowett] recognized the urgent necessity of lifting British thought out of its narrowness and ser-vility to its own tradition and leading it back to the great stream of Euro-pean philosophy."[15] For Metz, idealism developed in Britain because a number of literary and philosophic trends coincided with a religious crisis to which idealism seemed to provide a complement and solution. Quinton argues that the idealists were attempting to adapt the idealism of Hegel to quite specific British circumstances because it

> met two ideological needs. . . . The first of these was for a defence of the
> Christian religion sufficiently respectable to confront the ever more formi-
> dable scientific influences that were working to undermine religious belief.
> The second was the need for a politics of social responsibility to set against
> the triumphant *laisser-faire,* of political altruism to counter the idea that unin-
> hibited competition between individuals was the indispensable engine of
> human progress.[16]

Following Metz, Quinton suggests that British idealism began and grew as a response to scientific naturalism, specifically Darwinism, and the religious crisis it precipitated. Quinton, however, neglecting the revival of Greek philosophy, focuses on the social, political and economic issues that ideal-ists responded to.

In contrast, W. H. Greenleaf suggests that British idealism arose "from dissatisfaction with the two main, and contrasting traditions of philosoph-ical speculation which had grown up since classical times."[17] Greenleaf labels the first of these traditions "transcendental realism," in which he places Christian thinkers and Plato, among others. He uses Plato's terms to describe how this tradition "stressed the deceptiveness of what we learn from our senses and asserted the need to transcend this world of Becom-ing, to get beyond it to the real world of Being . . . [a] sphere of universal essences."[18] Greenleaf labels the second tradition "empirical nominalism."

Theorists of this tradition "asserted that all we know is ultimately derived from the organs of sense. [They] reputed transcendental metaphysics as moonshine, arguing that the so-called universal forms or essences were names"; for empirical nominalism, "The characteristic procedure was the classification of things in terms of features selected because of their typical or prominent nature."[19] Greenleaf saw British idealism as an attempt to overcome what it understood as the limits and abstractness of each of these two opposed philosophical views.

It is not of great importance here to establish exclusively that British idealism rose as a development of literary influences, as a response to crises in Christianity, as a reaction to *laissez-faire* economics, or as an attempt to address conflicts and lapses in the great traditions of philosophy. Among the writings of T. H. Green and F. H. Bradley and other idealists are works that offer responses both to social problems and to the philosophical difficulties that accompanied and perhaps compounded them. It is important to note, however, that idealism found a home in the land of empiricism and was the ascendent school of philosophy for two generations beginning sometime in the mid-nineteenth century.

Idealism in its many manifestations is a difficult and complex philosophy. Its usage can be arcane and attempts at clarity often seem to result in further obfuscation.[20] But again, to gain an appreciation of Oakeshott's philosophical starting point, some examination of its tenets is important. In an attempt to capture the essence of this school of thought and recount some of the main themes of British idealism, I will take recourse to a convenient précis Quinton provides of five of what he calls "the more specific doctrines of the school."[21] Since it is with his English forebear Bradley that Oakeshott claims heritage, I will substantiate Quinton's summary by illustrating these five doctrines though passages from *Appearance and Reality*. When I discuss Oakeshott's version of idealism, it will then be possible to see how much he had "learnt" from this school and specifically from Bradley.

The first of the doctrines of idealism Quinton discusses is "monism, . . . the theory that there is only one true substance, the absolute or reality as a whole."[22] Monism, which really gives rise to the other aspects of idealism I will discuss, is the contention that all of reality together forms one system. Nothing that is real, in other words, can be excluded or segmented in such a way that it is less a part of reality; thus all that is real combines to form a single, complex whole of reality. Bradley puts it this way: "The character of the real is to posses everything phenomenal in a harmonious form. . . . The real is individual. It is one in the sense that its positive character embraces all differences in an exclusive harmony."[23] Following idealist tradition, Bradley uses the term "Absolute" for this all-inclusive, harmonious reality. The driving question for Bradley is whether humans can come to know the Absolute in all its complexity or understand its harmony, and if so how? However, whether or not it can be fully comprehended, Bradley contends that the Absolute is implicit in all human experience.

In discussing the monism of the Absolute, Bradley also emphasized its "harmony," which leads then to the second of Quinton's doctrines of idealism: "the coherence theory of truth. A proposition cannot be considered true on its own, abstracted from its involvement with other propositions."[24] In fact, Bradley equates reality and truth, since the criterion of reality—harmony or consistency—is also that of truth. "Perfection of truth and of reality has in the end the same character. . . . Truth must exhibit the mark of internal harmony, or again the mark of expansion and all-inclusiveness."[25] This rejects a correspondence theory of truth, replacing the criterion of accuracy or alignment for that of consistency. The coherence definition of truth, one that emphasizes "internal harmony," also distinguishes itself from a correspondence theory by admitting of degrees of truth. A judgment that is completely true is one that is internally self-consistent and coheres with the all-inclusive harmonious reality; in this sense, it fully partakes of the absolute. However, there are greater and lesser degrees of consistency and harmony and thus of truth as well. "To be more or less true," Bradley states, "is to be separated by an interval, smaller or greater, from all-inclusiveness or self-consistency."[26] To speak of this in different terms, truth is both absolute and relative. Truth is absolute in that a proposition may be wholly self-consistent. In this case it would be absolutely true, internally self-consistent and cohering in the "Absolute." However, truth may also be relative because a proposition may exhibit an "internal harmony" of a sort that from the perspective of the Absolute is still dissonant. This "internal harmony" is evidence of truth, but not as complete as one that coheres with the harmonious totality of reality. Thus a proposition may be true to a certain degree and even evince a limited coherence together with other truths of the same character.

Quinton points to a third idealist doctrine: "the theory of the concrete universal which is put forward to replace the Aristotelian conception of an object as the instantiation by a bare particular of a cluster of abstract universals."[27] The concept of the "concrete universal" is surely a difficult one and perhaps best understood in contrast to the "abstract universal" against which it was offered. Recall Greenleaf's discussion of "empirical nominalism"; this tradition, he suggested, organized reality by "the classification of things in terms of features selected because of their typical or prominent nature." This procedure produces classes that are abstract universals in that they literally draw out or pull away from reality certain "features" around which the categories are organized. In the concept of "the concrete universal," however, particulars are not related merely because they have certain external features in common; instead, a concrete universal makes explicit the internal relations between particular ideas as they cohere in the Absolute. Although in *Appearance and Reality,* Bradley does not invoke the specific term "concrete universal," he does criticize abstract universals in a fashion that resembles the argument Quinton suggests the term makes. Bradley argues, for instance, against the suggestion that "by Comparison we learn the truth about things."[28] Again, by mere comparison we are lead to believe that individual things are related because they share particular features that are drawn out and focused upon; this implies that because some arbitrary, external feature is shared, they are related in a common identity as well. Against this, Bradley contends, "For myself I am convinced that no such relations exist. There is no identity or likeness possible except in a whole, and every such whole must qualify and be qualified by its terms. And where the whole is different, the terms that qualify it and contribute to it must so far be different, and so far therefore by becoming elements in a fresh unity the terms become altered."[29] Here, the features of the concrete universal are manifest in *Appearance and Reality* even if Bradley does not use the term, since he understands an identity as that which is related to a whole, both qualifying and being qualified by it. A whole and its parts exhibit a unity and difference together, the particular and the universal joined and mutually qualifying.

The fourth of the doctrines of British idealism that Quinton suggests is "the theory that reality is essentially mental or spiritual in nature."[30] Bradley's work is so thoroughly imbued with this idea that it is difficult to point to one or two passages that best exemplify it. Bradley explicitly argues that "to be real, or even to barely exist, must be to fall within sentience."[31] Sentience for Bradley is not merely a physiological phenomenon, it is rather "that which is called psychical existence. Feeling, thought and volition are all the material of existence, and there is no other material, actual or possible."[32] Bradley marshals this contention in direct opposition to the notion that there is a distinction between experience and what is experienced, a separate subject and an object in reality in which the subject or the one who experiences is the spiritual aspect of the world and is separate from the object or experience that is something else. For Bradley, reality is nothing separate from mental existence, and so, he argues, to be real "is to be something which comes as a feature and aspect within one whole of feeling, something which, except as an integral element of such sentience, has no meaning at all. And what I repudiate is the separation of feeling from the felt, or of the desired from desire, or what is thought from thinking, or the division of anything—I might add—from anything else."[33] This also supports the rejection of the correspondence theory of truth, since the correspondence implies a fundamental separation of judgment from what is judged. Bradley also recognizes the possible objection that such an understanding of reality may imply solipsism. Thus he dedicated an entire chapter of *Appearance and Reality* (Chapter XXI) to confronting and attempting to dismiss the anticipated accusation of solipsism. Regardless of his success in that defense, it is clear that for Bradley reality is primarily mental in nature.

The fifth and final doctrine of British idealism that Quinton suggests is "the theory that mind and its objects are internally and thus necessarily related."[34] This is perhaps not a separate theory, but a combination of the first—monism—with the fourth—the mental nature of reality. Yet, Bradley does make an explicit point of stating that relations within the diversity of Absolute are internal, and that includes the mind and its objects. Bradley argues that "any attempt again to take their [the Many of reality] togetherness as unessential seems to end in unmeaning."[35] Here again he wants to reject the notion that universals are merely categories created by the human mind of otherwise unrelated objects separate from humans. Bradley asks, "Can we then have a plurality of independent reals [sic] which merely coexist?" To which he resoundingly replies, "No, for absolute independence and coexistence are incompatible. Absolute independence is an idea which consists merely in one-sided abstraction. It is made by an attempted division of the aspect of several existence from the aspect of relatedness; and these aspects, whether in fact or thought, are indivisible."[36] Again, recourse to Greenleaf's category of "empirical nominalism" is helpful here. The empirical nominalist rejects—or at least remains agnostic about—the idea that the categories and relations humans establish are essential or natural. Instead, they are understood as mere human inventions to make sense of a world of independent particulars encountered externally by the senses. By contrast, relations, for Bradley, are internal and necessary to reality as a system, as elements of the Absolute. The diversity of reality, which includes the mind and its objects, are all related harmoniously within the Absolute, although Bradley would admit that this not does mean humans fathom the nature of their relation and harmony.

Monism, the coherence theory of truth, the concrete universal, the mental nature of reality, and the internal relatedness of reality, as suggested by Quinton and seen in Bradley's *Appearance and Reality,* each have a place in Oakeshott's work. Although, as I will show, each does not have the same career. Even though *Experience and Its Modes* is his most explicitly idealist work, Oakeshott draws upon this tradition in different ways and with different emphases even when in later essays his formal allegiance to idealism with all its "doctrines" dissolves. Oakeshott works to lay out many of these principles in idealist fashion, but even when he leaves idealism behind, the impress of these ideas on his thought is clear.

III

Experience and Its Modes was not Oakeshott's only philosophical endeavor in the late twenties and thirties. However, it was the most ambitious book of his whole life and also the primary, although not exclusive, source for his early philosophy. I take up that work now, but neither to show that Oakeshott was an idealist in every respect nor to argue that—contra Metz and Quinton—his is an under-rated contribution to idealist thought. Instead, I attempt to reveal how close his thought was to the idealist tradition in this early period but also to examine the variations from that tradition in his presentation. Most importantly, I separate out two different themes or elements in his work, a more whole or absolute idealism and a skeptical idealism.

In a single sentence near the beginning of *Experience and Its Modes,* Oakeshott displays the proximity of his thought to the tradition of idealism. He maintains, "And the view I propose to maintain is that experience is a single whole, within which modifications may be distinguished, but which admits of no final or absolute division; and that experience everywhere, not merely is inseparable from thought, but is itself a form of thought."[37] In this passage Oakeshott reveals his allegiance to the monism of idealism when he contends that experience is a "single whole," and certainly also to the idealist thesis, as Quinton put it, that "reality is essentially mental or spiritual in nature." Oakeshott recognizes that "This view of the character of experience is not so well established as to require no argument in its support."[38] However, I am not concerned here to examine his argument in support of this claim, but rather to explore the different features of this contention in his thought.

Oakeshott expressed the monism and the mental nature of reality, and following another of the doctrines of idealism that Quinton highlighted, he also held a coherence theory of truth. Again, in this philosophy, the model for truth is not a correspondence of ideas with the outside world, for there is no outside world for humans that is not also part of their thought. Instead truth is a matter of coherence. "Truth," Oakeshott suggests, "is the coherence of the world of experience: a world of ideas is true when it is coherent and because it is coherent."[39] Oakeshott has already claimed that experience is a "single whole," and that truth is the character of an expression that recognizes this single whole, one that reveals the relations of that coherent reality. As with Bradley, this means that there are greater or lesser degrees of truth as a greater unity and coherence in experience is achieved. Also with Bradley, Oakeshott formulates this as a direct rejection of a correspondence theory of truth. Oakeshott calls such a theory a "melancholy doctrine, as common as it is crude," for it does not recognize that there is no world of "facts" independent of experience to which judgments—to be true—must correspond.[40] Instead, Oakeshott insists, "Fact, then, is not what is given, it is what is achieved in experience. Facts are never merely observed, remembered, or combined; they are always made. We cannot 'take' facts, because there are none there until we have constructed them."[41] Since all experience is thought, there is literally no meaning to the suggestion that there is some datum outside of thought to which judgments must align to be true; as soon as data are sensed or perceived a judgment has been made and it is already within thought. Instead, since it is postulated that experience is a single whole, truth is understood as that which expresses the coherence of that unity.

Oakeshott's rejection of the idea that there are external data that the mind organizes by abstracting external features reveals not only his adherence to the coherence theory of truth but connects it to a notion of the concrete universal. Oakeshott repudiates the notion of a universal in which "The universal has been taken to mean that which is common to a set of particular ideas; . . . That which is common is merely that which is left over when particularity of particular ideas has been removed and it cannot pretend to be anything but an abstraction."[42] Instead, he offers a different notion of universality that reflects the concept of the concrete universal, although he, like Bradley, does not use the term. He recognizes that one way of conceiving the "single whole" of experience is as a universal: "experience is always a coherent world of ideas, and in that sense it may be said to be universal. The universality of experience is implied in, and belongs to its unity."[43] This universality, however, neither is one that is achieved only at the expense of the recognition of particulars, nor does a recognition of particulars or the individual prevent a concept of universality. Instead, Oakeshott claims, "universality and individuality, so far from being contra-

dictory notions of what is achieved in experience, depend for their significance upon being held together. Either without the other is a vicious
abstraction."[44] As with Bradley, the whole or universal qualifies and is qualified by its terms or particulars; an individual is not recognized in contrast
to a universal but together they contrive to form the whole of experience.

Finally, *Experience and Its Modes* also expresses aspects of the fifth of
Quinton's doctrines of idealism, that "mind and its objects are internally
and thus necessarily related." Oakeshott contends that the characteristic
unity of the single whole of experience is a necessary unity of all that is
contained in experience. "The unity of experience . . . is neither a unity
which revolves around some fixed point, nor one derived from conformity
to some original datum, nor one which involves mere abstractions, whether
these be essences or common elements. It is a unity congenial to a world
or system in which every element is indispensable, in which no one is more
important than any other and none is immune from change and rearrange-
ment."[45] Each of the first two types of unity he mentions would be a false
unity of abstract external relations, a unity imposed upon a diverse world
of particulars by drawing out certain commonalities. Instead, Oakeshott
understands the "single whole" to express a unity where "every element is
indispensable." A conception of unity that relied on abstractions of
"essences or common elements" would bleed away the particularity of
identity. Oakeshott instead conceives of a coherent unity in which all particularity is recognized as part of unity of experience, not neglected.

In the "Preface" to *Experience and Its Modes,* Oakeshott set for himself
the task of providing "a restatement of [idealism's] first principles." His
book does seem to achieve that goal, and it is this achievement that I have
labeled, following Quinton, Oakeshott's absolute idealism. In fact, however,
he even adds to the list drawn from Quinton in the previous section. The
first such addition has to do with philosophy itself. Oakeshott conjectures
that not only is there a fully coherent, internally related, single whole of
reality, but also that philosophical experience is experience of this world.
Philosophy alone takes for its world of ideas the single whole of experience. Thus Oakeshott claims, "Philosophical experience, then, I take to be
experience without presupposition, reservation, arrest or modification."[46]
Philosophy here is clearly something special: it is pure unfettered experience. Oakeshott takes the common criticisms of philosophy being abstract
or distracted from the real world and, in a table-turning move worthy of
Plato, he suggests that philosophy alone travels in the world of the concrete
and the real. Or conversely, that which is concrete experience of the coherent totality of experience is what Oakeshott labels the philosophical.

Oakeshott takes the constellation of claims about experience and reality of the idealist tradition, and links them directly to philosophy.

Of course, not all experience is philosophical experience. In a second addition to Quinton's list, most of Oakeshott's writing in *Experience and Its Modes* is concerned not with the whole of experience but with the way humans usually restrict and constrain their thoughts, comprehending experience by limiting it with the aids of constriction and modification.[47] Here we begin to see the skeptical moment of Oakeshott's early idealism. He gives his description of philosophical experience in the negative ("experience without presupposition, reservation, arrest or modification") because humans mostly do approach experience with reservations and presuppositions, by modifying or arresting it. The "modes" of the title of the book are worlds of such ideas; they are sustained modifications of experience. The particular modes Oakeshott examines are those of "Historical, Scientific and Practical experience . . . [which] represent the main arrests or modifications in experience."[48] Each of these, like philosophy, strives to achieve a coherent world of experience, but because they circumscribe the totality of experience in order to comprehend it, viewing reality from a "limited standpoint," their attempts are at best restricted and in the end self-defeating.[49]

The difference between the modes of experience and philosophical experience is fundamental. Philosophy rejects the modal experience not because it is not real experience, but because it is limited experience. Oakeshott does not, for example, reject practical experience, but the notion that it provides a complete, coherent, and thus fully satisfactory expression of reality. Neither is philosophical experience a super-mode that consists of all the modes put together, nor is it an arranger of the various modes to form complete experience like the pieces of a puzzle. While Oakeshott recognizes it would be surprising if "we should not be tempted to take up with the idea of philosophy as, in some sense, 'the fusion of the sciences,' 'the synthesis of the sciences' or the *scientia scientarum,*" he encourages the reader to hold firm against such temptation.[50] Instead, philosophy rejects limited and incomplete experience, but not "merely by ignoring it or dismissing it"; rather philosophy refutes modified experience by "exhibiting the principle of the fallacy or error in virtue of which a form of experience falls short of complete coherence."[51] This is the heart of what I call below his skeptical idealism.

Oakeshott claims the need for philosophy to study not only the modes, but also the relationships of the various modes to each other and to philosophy. In *Experience and Its Modes,* Oakeshott maintains that "unless these forms of experience [are] separated and kept separate, our experience would be unprotected against the most insidious and crippling of all forms of error—irrelevance."[52] Because the various "modes" are each based upon different presuppositions, whatever is accepted as true for one is idiosyncratic to it and therefore irrelevant for any other. For this reason then, each mode may claim a type of knowledge and each its own truth, but none is absolute and able to dictate to another. Each mode has a different way of conceiving the world, and thus what counts as a successful argument, and even whether argument is important, varies among the modes. To forget or ignore these distinctions, according to Oakeshott, is to be confused in our experience. Oakeshott claims "the view which I have to recommend is that confusion, *ignoratio elenchi,* is itself the most fatal of all errors, and that it occurs whenever argument or inference passes from one world of experience to another, from what is abstracted upon one principle to what is abstracted upon another."[53] Why is confusion the most "insidious" and "fatal of all errors?" Oakeshott does not explicitly say why, even though it seems fundamental to him. In this case it appears to be a particular form of confusion, category error, that concerns him. Modes themselves are human attempts to resolve some of the confusion of experience. If, however, those various attempts become confused, humans are in worse shape than before, because confusion is compounded by a false sense of clarity, and there is no means to recognize or resolve this error.

Oakeshott is not only concerned that the distinctions among modes be preserved, but also that the modes be kept distinct from philosophy. He admonishes that experience in full—concrete, philosophical experience— be kept separate from these modifications of it. I have already noted that Oakeshott does not intend for philosophy to order or arrange the modes, but neither can it nor should it dictate to them. In *Experience and Its Modes,* it is philosophy's goal to reject the modes' implicit claim to full experience; this is not, however, to purify the modes of their reservations. If a mode were to relinquish its presuppositions, it would not be a purified mode; rather it would lose its modal quality and become complete experience. Thus philosophy does not bring the modes closer to itself; instead it separates itself as experience from the modes. "In philosophy there is the explicit pursuit of what is ultimately satisfactory in experience," Oakeshott contends, "and, *ex hypothesi,* this must be irrelevant to practical experience; and wherever it enters practical life, that irrelevance must turn to error and falsehood."[54]

In a posthumously published essay, "The Concept of a Philosophy of Politics," Oakeshott reprises this theme directly in terms of the philosophy of politics and the activity of politics.[55] Following themes he began in

Experience and Its Modes, Oakeshott claims that "a philosophy of politics is an attempt to get away from what political life appears to be for common-sense—activity for the achievement of some end—to a view of the character of political life from the concrete standpoint of the totality of experience."[56] Oakeshott separates political philosophy from the practice of politics, but again it is based on the idealist conception of philosophy as "the concrete standpoint of the totality of experience." While political implications may arise from this position, they are not clear. On the one hand, Oakeshott may be attempting to protect politics from the overbearing demands by philosophers for consistency within a world typified by contingency. On the other hand, he may be trying to disabuse those in politics from the mistaken belief that certain principles or ideas like natural right, which belong to philosophy, are available to them or obligate and constrain them. His position could be used to criticize those who would insist upon the possession of special theoretical knowledge to participate in politics; or it could deny anything resembling critical theory by exempting practice from exposure of particularly oppressive inconsistencies. However, in this early stage, Oakeshott seems not to be concerned much with politics but primarily with philosophy. His counsel is that one cannot achieve true philosophy if one sets out to guide politics. The goal of the concrete experience of the single whole cannot be attained if one is detained by the practical world of politics.

All of this discussion of modes may seem to discredit Oakeshott's earlier allegiance to the unity of experience, based upon internal relations. Are modes and their "limited standpoints" outside of this? If politics and philosophy are distinct and separate, how are they yet also related to the totality of experience? Oakeshott anticipates this concern and maintains that a mode, as a world of ideas, does not disrupt the unity of the single whole of experience. He is quick to point out that a mode is not a distinct region or area of experience: "A mode of experience is not a separable part of reality, but the whole from a limited standpoint. It is not an island in the sea of experience, but a limited view of the totality of experience. It is not partial (in the literal sense), but abstract."[57] A mode then for Oakeshott is a fully conceived, if not fully coherent, view of the totality of experience; it is a view of the whole of reality from a limited perspective, a particular stopping place, standpoint or arrest. Thus to speak of an arrest is to recognize a condition where full experience has been modified; instead of "the pursuit of what is ultimately satisfactory in experience," such an arrest is the pursuit of limited, more certainly achievable satisfactions; it is experience that is held in check, based upon a presupposition that abstracts from experience instead of experiencing concretely. A mode, again, is not merely a part of reality nor is it experience that focuses upon one part of reality to know particular things. In reality, there are no fiefs of science or history or practice; rather each of these for Oakeshott is a manner of viewing reality in full, but from a "limited standpoint." Thus history is neither the world of the past nor the study of just what has occurred, science is not the study of that part of reality we call nature, and finally practice is not that part of life concerned solely with quotidian experiences. Instead, each mode views the whole of experience, but from its particular perspective, arrested by the presuppositions of each of these endeavors, and abstracting from experience according to it. These perspectives are not limited by *what* they view, but by *how* they view, because of the presuppositions of each particular modification of experience.

In this review of Oakeshott's early conception of philosophy two separable elements can be discerned that are represented by the elements of the title of that first book: there is a conception of "experience" and then also of "its modes." The first of these that I call Oakeshott's absolute idealism and the second skeptical idealism. The first is founded on the idealist notion of complete experience, the coherent whole of reality that is the world for philosophy. In this early period, Oakeshott is ambiguous as to whether philosophy is concrete experience of the whole or is only the pursuit of concrete experience. His insistence, however, that there is an absolutely coherent totality of experience diffuses this ambiguity, for that is the world philosophy calls its own and retains as a regulative principle. In a typically ambiguous passage, Oakeshott claims, "What is achieved in experience is an absolutely coherent world of ideas, not in the sense that it is ever actually achieved, but in the more important sense that it is the criterion of whatever satisfaction is achieved."[58] At times Oakeshott writes as if philosophy can and does achieve this concrete experience, at others as if it were its exclusive goal. Nonetheless, what makes philosophy unique, what separates philosophical experience from the "modes," is its unmatched relation with the unmodified and absolutely coherent totality of experience, its pursuit of what is ultimately satisfactory.

Following Quinton, I have chosen to call this aspect of Oakeshott's thoughts absolute idealism: it is that which is dependent upon a conception of philosophical experience that recognizes the "single whole," and thus is "positive and complete."[59] Oakeshott himself is wary of using the term "absolute," and of calling his notion of full experience "a world of absolute ideas," for he recognizes that the term absolute "has been the victim of dogma and the subject of a jargon which none but initiates pretend to understand."[60] However, while hesitant about its use, he still suggests "The end in experience . . . is a coherent world of ideas, a world or system of ideas which is at once unitary and complete; and it is difficult to know what, if not to this, the word absolute might be appropriate."[61] So I find it appropriate to label absolute idealism the aspect of his thought that is dependent upon the conception of "a world or system of ideas which is at once unitary and complete," and which it appears understands complete philosophical experience to be the achievement of that world. Oakeshott recognizes setting the goal of a "unitary and complete" world of ideals is no simple task. He acknowledges, "the attempt to find what is completely satisfactory in experience is so difficult and dubious an undertaking, leading us so far aside from the ways of ordinary thought, that those may be pardoned who prefer the embraces of abstraction."[62]

Skeptical idealism, the second element of his thought at this stage, calls attention to Oakeshott's focus upon "the embraces of abstraction."[63] Oakeshott reveals this skeptical moment of his idealism in his recognition that there are forms of experience, each of which limits experience in a particular way in order to comprehend it; while each of these may claim to express the totality of experience, none can actually accomplish this. A version of this skepticism was seen in Oakeshott's concern with the *ignoratio elenchi* and his insistence that what appears to be certainty within one mode should not be taken as universal truth, transportable to others. This form of skepticism actually predates his specific formulation of the absolute idealist position. In his earliest published works, for instance, Oakeshott examines the relationship between moral philosophy and religion and also that of history to spiritual needs.[64] He argues that claims made by each are irrelevant to any other, and so the various engagements, because they have different standpoints from which they build their worlds, cannot logically and should not be allowed to disrupt each other. He establishes this claim by exploring the character and presuppositions of the various endeavors to reveal the fundamental distinctions between these separate engagements.

An example of this early concern and strategy can be seen in an essay Oakeshott published in the late twenties, "The Importance of the Historical Element in Christianity." There Oakeshott concluded that the dismissal by historians of the accuracy of the Christ story has little to do with faith. It is simply irrelevant where faith is concerned that historians can prove the story of Christ to be inaccurate, because it is only shown to be historically inaccurate. He states "The conclusion, then, at which I arrive is that the historical element of our religion is not necessarily historical at all; that is, its essential characteristic lies not in the necessity of the *prima facie* historical [i.e. the necessity of an event like Christ's death and resurrection]."[65] He concludes, that is, that historical research and faith as the religious engagement of Christianity each have a different "essential characteristic." What appears to be a historical necessity for Christianity is really not such, for religious experience and historical experience are fundamentally different; they are each based upon different presuppositions about reality. This, in a sense, insulates religious experience against any but religious criticism—if matters of faith allow criticism—because a historical claim cannot logically, and thus should not actually attempt to, dislodge religious faith.

Still, the skepticism of *Experience and Its Modes* is not simply skepticism. What keeps this from being an entirely skeptical view is the idea of philosophical experience described in the other element in his thought: absolute idealism. At this stage, Oakeshott's ideas are guided by a conviction about philosophical experience and its relationship to an internally coherent, unified whole of reality, about which he brooks no skepticism. Similarly, the reason he gives for the critical venture of examining the modes is the task of gaining some ground toward "complete satisfaction." Oakeshott suggests, "unless we are exceptionally fortunate, a clear and unclouded experience is to be realized only through a process of criticism and rejection."[66] This is a complex image because of how he describes this "process of criticism and rejection." On the one hand it is tied to an image of "clear and unclouded experience," the teleological ideal of his absolute idealism and a belief that philosophy disposes of modes "from the concrete standpoint of the totality of experience." On the other hand, Oakeshott claims he does not want to reject "arrested" experience as experience, but instead to reject the implicit claim that such limited experience is actually complete experience. Again, this side of Oakeshott's skepticism does not criticize and reject incomplete experience "merely by ignoring it or dismissing it," but rather the skepticism is an attempt "to exhibit the principle of the fallacy or error in virtue of which a form of experience falls short of complete coherence." Philosophy, for Oakeshott, exposes the limits and the differing sources of the limits of different types of experience.

It is from this position of skeptical idealism that many of Oakeshott's later interests may begin to become clear: Oakeshott's famous concern that politics be safe not only from philosophy but also from the impress of scientific rationality, or that the claims of practical experience not disrupt the work of the historian, or that poetry not be overwhelmed by either science or practice, among others. It is also from this skeptical idealism that Oakeshott's conservative disposition can be appreciated: he is suspicious of all the absolute claims and attendant projects put forth by ideologies that neither recognize nor admit their own necessary limits. What remains as a curiosity is that Oakeshott exempts philosophy from this caution to respect limits. If, however, Oakeshott's understanding of philosophical experience were to change, if the presumptions of this view of philosophy—that there is a single, unified whole that expresses absolute coherence and that philosophy is experience released from the modes—were abandoned, then the skepticism would dominate. Coherence would remain as the criterion of truth, but not because it reflects the absolute coherence of the totality; the assumption of a unified coherent whole would have been foresworn. Coherence remains because nothing else is available; it is an internal, not an external—and thus unavailable—criterion. This is something like the position that Oakeshott takes up after his early stage, and I will explore below the changes it effects in his understanding of the relationship of theory and practice. In the thirties, however, Oakeshott held that philosophy was capable of fully coherent and concrete experience; thus he was able to argue in an essay published a few years after *Experience and Its Modes,* "a philosophical explanation is one which, in principle, is the relation of its subject to what I have called the totality of experience because this alone is a self-complete context, a context which criticism cannot turn into a text itself requiring a context."[67]

IV

I have portrayed the idealist background of Oakeshott's earliest works and the different emphases in Oakeshott's form of idealism. Following upon idealist predecessors, Oakeshott develops a conception of reality in which all experience is thought and is encompassed within a concrete, coherent, single whole. In Oakeshott's work, this commitment entails two different elements. First there is the absolute idealism, his insistence that philosophical experience is in fact that experience that is "without presupposition, reservation, arrest or modification." But there is also a skeptical idealism, which investigates the implicit and often unrecognized presuppositions that limit each of the modes, undermining their claim to absolute certainty. Skeptical idealism is concerned to reveal the limits of the different worlds of experience, not in order to deny that they express truth, but to understand the partial and relative quality of that truth. At this stage in his thought, these two elements are not contradictory, but in fact are closely connected.

That these two aspects of idealism exist in Oakeshott's early and prominently idealist writings is perhaps not surprising, for it has been observed that Bradley, from whom he claimed to have "learnt much," exhibited these same tendencies. In *Scepticism and Dogma,* Ralph Ross argued that "Francis Herbert Bradley, one of the most profound of modern sceptics, . . . was at the same time an absolutist in systematic philosophy."[68] Ross pointed to how the first book of *Appearance and Reality* "is characterized by the use of a sceptical method," as Bradley examines various claims to reality and rejects them as mere appearances.[69] Yet Bradley's own discussions of the Absolute simply asserts the validity of his conclusions as necessary. "It is this knowledge [Bradley claims] of 'the main character of the Absolute' that I am calling dogma."[70] Bradley, in the passage referred to by Ross, claims, "With regard to the main character of the Absolute, our position is briefly this. We hold that our conclusion is certain, and that to doubt it is logically impossible. . . . Outside our main result there is nothing except the wholly unmeaning, or else something which on scrutiny is seen really not to fall outside."[71] However, Bradley himself says that he wants his reader "to credit me with a desire to do justice to scepticism; and indeed, I might claim, perhaps, to be something of a sceptic."[72]

There are some similarities between my judgment of Oakeshott and Ross's of Bradley, but also at least two differences. First, Ross finds both skepticism and dogma in an idealist and considers this a fundamental contradiction; I, however, consider Oakeshott's maintenance of these two positions coherent—if confining—at least as expressed in *Experience and Its Modes.* What Ross finds unsettling is that Bradley begins as a skeptic and ends as a dogmatist. While I am not attracted to Oakeshott's absolute idealism, in *Experience and Its Modes* and the essays "The Concept of a Philosophical Jurisprudence" and "The Concept of a Philosophical Politics," he approaches these from the position of an idealist conception of complete experience and the skeptical judgements about other forms of experience are results. Thus Oakeshott assembles his argument with a different logic than Bradley, leaving himself less open to the criticism of Ross.[73]

The second difference of my observations from Ross is more important. If Ross's critique of Bradley were also attendant to Oakeshott of the thirties, I will argue in the next chapter, it would not matter because Oakeshott surrenders the absolute or dogmatic idealism. I emphasized the logical progression of Oakeshott's argument above because temporally skepticism possibly precedes, and definitely succeeds his idealism. Bradley is known as an idealist philosopher, perhaps the dean of the British idealists. However, only those who have paid close attention to Oakeshott's work recall the idealist forays of his prewar period, while to most this stage is a surprise. I have discussed "The Importance of the Historical Element in Christianity," to reveal that Oakeshott's skeptical concerns seem possibly to precede his commitment to idealism. Perhaps, he turned to idealism because it provided a means to explore these concerns. But even if not, as I argue below, the skepticism that was dominated by the absolute idealism in this period comes to eclipse the latter in turn.

Chapter Two

Skepticism in Conversation

I

In 1938, the view of Michael Oakeshott to a reader familiar with his writings may have been something like this:

Here is another last envoy of British idealist philosophy—that used to be Collingwood. Five years ago Oakeshott published his major philosophical work, *Experience and Its Modes,* which he himself considered "a restatement of [idealism's] first principles."[1] And now, in 1938, he has reaffirmed his idealist stance in a lengthy consideration of the study of law from an idealist perspective, "The Concept of a Philosophical Jurisprudence," where he again claims that "Philosophical thought and knowledge is simply thought and knowledge without reservation or presupposition."[2] He has shown some eclectic interests in subjects ranging from religion to politics to history to horse racing; but it is not clear if he has interests in these on their own, or to reveal the view of them through the lens of the idealist major work.[3] It seems likely that Oakeshott will continue the effort of working out the implications of philosophical idealism—probably in intellectual isolation—and will continue to broaden his purview, attending to other areas of interest from that perspective. We should expect a book on history next, expanding and defending the idealist conception from the chapter Collingwood liked so much in *Experience and Its Modes.*[4]

While this is a reasonable reconstruction of the view of Oakeshott in the late thirties, I suggested in the last chapter that some reviewers of Oakeshott, more familiar with his political philosophy, have neglected this period of his ideas. However, those who have attempted a full review of his works have not only paid attention to this stage, but have come to a view not dissimilar to that which might have been predicted in the late thirties. For instance, in the first book-length study of Oakeshott's ideas, W. H. Greenleaf suggested that "Oakeshott's political ideas are . . . very definitely the reflection of a philosophical standpoint. . . . So far as I can judge, his general philosophical position has remained constant throughout."[5] As I suggested in the last chapter, I do not agree with this interpretation, at least not as it stands. Part of the reason I consider it important to separate the elements of absolute and skeptical idealism is to gain a perspective on what are subtle but fundamental shifts in Oakeshott's philosophical outlook, from one dominated by idealism to one that is primarily skeptical. This change has an important affect upon Oakeshott's conception of philosophy and the manner of interaction between various forms and expressions of experience; it also influences his political philosophy, which he had only begun to develop in the thirties.

I describe this change as subtle as well as fundamental, because while it has a profound affect on Oakeshott's thought, he nowhere announces such a change. It is the burden of my argument in this chapter to demonstrate that regardless of the lack of such a confession, Oakeshott's work reveals such an alteration. I do not pretend to account for this change in Oakeshott's thought. It may be that his interest in Hobbes, which seems to have begun in the early thirties, was actually based in a more fundamental attraction to that skeptic, and that as he spent more time with Hobbes's work, his own skepticism, intimated in *Experience and Its Modes,* is drawn out and developed. It may be that the experience of serving in the Second World War caused him to doubt his own earlier claims about philosophy and a coherent world of absolute ideas. Before having the luxury of considering what might have brought this about, I have the task of substantiating the claim that such a change even occurs, against the claims of most, although not all, of Oakeshott's interpreters. To accomplish this, I focus upon Oakeshott's essay "The Voice of Poetry in the Conversation of Mankind."[6] This essay, originally published as a monograph in 1959, most clearly reveals the changes in his thought in the twenty years between it and the publication of "The Concept of a Philosophical Jurisprudence." These changes became increasingly clear over this period, but in "The Voice of Poetry" Oakeshott resumes, in a limited way, the task of *Experience and Its Modes,* considering human engagement and experience generally in order to examine poetry's voice within it. This does present the difficulty of comparing an essay, almost lyrical in tone, to the more formal and technically philosophical work of *Experience and Its Modes,* but this is a quandary that cannot be avoided. Oakeshott published no sustained work of formal philosophy after *Experience and Its Modes,* and no article in such a formally philosophical style after "The Concept of Philosophical Jurisprudence."[7]

There are many interesting aspects to "The Voice of Poetry," but there is one image that I will return to again and again to highlight the change in Oakeshott's thought: the image of voices in conversation he refers to in the title. Oakeshott had earlier relied upon the metaphor of conversation in discussing education. In fact, he described education as the introduction into a conversation in "Political Education" and "The Study of 'Politics' in a University."[8] But it is in "The Voice of Poetry" that Oakeshott most thoroughly develops this metaphor. My intention is not to defend this image, for it is as problematic as it is alluring. Instead, I focus on it because the image of voices in conversation reveals the change in Oakeshott's thought that I suggest is so important to grasp. Most significantly, it shows Oakeshott to have abandoned the absolute idealism, with its particular conception of philosophical experience and its rigid proscriptions against the interaction of philosophy and other forms of experience and their expression. The skepticism, which earlier existed but in terms of idealism, now obtains a more full expression. Earlier modes could have a provisional or contextual certainty, but only philosophy had such at a universal or absolute level; philosophical experience, emphatically, was not a mode (i.e. modified experience) but full, concrete experience. Now, with the image of conversation, philosophy is reconceived as a voice among voices. Philosophy has by now become subject to the same cautions and limitations as only the modes were earlier. Both a sign of change and a substantive alteration, the recognition of philosophy in a conversation with other voices is fundamentally important—and it is an issue of contention with interpreters of Oakeshott. The relationship of philosophy to practice is a difficult issue, and, as with the image of conversation, I am less concerned to defend Oakeshott's ideas about it than to interpret that relationship, as a sign of his skepticism, differently than other interpreters.[9]

The suggestions that I have just made, that Oakeshott changes some fundamental elements of his philosophy and that among those changes is a different, more open understanding of the relationship of philosophy and practice, go against the grain of most Oakeshott scholarship. For instance, Greenleaf's book is premised upon the judgment that Oakeshott's "general philosophical position has remained constant throughout. There have been changes of course, but they are modifications of detail rather than vital alterations."[10] Because idealism is prevalent in Oakeshott's early work, and it is from that part of his thought that the separation of theory and practice comes, Greenleaf is left to maintain that for Oakeshott the philosopher "contributes nothing himself to the modal undertakings of mankind and does not prescribe practical or other courses of action."[11] More recently, Paul Franco has provided an even more complete account of Oakeshott's thought, again returning to the early works and the idealist tradition where Greenleaf and I focus. Franco, in *The Political Philosophy of Michael Oakeshott,* contends that "at the heart of Oakeshott's political philosophy lies a doctrine about the nature of philosophy."[12] Also like Greenleaf, Franco argues that there is a central coherence to Oakeshott's works, from *Experience and Its Modes* through the essays *Rationalism in Politics* and continuing even past *On Human Conduct.*[13] In fact, Franco claims that when it comes to Oakeshott's idea of philosophy, the "account [in *On Human Conduct*] in many respects parallels the account of experience in *Experience and Its Modes,*" although he does admit that "it contains nuances and even some slight deviations."[14] This results in another central agreement between Franco and Greenleaf; for Oakeshott, philosophy and politics or theory and practice are entirely separate and should be kept that way. In discussing the relationship of theory and practice Franco refers to "the distinctively Oakeshottian gulf between theory and practice."[15] In fact, according to Franco, not only does Oakeshott suggest that philosophy is irrelevant to the practical concerns of politics, but he also insists upon the "inimicality of philosophy to practice."[16] Franco, by emphasizing one aspect of the idealism that Oakeshott expressed in *Experience and Its Modes,* produces an Oakeshott who, in all his works, consistently shears philosophical reflection from the practical engagements of life, especially that of politics.

I certainly agree with each of these writers that attending to Oakeshott's early work provides a requisite background for understanding his later work. And I do not disagree with them over whether there are parallels and consistencies throughout his work. However, I differ in my view of the character of that consistency and about what remains constant. Having developed the idea of Oakeshott's absolute and skeptical idealism it is possible to see how in fact some of his ideas grow and others fall away.[17] Oakeshott's skeptical and absolute idealism are not like sides of a coin that retains its currency over the years; instead they are like different shoots from a common root, one of which thrives while the other withers—or is pruned away. It is, I argue, the absolute idealism that Oakeshott quietly abandons, and in doing so he provides fresh attention to the skeptical idealism. It is this skepticism as it is redeveloped in the image of the conversation that allows for an open and contingent relationship between theory and practice.

II

"I do not myself know where to place an experience released altogether from modality or a world of 'objects' which is not a world of images and is governed by no considerabilities."[18]

This confessional passage from "The Voice of Poetry," reveals Oakeshott to have changed remarkably his understanding of philosophy and experience. Twenty years earlier Oakeshott would have had no doubt where to place an experience "governed by no considerabilities": it would be a philosophical experience. Such an unmodified experience would be a concrete example of the absolutely coherent totality of experience. In claiming not to know "where to place" such an experience, Oakeshott divulges that he has renounced much of his earlier idealism. In *Experience and Its Modes,* he understood philosophy as the "logical end" of experience.[19] Conversely, in "The Voice of Poetry in the Conversation of Mankind," he claims that philosophy is only another voice—a voice that is "unusually conversable."[20] Oakeshott no longer holds that "philosophical thought and knowledge is simply thought and knowledge without reservation or presupposition." Instead, by the writing of "The Voice of Poetry" Oakeshott contends that "philosophy, the impulse to study the quality and style of each voice, and to reflect upon the relationship of one voice to another, must be counted a parasitic activity; it springs from the conversation . . . but it makes no specific contribution."[21] "Parasitic" is perhaps precisely accurate as he describes philosophy, but the pejorative lingers with its use. What is more, consider Oakeshott's claim that philosophy "makes no specific contribution" to the conversation. By this, he must mean that while philosophy may "study the quality and style of each voice," which could be considered a contribution of a secondary sort, philosophy makes no *substantive* contribution to the conversation as a whole. Earlier, Oakeshott would likely have agreed that philosophy makes no contribution to any of the modes as modes; but its contribution to experience was fundamental, nothing less than the provision of "a clear and unclouded experience."[22] Oakeshott has clearly reined in his conception of philosophy, and this is certainly a "vital alteration," more than a mere modification of detail or nuance as suggested by Greenleaf and Franco.

Oakeshott had begun this change in thinking about philosophy at least by the late forties, as evidenced in an essay that has only recently been published, "Political Philosophy."[23] For instance, in the early period, Oakeshott had maintained that "the business of a philosophy of politics is to persevere with [the] task of continual redefinition of concepts until a comprehensively concrete result is achieved."[24] In "Political Philosophy," however, Oakeshott describes the character of philosophy as "a reflective enterprise . . . [which] would not improperly be called *radically* subversive."[25] Philosophy here is not "simply thought and knowledge without reservation or presupposition," but a skeptical disposition. Significantly, Oakeshott claims, a person "is a philosopher not in respect to something he achieves at the end, but in respect of his predisposition. . . . Indeed, it might be said that his only tangible achievement is the maintenance of this predisposition."[26] Philosophy is skeptical not because of its "logical end" of complete experience or because it can refute experience from such a position; instead it is the adoption of a disposition. At this point, however, even though Oakeshott has dropped many of the vestments of the idealist conception of philosophy, he does maintain the separation of philosophy and politics. He argues "if we expect from political philosophy conclusions relevant to politics, the result will be either a political philosophy in which the reflective impulse is hindered and arrested by being made servile to politics, or a political activity in which the reflective impulse, disengaged from the necessary limits of politics, has lost its virtue."[27] In both "Political Philosophy" and "The Voice of Poetry," Oakeshott has lost faith in the notion of "experience without reservation" and so also in philosophy as that experience. That is to say, Oakeshott has begun to direct his skepticism to the claims of philosophy itself. Implied with this alteration is also a change in the skeptical aspect of Oakeshott's philosophy. Oakeshott neither any longer claims that all nonphilosophical experience is "confused and distracted," nor does he insist that forms of experience must be kept completely separate.

The most significant indication of this change, a shift begun but not completed in "Political Philosophy," is that Oakeshott relinquishes the stiff and formal concept of modes for the metaphor of voices in conversation. And what is most notable about voices in conversation is that they, of course, converse—an activity difficult to orchestrate among modes that are separated by gulfs. In "The Voice of Poetry" Oakeshott claims that "the diverse idioms of utterance which make up current human intercourse have some meeting-place and compose a manifold of some sort. And, as I understand it, the image of this meeting place is not an inquiry or an argument, but a conversation."[28] Before discussing the relationship of voices indicated here, it is important to note how different this image of the "manifold" of "diverse idioms of utterance" is from the contention of a single coherent whole of experience that Oakeshott maintained in *Experience and Its Modes*. Oakeshott makes no claim about the "absolute coherence" of this "manifold" or "meeting-place"; at best it would seem to exhibit the rough mix of dissonance and harmony of the bazaar.

As to the relationship between voices, this passage appears to be a revision of his earlier contention that "forms of experience [be] separated and kept separate."[29] Nevertheless, Oakeshott remains concerned with the distinctiveness of each voice and with the conditions of the manifold they compose. In this reformed understanding Oakeshott views philosophy as a voice continually interested in the "style of each voice" and the "relationship" of voices to each other. Still, while revealing how these voices mix, in these passages Oakeshott manifests the reconstituted aspect of his skepticism: he retains the concern with the limited character of each voice and the restricted relations between the various voices. In *Experience and Its Modes,* Oakeshott had admonished that any mixing of modes was ill-advised, suggesting for example, "Between the worlds of history and practice, as specific worlds of experience, there is an impassable gulf."[30] When later Oakeshott suggests conversation as a metaphor, the gulf between modes becomes passable, as voices converse with each other, not shout at each other. But while admitting conversation, Oakeshott preserves a concern about irrelevance. In fact, "The Voice of Poetry" can be seen partially as the defense of poetry from the irrelevant claims and immoderate influence of "science" and "practice." More notably though, by using the image of conversation, Oakeshott provides a manner of interaction that can be meaningful and yet with conditions to protect against irrelevant claims of supposed authority.

Oakeshott had earlier contended that it is irrelevant—and improper— to carry a "fact" from one mode to another. With the metaphor of conversation he retains this concern, proposing that it is inappropriate to impress truths spoken in the idiom of one voice upon that of another. Now, however, voices can respond to other voices in a way that his earlier modes precluded. This is how Oakeshott describes the character of this interaction:

> In conversation, "facts" appear only to be resolved once more into the possibilities from which they were made; "certainties" are shown to be combustible, not by being brought in contact with other "certainties" or with doubt, but by being kindled by the presence of ideas of another order; approximations are revealed between notions normally remote from one another. Thoughts of different species take wing and play around one another, responding to each other's movements and provoking one another to fresh exertions.[31]

This passage illuminates the character of the alterations Oakeshott made in the relationship between what he had called modes but has now reconceived as voices. Voices have no claim over one another and there is no single idiom of speech in which they all converse, but they may respond to and "provok[e] one another." "Certainties" lose their apodictic quality, and yet they remain as "possibilities." To extend his metaphor, a voice may expand its vocabulary or alter its mood of expression, not because it adopts another idiom, but because "in the presence of ideas from another order" it can be "provok[ed] . . . to fresh exertions." It is even possible to express this in the manner of the argument of *Experience and Its Modes,* though Oakeshott envisioned no such interaction there: a world of ideas, through encounter with another such world, may be provoked to explore different contributions to the coherence of its own world.[32] When understood as voices in conversation, however, there is nothing necessary or restrictive about this interaction, except the paradoxical recognition that there are no certainties within it. The sorts of provocations and responses depend only upon the character of the conversation at the time and the desire, need, or ability of each voice to "respond to each other's movements." This is certainly a fundamental change in Oakeshott's conception of human experience and expression. Yet it is an alteration in which the character of Oakeshott's concern remains. The skeptical element of his thought is evident in his rejection of the certainties of any voice in the manifold of human utterance.

In discussing *Experience and Its Modes,* I labeled Oakeshott's skeptical idealism those aspects of his thought that were concerned to reveal the peculiar limits and unique standpoints of the various modes. This aspect of his thought focused on these limits in order to rebut any claim to universal experience or knowledge by any mode, or even the claim that any given mode is somehow necessary to experience—such claims were reserved for philosophical experience. The skeptical element of his thought is now re-articulated in "The Voice of Poetry" in his rejection of the certainties of any voice within the manifold of human utterance. "Facts" may exist in and for a particular voice, in a particular "universe of discourse," but Oakeshott rejects the idea that they are or can be natural or absolute, existing as "facts" outside of their peculiar form of expression. So also, the certitude concerning "certainties" is established only within their own order of expression. Oakeshott's skepticism thus acts to facilitate conversation by providing the space for a variety of interlocutors and rejecting any claim by a voice that it is the only way to converse. The skepticism of "The Voice of Poetry" can then be seen partially as a development of his earlier skeptical idealism, no longer concerned to keep experiences separate, but to attend to the quality of their interaction. Also noticeably new in this reformulated skepticism of "The Voice of Poetry" is the seeming recognition that philosophy is also subject to skepticism and that it partakes in conversation with its own limits. Skepticism itself, however, is not new, but the development by Oakeshott of an aspect of his earlier thought, the pursuit of an evident intimation. Earlier, skepticism about the certainties of the modes came from the idealist commitment to an understanding of philosophical experience exclusively being concrete experience; that earlier skepticism was bounded by idealism and thus my label skeptical idealism. Now, however, skepticism becomes a disposition against the final or absolute certainty of any voice, including that of philosophy.

Oakeshott himself recognizes the skepticism of the metaphor of conversation. He suggests, "The image of human activity and intercourse as a conversation will, perhaps, appear both frivolous and unduly sceptical."[33] For example, this image might seem to negate or diminish achievements of practical or scientific enterprises, especially to those who consider them to be laudable or even wondrous. He goes on, "And the denial of a hierarchical order among the voices is not only a departure from one of the most notable traditions of European thought (in which all activity was judged relative to the *vita contemplativa*), but will seem also to reinforce the scepticism."[34] In *Experience and Its Modes,* Oakeshott explicitly judged as inferior all experience that did not have the concrete character of philosophical experience. There was no hierarchy of the modes, but there was a hierarchy between philosophical experience and all modal experience. In this passage, Oakeshott indicates a change in his assessment of philosophy. Previously, both for him and for "one of the most notable traditions of European thought," philosophy was the height of thought or the "logical end" of experience; now it is reduced as are all other "universes of discourse" to the position of voices in conversation in which there is no hierarchy.

One more alteration, perhaps more subtle but worthy of note, exists from *Experience and Its Modes,* in the characterization of the relationship of voices. In *Experience and Its Modes,* the fallacy of irrelevance, *ignoratio elenchi,* was the most fatal and grievous of all errors. In "The Voice of Poetry," a variation of this fallacy concerns Oakeshott most: the irrelevance that exists when one voice presumes to speak with authority over the concerns of all other voices, assuming its voice and idiom to be the only one with importance or meaning. In *Experience and Its Modes* the source of the error or irrelevance was confusion; in "The Voice of Poetry" the source of irrelevance is a pointed form of confusion, *superbia* or pride. Oakeshott explains, "For each voice is prone to *superbia,* that is an exclusive concern with its own utterance, which may result in its identifying the conversation with itself and speaking as if it were speaking only to itself."[35] This *superbia* relates to the error of irrelevance in that in *ignoratio elenchi* one fallaciously ignores the different "limited standpoints" of various modes of experience, and thus passes inappropriately in argument from one to the next. Here, the particular manner of irrelevance that concerns Oakeshott is when a voice consciously dismisses other voices, assuming that all meaning is capable of being expressed in its idiom. Such a voice either does not recognize or ignores that it, in fact, speaks in a particular idiom. It recognizes other voices—if at all—only as idiomatic, partial and incomplete. *Ignoratio elenchi* identified a situation of confusion; *superbia* identifies a situation where confusion is sadly and dangerously compounded by arrogance. Earlier, when limited experience was understood as modes, they were only to be concerned with themselves; when Oakeshott reconceives what he had understood as modes as instead voices, such a voice is at fault if it is so self-centered. This, however, does not undermine the importance of the matter of irrelevance. In fact, it heightens the need to be wary of it. Because voices do interact, now the manner of that interaction is a concern for Oakeshott. Here, Oakeshott's skepticism is particularly clear; first it was exhibited in a denial of the certainty of one voice—including philosophy's—to preside over others; now its is seen in a warning against those voices that feign such certainty.

I have suggested that there are at least three notable changes from *Experience and Its Modes* to "The Voice of Poetry." First, and most significantly, Oakeshott abandoned the absolute idealist element of his conception of his philosophy even while retaining and reforming the skeptical element. Philosophy no longer has a unique relationship to absolute, complete, and unmodified experience; it is now a voice among voices. Not only is the idea of such fully coherent experience, idealism's monism, abandoned, but the faith in philosophy to free itself from modification is as well. In its skeptical vocation, however, philosophy does continue to examine the characteristics, quality and style of the voices, enhancing conversation by discounting claims to absolute experience. Second, Oakeshott cashiered the notion of modes that can have no meaningful form of interaction, offering instead the idea of forms of experience and expression related as voices in conversation. Finally, the emphasis of Oakeshott's concern with irrelevance changed from one of simple confusion to that of *superbia*. He is anxious in the later essay not only that we humans find ourselves in a muddle, but do so because of the overwhelming and arrogant posture of certain voices.

III

Without a doubt, in *Experience and Its Modes,* Oakeshott was greatly concerned that types of experience be kept separate and also that philosophy, as
pure experience, not be distracted by the concerns of practice, science, or
history. I have argued, however, that Oakeshott changes his conception of
philosophy as, in effect, he directed his skepticism at the claims of philosophy itself. The result is that by "The Voice of Poetry" philosophy is a voice
among voices. The relationship of philosophy to other voices is no different
from that among all the other voices: it is conversational. And philosophy has
no rulership over other voices, for in conversation "there is no symposiarch
or arbiter; not even a doorkeeper to check credentials."[36] However, none of
this precludes philosophy from interacting with the other voices and the
other voices from conversing with it. In the case of philosophy and politics,
clearly the two do not share a common idiom. They do however share a
conversational meeting-place where ideas may intermingle. Now that
Oakeshott has left behind his absolute idealism, philosophy, as the other
voices, partakes in the manifold of human utterance. Now also, instead of
philosophy simply rejecting any except full experience, Oakeshott is appre-
ciative of the variety, even encouraging it in his paean to poetry. If there is
anything distinctive about the philosophical voice in the manner in which
it participates in the conversation it is, Oakeshott claims, that "the voice of
philosophy . . . is unusually conversable."

Greenleaf, in acknowledging such changes as these, suggested they be
understood as a mere "change in expression . . . affect[ing] rather the way
in which [Oakeshott's] epistemology is described than the essence of the
doctrine itself."[37] I have argued that in dropping his absolute idealism,
Oakeshott has altered an essential component of what Greenleaf calls his
"doctrine." Franco aligns with Greenleaf in contending that Oakeshott's
philosophy remains throughout essentially the same and that a central element of this consistency is the complete separation of philosophy and practice, and he pursues this consistency through *On Human Conduct.* If in *On
Human Conduct* Oakeshott were perhaps to have re-adopted the commitment to philosophy as "experience without reservation" and rejected in his
conception of conversation between diverse idioms, then Franco may be
correct and Oakeshott may maintain a complete separation of philosophy
from practice throughout.[38] However, I contend that in that later work
Oakeshott reveals another rearticulation of his skepticism and of the notion
of contingent relations between types of experience that he established
with the metaphor of conversation.

In the opening chapter of *On Human Conduct,* Oakeshott once again considers the nature of philosophy that he here describes as the "unconditional engagement I shall call theorizing."[39] It is, it appears, to these early pages that Franco looks when he suggests Oakeshott's conception of philosophy remains essentially the same as that in *Experience and Its Modes.* Time and again Oakeshott describes how theorizing is "unconditional" and that what "distinguishes a theorist is his undistracted concern with the unconditional, critical engagement of understanding."[40] Statements such as these certainly bear a similarity to those forty years earlier when Oakeshott described philosophy as "experience without presupposition, reservation, arrest, or modification."[41] The "unconditionality" of theorizing in the later work seems to mirror the philosophical rejection of "presuppositions" and "modifications" found in the earlier work. However, in *On Human Conduct* Oakeshott uses "unconditional" differently than he did these other terms. As I suggested earlier, Oakeshott now points his skepticism toward philosophical knowledge itself; and what Oakeshott means here by "unconditional" is the ongoing criticism of all claims, even those made by the theorist.

In *On Human Conduct,* as in *Experience and Its Modes,* Oakeshott takes theory to be focused upon the examination of the presuppositions and conditions of various forms of understanding. In *Experience and Its Modes,* Oakeshott contended that philosophy was concerned with modes in order to reveal the presuppositions that created the limited standpoints by which they viewed reality; he suggested in "The Voice of Poetry" that philosophy studied the quality and style of each voice. Now in *On Human Conduct,* Oakeshott claims that for the theorist, "His enterprise is to make identities more intelligible, . . . by seeking to understand them in terms of their postulates; that is, in terms of their conditions."[42] The result, however, of such an examination has changed. In *Experience and Its Modes,* Oakeshott had claimed, "Philosophical knowledge is knowledge which carries with it the evidence of its own completeness." He thus considered philosophical knowledge to be "positive and complete."[43] Oakeshott echoed this in "The Concept of a Philosophical Jurisprudence," where he contended that philosophical knowledge is that set in a "context which criticism cannot turn into a text requiring a context."[44] However, *On Human Conduct* does not show Oakeshott to have returned to the notion of absolute idealism that he had abandoned by "The Voice of Poetry." Instead, in *On Human Conduct,* he claims that "theorizing has revealed itself as an unconditional adventure in which *every achievement of understanding* is an invitation to investigate itself."[45] Oakeshott now argues that every understanding, even those of philosophy, must be seen as a context that criticism *can* "turn into a text requiring a context." The unconditionality of the engagement of the theorist is not the achievement of knowledge without conditions, the attainment of "knowledge which carries with it the evidence of its own completeness"; instead it is the relentless endeavor to reveal conditions that always exist. Theorizing, or philosophy, is not the achievement of "what is ultimately satisfactory," but the engagement never to be satisfied. "The irony of all theorizing," Oakeshott claims, "is its propensity to generate not an understanding, but a not-yet-understood."[46]

What is retained then from *Experience and Its Modes* is a concern that Oakeshott has revised, developed, and expressed in different ways: it is the skeptical engagement to reveal the unique characteristics, the particular points of arrest, the quality and style, and the postulates and conditions of modes, voices, and identities. What Oakeshott has left behind is the contention that the product of this effort is "a comprehensively concrete result." Along with this relinquishment, Oakeshott also has forsaken the strict separation of what is complete from what is partial, and this because he no longer holds that philosophy can achieve what is complete: "Nevertheless, the engagement of understanding (i.e. theorizing or philosophy) is not unconditional on account of the absence of conditions, or in virtue of a supposed terminus in an unconditional theorem; what constitutes its unconditionality is the continuous recognition of the conditionality of conditions."[47] Oakeshott here could hardly be more explicit; the character of the "unconditional" is "not the absence of conditions," while earlier the absence of conditions, modifications, and presuppositions had been precisely the character of philosophical experience. In *On Human Conduct,* theorizing or philosophy is a maintenance of "the continuous recognition of the conditionality of conditions." It is the recognition that all experience, knowledge, and expression is conditional, in which the criterion of an unconditional, absolute, coherent system of universal coherence would be meaningless. It is this aspect of Oakeshott's conception of theory, in which "temporary platforms of conditional understanding are always being reached, . . . but each is an arrival, an enlightenment, and a departure," that I suggest other interpreters undervalue.[48] Every achievement of theory is only a temporary achievement. Each is a context of understanding soon to be turned into a text needing a context itself by the skeptical engagement of the theorist because Oakeshott no longer posits a "self-complete context" of the totality of experience. This is why Oakeshott claims "there is no body of philosophical knowledge to be detached from the activity of philosophizing"; for Oakeshott, philosophy has become understood to be a continuing engagement, not an achieved state or set of contents. Once again, he has forsaken the absolute idealist postulate that unhindered experience is unique to philosophy, which he held in *Experience and Its Modes* and "The Concept of a Philosophical Jurisprudence." It is difficult to see how Oakeshott's account of philosophy and experience given in those earlier works parallels that in *On Human Conduct* with his reformed conception of theory and the meaning of "unconditionality" he gives there. If one misses the evident changes in Oakeshott's conception of philosophy, then one can also easily misconstrue Oakeshott's concern about the relationship of theory and practice. If philosophy is unconditional experience denoting "experience without presupposition, reservation, arrest or modification," then perhaps it would be separated from practical experience by an impassable gulf. If, however, philosophy is an "engagement to be perpetually *en voyage,*" and if it is a voice among voices in conversation, then there can be a relationship between philosophy and practice as between all voices.[49]

Before I discuss the relationship of theory and practice in *On Human Conduct,* it is important to recognize another alteration, this time in Oakeshott's usage of the term practice. Earlier, in *Experience and Its Modes,* he understood practical experience to be a separate world from those of history and science. It was a mode in which "the alteration of existence is undertaken," it is the constant engagement to reconcile "'what is' with what we desire shall be."[50] In *On Human Conduct,* however, Oakeshott does not see practice as a unique world, but uses the concept of practice to denote the aspect of every human engagement that makes it an activity shared between individuals.[51] A practice is not the set of postulates and conditions of a platform of understanding, but the relationship of those joined in such an engagement.[52] When Oakeshott speaks of the distinction of theory and practice, it is of the distinction between the theoretical postulates and conditions of a type of understanding and the shared, prescriptive relations between those engaged in an activity. To be sure, Oakeshott was wary of the relationship between theoretical understanding and practical activity. Oakeshott, for instance, has some particularly nasty words for the type he calls the "'theoretician,' . . . this deplorable character who has no respectable occupation. . . . In virtue of being a theorist he purports to be concerned with the postulates of conduct, but he mistakes these postulates for principles from which 'correct' performances may be deduced or somehow elicited."[53] As in the earlier works, Oakeshott is concerned here that the certainties of one type of engagement should not be taken as certain in another type. The "theoretician" suffers from the *superbia* Oakeshott warned against in "The Voice of Poetry." In that essay, however, Oakeshott did not caution against *superbia* in order to reject all relationships between voices, but to enhance conversation among them.

Paul Franco points to Oakeshott's reworking of Plato's allegory of the cave to support his contention that *On Human Conduct* maintains "the distinctively Oakeshottian gulf between theory and practice." He explains that Oakeshott's criticism "concerns Plato's contention that the understanding of the philosopher (alleged to be unconditional) is not only superior to, but a substitute for, every other conditional understanding."[54] There is nothing surprising here; Oakeshott would always disagree with a claim like Plato's: one type of understanding can never be substituted for another. However, Franco cites this as merely another example of what he earlier called the "inimicality of philosophy to practice." In dismissing the "Voice of Poetry," Franco has not recognized that Oakeshott conceived of a relationship that neither is the "substitution" of one form of understanding for another nor the imposition of an impassable gulf between them. When Oakeshott jettisoned the absolute idealism, with it went the language of complete separation of philosophy from the modes. However, in reconfiguring his skeptical idealism, Oakeshott maintained the commitment that no voice—including that of philosophy—expresses an absolute certainty; rather truth is always dependent upon certain conditions.

In Oakeshott's reinterpretation of the allegory of the cave, it is quite true that he warns against "the 'theoretician,' the *philosophe,* the 'intellectual,'" and against the consequences of a theorist presuming to speak with authority in matters of practice.[55] He does not say, however, that the philosopher can have no interaction with the cave dwellers. In Oakeshott's account of the allegory, when the philosopher returns to the cave, the dwellers there most likely treat him as an amiable and knowledgeable fellow, even if they grant him no authority based on his travels. Oakeshott suggests,

> The returned theorist . . . is recognized as a man with an unusual store of surprising information and also a fresh, questioning, unconventional intelligence. When he tells [the cave-dwellers] that what they have always thought of as 'a horse' is not what they suppose it to be . . . , but is, on the contrary, a modification of the attributes of God, he is clearly recognizable as a clever fellow from whom there is much to be learned.[56]

We may note a smirk here as we can imagine a cave-dweller's eyes glazing over at this depiction of a horse, although the handler who loves her horses may be found nodding her head. Nevertheless, while there may be some irony in the assessment of him as "a clever fellow," Oakeshott describes a relationship between the philosopher and the dwellers in the practical world that suggests neither the complete separation of the two, nor the substitution or dismissal of one for the other. Instead, Oakeshott suggests the possibility that those who live exclusively in the practical world may interact with and even learn much from the philosopher; they may be challenged, intrigued, surprised, or amused by the philosopher—and of course, they might not be.

In his detailed discussion of politics and political deliberation in *On Human Conduct* Oakeshott no more rejects a contingent, conversational relationship between theory and practice than he did in his account of the allegory of the cave. For Oakeshott, "Political engagement . . . is an exploration of *respublica* in terms of the desirability of the conditions it prescribes, and this entails a relationship to *respublica,* which is at once acquiescent and critical."[57] I am concerned here with the critical aspect of this relationship, for as Oakeshott describes it, "The ingredient of criticism, of questioning, and of non-acceptance is concerned with approval or disapproval and with desirabilities. Thus, engagement in politics entails a disciplined imagination."[58] We can glimpse already that the philosopher with his "unusual store of surprising information and also a fresh, questioning, unconventional intelligence," might here be an interesting character to have around. With the description of deliberation though, Oakeshott remains consistent in his admonition that the philosopher's seeming certainties lose that quality when it comes to politics. "A civil prescription then," Oakeshott contends, "cannot be shown to be desirable . . . by purporting to connect it inferentially with a superior norm of unquestionable or acknowledged desirability, a moral rule, a prescriptive law of reason or of Nature, a principle of utility, a categorical imperative or the like . . . no civil rule can be *deduced* from the Golden rule or from the Kantian categorical imperative."[59] Once again Oakeshott shows a concern with *ignoratio elenchi* and warns that in political deliberation we would be wrong to assume that we could "deduce" a civil rule from a philosophical system. This would mistakenly give authority to philosophical reasoning in the practical engagement of politics.

However, the engagement of political deliberation, "the exploration of *respublica* in terms of the desirability of the conditions it prescribes" and the "criticism . . . concerned with approval or disapproval and with desirabilities," is not an activity that exists on its own or is created *de novo.* Instead, Oakeshott suggests that "Every proposal for deliberate innovation in the conditions of conduct specified in a *respublica* is both an appeal to current achievements in civility and an exploration of the intimation of these achievements; and there is no mistake-proof manner of doing this."[60] There is little reason here to suppose that neither the philosopher, nor the achievements of philosophy, nor the engagement of philosophical reflection can contribute to this exploration of intimations. On the contrary, it is quite reasonable to assume this is one of the places in which there might be "much to be learned" from the philosopher. This is not because the philosopher has a "mistake-proof manner of doing this," but because the philosopher—not the theoretician—is likely to recognize the limited, circumstantial, and conditional nature of political proposals and achievements.

It is also quite likely that among "the current achievements in civility" are contributions of philosophers of the past: the characterization of a dilemma or concern, the coinage of a particular term or phrase, the style of types of arguments. For example Oakeshott includes many things in his discussion of education in *On Human Conduct*.[61] He claims that in practical activity "agents as historic persons composed of acquired beliefs, understandings, sentiments, imaginings, aptitudes, arts, skills, . . . themselves emerge in a transaction between the generations called education in which new comers to a local human scene are initiated into its 'mysteries.'"[62] Oakeshott is not explicit about the place of philosophy in "a local human scene," but certainly there is a place for philosophy in the composition that makes up an agent. This need not, however, conflict with his argument against the authority of philosophy in matters of practice. Consider, for instance, Oakeshott's claim that "no civil rule can be deduced from the Golden rule or from the Kantian categorical imperative." Yet certainly, among the "understandings, sentiments, aptitudes . . . of a local human scene" may be either the saying "Do unto others as you would have them do unto you," or the more complex rendering of Kant's categorical imperative. Oakeshott places no restriction on an agent who would attempt to persuade others to consider a situation in terms of the Golden rule or to elucidate a discussion over a proposed civil prescription by means of the categorical imperative. Should such a contribution to deliberation determine the solution regarding the "approval or disapproval" of a civil rule? Oakeshott would, of course, answer no. Does Oakeshott preclude referring to "a prescriptive law of reason or Nature, a principal of utility, a categorical imperative, or the like" in political deliberation? Again, the answer is no.

Political philosophy of the past then would be available as a resource in political deliberation, but what of an individual who engages in contemporary philosophical reflection, searching for theoretical understanding? Because political deliberation requires "a disciplined imagination" those engaged in it may be able to look to the philosopher or to their own philosophical reflections to help illuminate the difficulties encountered. Again, there is nothing necessary, certain, or determinate about this possibility. It is wholly dependent upon a practitioner of political deliberation being intrigued, inspired, or challenged by interaction with philosophy—not with its seeming certainties, but with its curiosities and questions. It may be that there is seldom time for philosophical reasoning for those engaged in heady political deliberation. It may also turn out that the problem faced or prescription under consideration is one to which philosophical reflection—past or present—is of no help. Each situation, however, is individual: the various contingent circumstances and the desires and abilities of the practitioners of politics will determine whether politics is enabled, distracted, or disabled by philosophy. The attempt to re-define a political problem once one has engaged or encountered philosophical reflection begins with an individual deliberator. If other practitioners with whom such a deliberator is engaged in politics are not impressed, that is all there is to be said.

Oakeshott is not concerned to abet an inimical divorce of practice from philosophy, of practical understanding from theoretical, politics from theory, but to recognize that each has authority only for itself and that neither has any authority, natural or otherwise, in the conversational meeting-place they share. What the cave-dweller learns from the philosopher is up to the cave-dweller—not the philosopher. While what the cave-dweller learns may be wrong or naive philosophy, it may still be a fine contribution for addressing the needs of an activity. Whether it is a useful addition or an irrelevant distraction will be determined by the demands of the activity, the skill of the practitioner, but not by the philosopher. It is perhaps easy to be fooled by the certainty of the "theoretician" with a plan, but warning against such a character in politics ought not be read as proscription against reflection in politics, even philosophical reflection. To categorically deny a place for philosophical reflection in politics would smack of the very certainty that Oakeshott questions.

IV

In 1959, Neal Wood explained Oakeshott's conception of philosophy in the following way: "Philosophy, therefore, is the search for the systematic, the development of a world of ideas, each a part of which is necessary and sufficient. The creation of such a system is the 'self conscious' and 'self-critical' effort to allow multi-form experience with elemental organic unity. . . . The *raison d'etre* of philosophic creativity is a vision of things as an integrated unity."[63] Yet, without the advantage of having read "The Voice of

Poetry," Wood argued that even *Experience and Its Modes,* evinced a "profound skepticism," and that "Oakeshott's conception of philosophy is fundamentally skeptical."[64] For Wood, Oakeshott's skepticism is partially revealed in the final inability of philosophy to achieve and sustain such a world. I have also argued that Oakeshott revealed a type of skepticism in his earlier work, but that it was restrained by such a vision of philosophy and experience, not a product of it. Whether attainable or not, the belief in the criterion of "elemental organic unity" that is unique to philosophy reveals a limit to Oakeshott's skepticism. The skepticism of "The Voice of Poetry" and *On Human Conduct* is more profound because Oakeshott has "abandon[ed] the idea of a monistic system of absolute coherence."[65]

I have characterized the shift in Oakeshott's skepticism as seen specifically in his alteration of this idea of philosophy, as typified in his re-description of philosophy as one voice among others in conversation. The relationship of philosophy to practice is important in this instance. Earlier, when philosophy was understood as experience fundamentally different from the various modifications of experience, he used the imagery of the "impassable gulf" to typify the relationship of philosophy and the different modes. Reconfigured, Oakeshott subjects philosophy to the same scrutiny as of forms and expressions of experience. The result is the allowance of a form of interaction, yet one that is typified by skepticism. It is a skepticism that rejects universal claims to truth and forms of discourse. Oakeshott's adoption of the metaphor of conversation then is both a sign and the substance of a strengthened skepticism.

Wood also claims that "The skepticism of Oakeshott's philosophical perspective is even more apparent when he discusses political activity."[66] Like Oakeshott's philosophy itself, however, Oakeshott's political philosophy undergoes change. It begins in the world in which we found Oakeshott, that of the British idealists, yet again exhibiting a type of skepticism. However, Oakeshott's conception of political philosophy follows a similar trajectory to that of his understanding of philosophical experience. I turn now to Oakeshott's earliest writings about politics to reveal the commitments there that he retains and transforms along with his ideas about philosophy.

Chapter Three

Oakeshott's Idealist Political Thought

I

"I venture to think that the prospects of political thought to-day are darker than even those of theology. For the theory of politics has fallen on evil days, its ideas are for the most part misappropriated, its words mere jargon, and it is too far gone in decay to allow of any sudden rejuvenation."[1] From an essay titled "The Authority of the State" published in 1929, these were Michael Oakeshott's first published comments concerning political philosophy. Given their tone, it would not be surprising if they had been his last. However, in the twenties and thirties, Oakeshott had begun to think much about politics. The extent of his thought on politics has become more evident recently as some previously unknown works and notebooks relating to political philosophy have been discovered posthumously, and some of these published for the first time.[2] As with Oakeshott's thoughts on philosophy, these early political works share a continuity with his later, more familiar works, such as those in *Rationalism in Politics;* yet these are also primarily focused on the concerns of idealism and expressed in its idiom. The genesis of the concerns that mark Oakeshott's later work is here (e.g., the interest in authority, caution about democracy, dislike of contract theory), but the basis of those concerns is not a quiet reflection on English tradition, but once again philosophical idealism. It will take a developed appreciation for Hobbes to alter the character of Oakeshott's political thought, and before exploring that alteration in the next chapter, I will here examine what was there to be altered.

In the last two chapters I have reviewed various interpretations of Oakeshott that seem to result in a common two-part claim: 1) Oakeshott's philosophical outlook is substantially unchanged from his earliest writings to his last, and 2) Oakeshott's political philosophy is a reflection of this general philosophical outlook. I have challenged the first of these. The second part of this claim, however, is more complicated. Oakeshott's thought on politics is the reflection of a general outlook, but as that outlook changes, so do his conceptions of political philosophy. To appreciate how fully skeptical Oakeshott's later, better-known political philosophy is, it is important to see how closely connected his earliest political thought is to the absolute idealism of the early period. Just as elements of Oakeshott's later skepticism could be seen in this period, so also later aspects of his political philosophy can be glimpsed there. But just as it took the quiet abandonment of the idealism for the skepticism to bloom, so also with his thoughts on politics. I begin then by examining Oakeshott's consideration of the state and its authority, because "The Authority of the State," perhaps more than any other essay, reveals what a political philosophy dependent upon Oakeshott's early idealism would look like.

II

"The Authority of the State" was actually only the third essay that Oakeshott had published (and only the second for an audience wider than Cambridge University), and he says nothing to indicate why he would take up the authority of the state as a topic to investigate. He neither claims to be responding to any argument that has been made nor to situate himself in any debate. However, his concerns as a student of the British idealists in the twenties may not be too difficult to surmise. Recall that in *Experience and Its Modes* he had admitted that much "abuse" had been "reserved for philosophical Idealism, which (it is the common opinion) is dead."[3] The same mortal fate had befallen the idealist conception of the state.

The last great full-blown exposition of the state by an idealist had been Bernard Bosanquet's *The Philosophical Theory of the State,* originally published in 1899, but put out in a fresh edition with a substantial new introduction in 1909, and again in 1919.[4] In the years between the second and third edition of this work, L. T. Hobhouse responded to Bosanquet with *The Metaphysical Theory of the State,* which Stefan Collini argues "is still considered as the standard, and most devastating, criticism of Idealist political theory in English."[5] Closer to Oakeshott's writing, the Aristotelian Society in 1928 held a symposium dedicated specifically to the element of Bosanquet's theory that had caused Hobhouse such grief: the general will. As if to put another nail in the coffin of idealist political theory A. D. Lindsay and H. J. Laski each again struck out to dismantle the theory of the state and general will as found in Bosanquet.[6] By the late twenties, the idealist theory of the state was thus highly contested, even in ill-repute. In discussing the authority of the state, Oakeshott conveniently ignores the recent, rocky history of idealist political thought and ventures into the morass.

Oakeshott follows what seems to be a straightforward conceptual analysis in a subtle fashion by proposing to pursue three questions in "The Authority of the State": "First, What do we mean by authority? secondly, what do we mean by the state; and thirdly, where, then, is the authority of the state?"[7] I call this subtle because while he announces these elements of the inquiry as if they were separate parts to be assembled, actually each implies the other for Oakeshott. To get at this complex congeries of ideas then, we must follow Oakeshott through each of the concepts, and then to their combination; for while Oakeshott claims to be interested in what "we mean by authority" and "the state," it becomes clear right away that Oakeshott is really interested in what is implied by these concepts beyond what we usually mean by them. This strategy also allows for insight not only to his thoughts but also to his idealist method. Oakeshott first suggests two possible strategies for answering a question like "What do we mean by authority?" "It may be suggested that it is unnecessary to go beyond what is commonly understood by the word; or if, as we shall discover, the common meaning not be entirely unambiguous, all we require is agreement upon some definite meaning"; these, however, he rejects: "The common meaning, as such, will satisfy us no more than a merely agreed meaning; what we desire is a coherent and unambiguous conception of authority. We must, no doubt, start with the common meaning of the word, but we can escape its inconsistencies, not by agreeing upon some arbitrary definition, but by transforming them into a coherent whole. And that is what I propose to attempt."[8] Here we quickly see that Oakeshott is really less concerned with what "we mean" by authority than with pursuing what is implied by our incoherent but common usage of words like authority, "transforming them into a coherent whole." Now, this essay was published four years before *Experience and Its Modes,* but we can already see in it a way of thinking to be fully developed in that later work. There is an understanding of authority that is common, but also finally incoherent and unsatisfactory; the "inconsistencies" of such a concept must be escaped, however, not by mere rejection, but through transformation. A final important common element at this stage is the very idea that inconsistencies can finally be purged and that the result will be "a coherent whole," as he understood the transformative capacities of philosophy in *Experience and Its Modes.*

Oakeshott begins by suggesting that "there are two points in the common view of the meaning of authority," and these are that authority is "external and coercive."[9] He gives two examples of what he means by this "common view":

> Whenever a man adopts an opinion without himself going through the appropriate process of reasoning that would bring him to that conclusion, but because it is presented to him complete by some one who he thinks more competent than himself, his belief is said to be the work of "authority." And on the other side, whoever converses dogmatically, "like a law giver," forcing opinions into the minds of his audience speaks as an authority.[10]

In this understanding, there is an "external" source of authority, seen either in the expertise possessed by an individual in a certain engagement, or in the capacity of an individual who is able to compel beliefs, assent, or action. Authority, in the common view, is external to the individual over whom it is exercised, possessed by the person who exercises it. The problem with this conception of authority for Oakeshott is that by focusing on the external it confuses the "*cause* of belief, opinion, or action" with what he calls "its whole *ground,* and it would be absurd to maintain that the power which actually compels a belief belongs merely to its cause."[11] This is an important distinction, but one that Oakeshott does not fully explain. His complaint assumes there is such a thing as "the whole ground" that is identifiable by reflective inquiry. However, Oakeshott does not here explain what would constitute "the whole ground" or why this "common meaning" cannot satisfy for quotidian purposes.

Since authority does not rest—at least not exclusively upon an external element, Oakeshott looks to an internal capacity for the ground of authority: judgment. He provides examples:

> The cause of our belief that a certain man is guilty of murder may be the knowledge that he was convicted in a court of law; the ground of this belief, however, is not the bare consciousness of the verdict, but a judgement we make about the whole body of evidence brought against him, or (failing a detailed acquaintance with that), an independent judgement, resting upon and guaranteed by our whole world of ideas, that those who have sifted the evidence are competent to arrive at a true conclusion.[12]

In order for someone such as a "law-giver" or an expert or something like a verdict to possess authority, "an independent judgement" needs to be made about that body of evidence or the person accused and convicted or persons rendering the verdict. He maintains "that which compels us to hold a belief which was derived from some external source—a book, a person, or a tradition—is not the 'authority' of the source (for it can in itself have none) but *some judgement we make* about its reliability, or indeed, a reason utterly unconnected with the source of belief."[13] Here authority is grounded in the judgement that a "we"—yet to be identified—makes about the external source of belief. The authority of what is external is "derivative and dependent" upon that judgement.[14] Therefore, Oakeshott maintains, "We accept such an authority not on its own recognition, but for reasons which lie outside its jurisdiction."[15] He has reversed what is "external" in authority. Authority is not external to the person over whom it is exercised, but external to the exerciser of authority, since it rests in the judgment by the former about the latter, sustained by reasons independent of the claims of authority.[16] But notice also Oakeshott's invocation of the need for "the whole ground" of authority and his claim that this whole ground is "our whole world of ideas." He is not at all clear concerning what he means by such a whole world of ideas. We have seen that later, in *Experience and Its Modes,* Oakeshott will contrast the totality or whole world of ideas with the limited worlds of ideas—modes. Here, however, the two appear to be combined. I point this out because the examples he provides seem not to imply the exercise of judgment of the whole world of ideas, but a limited set of ideas or judgments about a particular verdict, person or belief. Such a judgment may cohere well, poorly, or not at all, and it might connect with only some or more or all of the ideas that act as the ground of authority. It might be that Oakeshott understands these two aspects to be combined; he simply does not reveal their connections.

I have been discussing the claims about externality, but Oakeshott's description of the "common view" of authority had two parts: authority was "external and coercive." He took pains to examine and transform the former, and now the latter element of coercion remains. However, Oakeshott advances, "I take it that only a measure of perversity which can expect no reply will question the supposition that coerciveness is inseparable from whatever is actually authoritative."[17] Given his earlier claims, this is surely curious. Here Oakeshott simply accepts the "common view" without transforming it in the manner he has suggested is necessary. If we merely accept the supposition that authority and coerciveness are inseparable, then we have a large portion of our definition simply provided for us, but without engaging the same critical faculties that Oakeshott used to question authority's supposed externality. Oakeshott continues, "that which does not actually compel belief or action, and from the command of which there is no appeal, is not in the full sense authoritative; and conversely, that which is really coercive of belief and action is the authority upon which they rest."[18] The difficulties of not examining this "common view" abound. First, his claim implies a circular definition: authority is coercive because without coercion it would not be authoritative. Second, Oakeshott does not explain what he means by coercive; does he mean only brute physical force, or other forms of the exercise of power? He has just argued that authority is not external, but then he leaves undeveloped the way in which coercion (or "that which actually compels" or "power," other terms he uses in this context) is internal or how it combines with judgment.

It is this unexamined coerciveness that increases the difficulty with Oakeshott's conception of authority. Having first based authority upon judgment, he goes on to speak of authority's coerciveness, which takes on the character of something independent of or external to any recognizable "us." He claims:

> an authority is always its own sanction. That which is authoritative is, thus, absolute and unlimited, not in the sense of embracing every detail, but because there can be no appeal from it. The real authority of all belief and action is that which can show itself to be absolute, irresponsible, self-supporting, and inescapable. Also, that which is authoritative is always single and indivisible; for a series of reasons which really compels a belief is the necessary foundation of that belief, and a foundation, as such, is always a unity.[19]

What begins as a recognition of the character of authority as limited to the judgment of those over whom it is exercised is now converted into that which is "absolute, irresponsible, self-supporting and inescapable . . . single and indivisible." Oakeshott does not simply reject the externality of authority, but externality altogether. In a preview of the language he uses so often in *Experience and Its Modes*, Oakeshott himself summarizes his discussion of authority: "In short, then, that which alone has the power to coerce belief or action, and which is consequently the only final authority, is our world of ideas as a whole."[20] This whole "world of ideas" lies behind and beyond the judgement which originally acted as the ground of authority, and it is this "which alone has the power to coerce." He does, however, seem to let externality in the side door in his discussion of the "cause" of belief.

Nonetheless, this conception of authority is dependent upon the idea of a "whole world of ideas" and a notion of the authoritative that is "single and indivisible," the contention that the set of reasons that would lead to a judgment about authority comprise "a foundation . . . [which] is always a unity." These are complex ideas, and once again resound with the absolute idealism that will characterize Oakeshott's conception of philosophical experience in *Experience and Its Modes.* However, at this stage, Oakeshott does not provide arguments for them. His ideas here reveal the monism, the coherence theory of truth, the desire for the concrete universal, and the ideas about internal relations that are the central elements of absolute idealism I discussed in Chapter One. Yet the skeptical aspect of Oakeshott's idealism is evident as well. Authority does not come from without, it is not based on an external claim like universal natural law that humans can know through reason and with certainty, but is instead built on the judgment of persons. As I have argued in Chapter Two, Oakeshott eventually abandons the conception of the coherent and absolute "world of ideas as a whole." In doing so, he will have to reconfigure his conception of authority, because it would mean also abandoning the "whole ground" he claims for it. The absolute idealist referral to the "whole world of ideas" as the "final authority" must and indeed does change as Oakeshott relinquishes his absolute idealism and with it the ground of the world of ideas as a whole. What does not need to change, at least not dramatically, is the skeptical recognition that authority does not rest upon something external but rather is merely based in the judgment or recognition about the capacity or office of authority related to the belief or action in question.

In contemplating authority, Oakeshott examined a concept that had not been central to the political theories of earlier idealists. In discussing the state, however, he takes up a concept that his immediate forebears in the British idealist tradition dwelled upon.[21] Oakeshott adds little to the conception of the state he inherits; however, his analysis is worthy of consideration for two connected reasons. First, it reveals that not just Oakeshott's conception of philosophy in *Experience and Its Modes,* but the political philosophy of this early period was closely linked to the British idealist tradition. Second, and more importantly, it also allows a perspective on the meaningful changes in Oakeshott's political philosophy once he abandons the absolute idealism of this early period. Oakeshott will later discuss the state, but quite differently from the way he does here.

As he had with authority, Oakeshott begins by reviewing common views of the state. Each of the conceptions that he examines, that the state is "a piece of territory," "a collections of persons," "persons organized for secular purposes," or "the political machinery of government in a community," is dismissed because each is "abstract."[22] That is, they draw out one set of relations and assume the state in all its manifestations are reflected in or subordinate to that set. As he will claim in *Experience and Its Modes* regarding the modes, abstractions may have some use within their abstract worlds, but in the end they are not fully satisfactory. He claims, "Many conceptions of the state are defective because they result not in facts, but in fictions, such as society as politically, or ecclesiastically, or industrially organized. The limitations of such conceptions as these make them useful in practical life, but if we set out to construct a complete conception, these and their like must disappear."[23] For example, referring to government and politics, Oakeshott claims, "Men as governed are abstractions, for no man is merely what the government as such thinks he is; and consequently the political whole which such 'persons' constitute is an abstraction also."[24] There may be an important use for such abstractions, but they do not reflect the entirety of social relations. Notice that Oakeshott has slipped into the assumption that the state must in fact be reflective of all these relations. That is, while "government" may be an abstract relation, by implication, "the state" is not. The state must be a concrete concept, for "the state . . . is a conception we may permit ourselves to call a fact only when we have made it clear to ourselves and complete in itself."[25]

In taking the state as an all-inclusive set of relations, the social equivalent of monism, and in dismissing the "political machinery of government" or "the political whole" as satisfactory for an understanding of the state, Oakeshott is again following closely the idealist understanding of the state. Following Hegel, Bosanquet understood "the Political Organism, or the state in the strict sense," to be only one element in a fully philosophical understanding of the state.[26] Only in combination with other social institutions, specifically the family and "Bourgeois society" can the political state be understood as the state as a whole.[27] The state then, in the idealist understanding, is inclusive of the whole of social relations, more than "the state in the strict sense." The political state is an abstraction, but from what is it an abstraction? An absolute or whole that precedes it, the notional monism of total social relations. It is in the depiction of this absolute, which is implied by and supersedes the various abstractions, that Oakeshott finally provides his conception of the state.

> If it is to be a concrete fact, the state must be self-subsistent, something which carries with it the explanation of itself and requires to be linked on to no more comprehensive whole in order to be understood. And it appears to me that nothing fulfills these conditions save the social whole which is

correlative to the individuals who are complete and living persons; or in other words, the totality in an actual community which satisfies the whole mind of the individuals that comprise it.[28]

Paul Franco has commented that "Oakeshott here seems to end up with a full-blown Hegelian definition of the state, an impression that is confirmed when he goes on to reject the separation of the state from society."[29] Franco is exactly right in this regard, for once again Oakeshott's claim follows directly on the heels of his idealist predecessors.[30] Consider, for instance, Bosanquet's claim, "The term the 'State' accepts indeed the political aspect of the whole. . . . But it includes the entire hierarchy of institutions by which life is determined, from the family to trade, and from trade to the Church and the University. . . . It follows that the state in this sense, is, above all things, not a number of persons, but a working conception of life."[31] Bosanquet's conception "the whole," of which the political only makes up a part that makes up the state, gets at the same idea that Oakeshott would later with his conception of the "social whole."[32]

Oakeshott later came to reject outright this loosely defined understanding of the state as "the social whole," construing what he here calls abstractions differently. He later conceived of these abstractions as conditions that provide meaning and distinction. For example, almost fifty years later in *On Human Conduct,* Oakeshott maintains, "Agents cannot be associated in respect of no conditions in particular; and there can be no unconditional association. . . . And of course, there can be no social consciousness which is not the consciousness of a *socius* that is, of a particular agent understanding himself to be associated with others in recognizing the conditions of some specific practice."[33] Oakeshott would have later considered the conception of the state from the earlier essay to be an ill-defined notion of the social whole. By not allowing of modification this conception also does not allow the actual practices of specific agents to be recognized, because each of these is viewed as an abstraction from the social whole. In fact, Oakeshott's negative appraisal of the association of the state with society as a whole that he develops in his later work is reflective of the criticism that Hobhouse made of Bosanquet's conception of the state. In criticizing the identification of the state with the social whole, Hobhouse asks,

Is the state then another name for the entire social fabric, for the family, for the mass of one's social interests, for science, art, literature, and religion? To the modern mind, at any rate to the non-German mind, the question answers itself in the negative. . . . Underlying Bosanquet's account, in fact, there is a serious confusion between state and society. The state is at present necessary to society, but it is only one of its conditions.[34]

Here Hobhouse argues that if there is anything like a social whole, it is only the contingent confluence of the variety of conditional associations of which the state is only one—a recognizably Oakeshottian idea. I have suggested there is a parallel between Oakeshott's early understanding of the state as a social whole and the monism of his understanding of philosophical experience in *Experience and Its Modes*. It is not surprising then that as the one is rejected so is the other.

In "The Authority of the State," Oakeshott rejects as incomplete the differing, limited conceptions of the state; still, as in *Experience and Its Modes*, he does not completely deny the practicality of limited or abstract understandings of the state and individuals so related. Again, he claims "the limitations of such conceptions as these make them useful in practical life." This attitude remains then through *Experience and Its Modes* and into the later *On Human Conduct*. What disappears is the idea of a "complete conception." With this much else will change as well; for instance, another manner in which he conceptualizes the state is surprisingly related to the satisfaction of needs. In "The Authority of the State," Oakeshott claims "All activity directed toward the satisfaction of the needs of concrete persons is state activity."[35] This might be a way to delve more deeply into Oakeshott's conception of the state, yet he swiftly moves past this claim, providing no discussion of what comprises "needs."[36] However, it is not important for him to have done so to see a contrast with his later more familiar work. As I discuss more fully in Chapters Five and Six, the understanding of the state as related to the satisfaction of needs is one Oakeshott recognizes as conceivable, but also one he explicitly rejects. In fact, satisfaction of needs is fundamental in his eventual development of the contrasting concepts of "enterprise association" and "civil association," the former of which he rejects as a model for the state because it may entertain any teleological goal including especially the satisfaction of needs.

Oakeshott admits that he is moving a bit quickly, not pausing to develop each claim he makes about the state. Concerning his conception of the state as "the social whole" Oakeshott concedes with some candor "I cannot now enter into all the implications of this conception of the state, and indeed I cannot pretend that they are all as clear to me as I should wish."[37] For a philosopher who had just claimed that "The state . . . is a conception we may permit ourselves to call a fact only when we have made it clear to ourselves and complete in itself," it would seem a hazardous strategy to continue. Nonetheless, he goes on to consider his third question about the combination of the two terms he has examined independently: "the authority of the state." Perhaps not surprisingly given his statement about the political state, Oakeshott rejects immediately the idea that the government might be where we can find the authority of the state, "For no government, as such, was ever a strictly sovereign power, or ever had more than derivative 'authority.' "[38] But what then of the social whole of the collected concrete persons that make up the state? He considers and then dispatches the idea that authority rests in the "consent" of "the people," and this for two reasons: "in the first place, consent can never create or maintain authority; . . . and secondly, what is this 'people' whose will as such is supposed to be the authority behind government? It is, in fact, never more than a class in a community, a fluctuating and elusive majority."[39] The first of these two objections rests uncomfortably on Oakeshott's earlier understanding of authority. On the one hand, the fact that there may be no actual historical experience of consent being given may be a reasonably good reason to reject it, although in other matters Oakeshott might consider this a mere confusion of the actual with the real. However, even if consent is or has been given, that could not be the basis of the authority of the state: "Mere consent may be given or withheld, but whatever is really authoritative is absolute and independent of acceptance and recognition."[40] A confusing claim, since in his first discussion, it was a "recognition" in the form of a judgment that was the ground of authority. But with the introduction of the need for authority to be "absolute and independent" this ground for authority is lost; it does not partake of the "whole world of ideas."

"Where, then, is the authority of the state?" Oakeshott asks.[41] It exists in a complex combination of certain elements of the two concepts he had defined as authority and the state.

> If actual authority belong [sic] only to the whole ground of a belief or action, if such an authority is absolute and inescapable, and if (further) the only conception of the state which escapes the tint of abstraction is that which considers it to be the totality of conditions which fulfills the needs of the concrete persons, the whole ground of their actions and beliefs, then the authority of the state can reside nowhere save in the state itself as such. . . . [It] resides solely in the completeness of the satisfaction which the state itself affords to the needs of concrete persons.[42]

Now indeed, Franco's claim that "Oakeshott here seems to end up with a full-blown Hegelian definition of the state" seems to be fully merited. The invocation of the "state itself as such," which is its own authority, as the only possible repository for the authority of the state rings true not only with that tradition, but with those idealist elements we have seen above. As for the latter, this passage, of course, depends upon the three "ifs" in order for its "then" to be convincing. Some of these have been more and some less convincing, and even Oakeshott admits his conception of the state is "less clear." Each of the elements, however, is an aspect of his discussion that reveals the assumptions of absolute idealism, and skepticism does not make it into these concluding remarks. For instance, in the understanding of authority as first laid out, the ground of authority was that of "an independent judgement" concerning whatever claimed authority, and thus authority was internal. At this later stage in the argument, Oakeshott claims "whatever is really authoritative is absolute and independent of acceptance and recognition." This latter, more fully idealist claim is what predominates in deciding where the authority of the state resides. The same is true of his emphasis upon the need for "the whole ground" and "the totality of conditions which fulfills the needs of the concrete persons." Each of these reveals the strong idealist elements of Oakeshott's discussion.

However, as closely as this discussion of the state resembles Hegel, and the British idealists influenced by him, there is an important and unannounced alteration: Oakeshott has no conception of the state in history. Oakeshott's conception of the state and its authority lacks entirely the teleological aspirations of Hegel. In Chapters One and Two, I observed that in *Experience and Its Modes,* Oakeshott explicitly denied that there was a set pattern of stages through which an individual or society must pass in order to achieve philosophical experience. There was no hierarchy or teleology for the modes. Here too, Oakeshott does not see the state as a social and coherent whole that is achieved over time. Rather, in examining the "common view" or "common meaning" of the authority of the state, Oakeshott wants to take up what is implicit and transform it "into a coherent whole." For Hegel, according to Charles Taylor, "man is the vehicle of cosmic spirit and . . . the state expresses the underlying formula of necessity by which the spirit posses the world."[43] Oakeshott does not explicitly dismiss this but ignores it, expressing nothing about the state's place in the history of spirit. However, it would seem that to ignore something so central to Hegelian political philosophy as the "theodicy" of the state is in fact to dismiss it.[44]

Oakeshott had admitted some anxiety about political philosophy, judging that "the theory of politics . . . is too far gone in decay to allow of any sudden rejuvenation." He however attempted at least a small element of rejuvenation by bringing a well-known tradition of thought, that of idealism, to bear on a fresh topic, that of authority. He adds little to that tradition in terms of its theory of the state, except by subtracting its teleology. Instead he shows himself adept at exercising the vocabulary and addressing the concerns of idealism. The importance of showing this close association with idealist political philosophy in this period is that, as I have argued, he abandons this tradition after the thirties. Elements of his thinking from this period remain, but as in his general philosophy, it changes as he rejects the absolute idealism in which it was first expressed. Of what remains, the most important element is the placement of the ground of authority in judgment of those over whom authority is exercised. That is, regardless of his concluding argument that authority is "absolute and independent of our acceptance and recognition," Oakeshott clings to a stronger claim that authority is not external, and in fact uses the term recognition to characterize the ground of authority. However, most of what Oakeshott outlines in "The Authority of the State" he leaves behind or even explicitly rebuffs when he returns in full force to political philosophy.

Oakeshott, perhaps inadvertently, provides a clue to what will help to sculpt these changes in the very last line of "The Authority of the State." Here not Hegel but Hobbes makes an appearance as Oakeshott appraises this "absolute and inescapable authority" of the state, professing "Of this authority, and of no other, can it be said: *Non est potestas super terram quae comperatur ei.*"[45] With these words of Job from the frontispiece of Hobbes's famous work, Oakeshott associates his conception of the authority of the state with that of the great Leviathan. But Hobbes here rests lightly on Oakeshott's thought about politics; in fact, when Oakeshott insists "of this authority and no other" can these word be said, it seems more a rebuff to Hobbes than an encomium. Hobbes will yet have his day, but only after Oakeshott spends another decade working through philosophical idealism.

III

The "prospects of political thought" must have been darker even than Oakeshott had first thought in 1929. For while "The Authority of the State" is one of his first publications, it is also his last in political thought for a while. Throughout the thirties Oakeshott wrote some book reviews of political works, and a few occasional pieces, but the bulk of his attention was given to philosophy proper, culminating in his opus *Experience and Its Modes.* It seems as though the complexities of the idealist theories of the state were sufficiently unclear to Oakeshott that he found it necessary to step back and examine the pre-conditions not only for politics but for a variety of conditional forms experience. What is the impact of this venture on Oakeshott's understanding of the activity and provenance of political philosophy? It has been clear in discussions of *Experience and Its Modes* that Oakeshott's concept of philosophy was centrally important. What then, for him, is political philosophy in this idealist stage?

In *Experience and Its Modes,* political philosophy actually plays a very small role, at least explicitly. In that work Oakeshott had depicted Historical, Scientific, and Practical Experience as the three established and sustained arrests in experience. Each of these, while limited from the perspective of full or complete experience, were worlds of ideas in their own right. Oakeshott maintains that there are also other arrests in experience, but these do not sustain worlds of ideas. These other arrests are a type of experience he calls "indeterminate modification of experience," in contrast to the "determinate modification experience" of the modes, and he labels it as "pseudo-philosophical experience."[46] It is "pseudo-philosophical" because while it is arrested experience, its world of ideas is actually the concrete world of ideas since it cannot maintain its own determinate world.[47] This sort of experience and fully or truly philosophical experience then share the world of concrete ideas. Oakeshott explains, however, "the difference . . . between a pseudo-philosophical idea and a philosophical idea is not that they belong to different worlds, but that while one is ignorant of its world, the other recognizes it."[48] Thus there are actually three types of experience, not two. So far in *Experience and Its Modes,* Oakeshott had emphasized the primary contrast between worlds of modified experience and the system of absolute and fully coherent experience. This third type of experience is part of the concrete world of ideas even though it does not recognize or accept this placement; thus, it is pseudophilosophical experience.

The discussion of pseudophilosophy comes very late in the book, and Oakeshott claims not to be interested in exploring the various indeterminate arrests, rather offering only a single illustration. This discussion of pseudophilosophical experience is the only place in *Experience and Its Modes* where Oakeshott mentions political philosophy—and he does not even use it as the illustration. Instead his focus is on ethics. "Ethical thought," Oakeshott maintains "as I understand it, is an indeterminate arrest in experience . . . it is a philosophical error; and I shall use it for the purpose of illustrating what I take to be the general character of all pseudo-philosophical experience."[49] Here, in a footnote to the discussion of ethical thought—not at all in the discussion proper—Oakeshott mentions political philosophy as one of the various examples of pseudophilosophical thought.

The name 'Moral Philosophy' indicates, I think, the character of ethical thought. It is philosophical thought, but qualified and limited philosophical thought. And where philosophical thought is qualified and limited, it at once falls short of its philosophical character. The same general character belongs to Theology, to so-called Political Philosophy, and (I think) to Psychology.[50]

Oakeshott's observations on political philosophy at this early stage, as with moral philosophy, show his fundamental concern about its character as a "pseudo-philosophical experience." Political philosophy may be philosophical, but it resides somehow in a purgatory between the limited, yet determinate worlds of experience of the modes and the unconditional, unqualified experience of the concrete world of ideas or true philosophy. Political philosophy, as Oakeshott says about ethical thought, "is incapable of constituting itself as a self-determined, homogenous world of its own."[51] Since on Oakeshott's own terms he considered *Experience and Its Modes* a philosophical endeavor, it is with caution that we should attempt to understand it, or any part of it, as political philosophy.

This caution is necessary because one might be drawn to view the long chapter on "Practical Experience" as an early form of Oakeshott's political philosophy; yet for Oakeshott, his consideration of practical experience is in the manner of criticism and rejection as it is with all the modes. Again, his comments upon ethics may resolve this paradox. On the one hand, ethical thought is philosophical because it belongs to the concrete world of ideas; on the other hand, it is limited and abstract because it is focused exclusively upon a limited world of experience, in this case the world of practical experience. Ethics is unsatisfactory, "pseudo-philosophical experience" because by attempting both to elucidate and to dissolve the character of an abstract world it contradicts itself. "In short," Oakeshott claims, "ethics is taken to be the attempt to define, to discover the ultimate character of the main concepts and categories of practical experience."[52] And yet, since this attempt at definition is within the concrete world of ideas, Oakeshott maintains, ethics cannot help but dissolve the very concepts it examines. "In short" he asserts,

ethics is the consideration of evaluation and practical judgement from the standpoint of the totality of experience, and since valuation and practical judgement are defective from this standpoint, *it is impossible to explain them without explaining them, as such, away.* . . . Ethical thought is simply the application of the solvent force of the totality of experience to the abstract world of practical experience.[53]

To reject what is limited is, of course, the goal of philosophy as Oakeshott had defined it. But the fault of ethics, as with all pseudophilosophical experience, is that it does not intend the rejection it achieves. Ethics "is not the attempt to find and maintain a world of experience wholly satisfactory in experience, but merely the attempt to see one particular mode experience—practical experience—from the standpoint of total experience."[54] Ethics is, in the end, self-contradictory or self-defeating because it destroys what it strives to explain; it is an arrest—if indeterminate—in the concrete totality of experience.

Again, what then are we to make of Oakeshott's own consideration of practical experience (or either of the other modes)? Is it ethics (or the philosophy of history or science)? Is he himself guilty of the very pseudophilosophy that he here condemns as "fail[ing] to provide what is satisfactory in experience?" At least as he outlines and understands his project in *Experience and Its Modes,* it would seem he is not. Oakeshott contends throughout that work that he examines the various modes not for their own sake, but to determine whether or not they provide what is wholly satisfactory; and he certainly has no hesitation in rejecting each world of ideas when it fails to offer what he seeks. Political philosophy, as pseudophilosophy, as an indeterminate arrest, would seem to have little attraction for Oakeshott. Trained as a historian, the limited, yet determinate world of historical experience, certainly would have its restricted satisfactions; and, of course, philosophical experience was what he understood to be finally and fully satisfactory. Yet Oakeshott does return to political philosophy, even in this early period. I turn next to another consideration of political philosophy by Oakeshott that reveals a development of the themes in *Experience and Its Modes,* in an essay that was written, I will suggest, not long after that work.

IV

"The Concept of a Philosophy of Politics" is an essay that Oakeshott chose not to publish during his life and has only recently become available. Timothy Fuller, the editor of the collection in which it is included, judges that the essay "was written in the mid-1940s, around the time that Oakeshott was producing his edition of Hobbes's *Leviathan.*"[55] I, however, want to use this piece as an example of Oakeshott's political philosophy in the thirties, and also argue that there are changes in his conception of political philosophy by the mid-forties. This, of course, throws Fuller's dating into question. His placing of the essay in 1946 appears to be based upon Oakeshott's introductory paragraph. There Oakeshott states, "Lately I have had occasion to consider the writings of Hobbes."[56] It is not unreasonable to assume that Oakeshott was speaking of his "Introduction to *Leviathan,*" which, it appears, was the source of Fuller's dating.[57] However, when Oakeshott writes that he has "had occasion to consider the writings of Hobbes," he may instead be writing in the mid-to-late thirties, referring to either or both an essay on Hobbes he published in 1936 simply titled "Thomas Hobbes" or to a rather lengthy review of Leo Strauss's *The Political Philosophy of Hobbes,* which he published in 1937.[58] Oakeshott's comments from the introductory paragraph of "The Concept of a Philosophy of Politics" are general enough that they could apply to the earlier pieces or the "Introduction," and so from it one cannot tell to which occasion of consideration he may be referring. Beyond this, there are some specific pieces of evidence that make it at least plausible, and perhaps likely, that Oakeshott wrote this piece in the thirties.

First, and most importantly, in the thirties Oakeshott did write several pages of this essay and publish them in 1938 as part of "The Concept of a Philosophical Jurisprudence." The pages numbered 127-131 in "The Concept of a Philosophy of Politics" were published almost word for word on pages 345-350 of "The Concept of a Philosophical Jurisprudence."[59] In both cases these pages contain a discussion of the character of philosophical "thought" (in "Philosophy of Politics") or "enquiry" (in "Philosophical Jurisprudence"). Several paragraphs are exactly the same, especially in the discussion of what he considers "the four characteristics or attributes of the philosophical concept."[60] Altogether, almost a quarter of "The Concept of a Philosophy of Politics" is included as part of "The Concept of a Philosophical Jurisprudence," an essay Oakeshott published almost ten years earlier than when Fuller dates the former. Second, there is also a notable similarity in the titles of these two essays. This may seem minor, but in each case the title of the piece reveals a particular and common approach to the subject. In both essays, Oakeshott is concerned with "The Concept of" a provisional philosophical inquiry, distancing his work from a consideration of the subject matter itself, exploring instead the presuppositions of such an endeavor of reflection. This similarity in title of the two pieces contrasts with the dissimilarity of the title of another previously unpublished essay, "Political Philosophy," which Fuller judges to have been written between 1946 and 1950.[61] Here Oakeshott reveals no reluctance as he had earlier about the notion of political philosophy. Finally, there are many distinctive similarities of locution between "The Concept of a Philosophy of Politics" and the "Concept of a Philosophical Jurisprudence" essay and other works written in the period I am discussing that increase the likelihood it was written then. It is always possible that the composition of the essay spread over many years, beginning at least in the period when he wrote the passages shared with "The Concept of a Philosophical Jurisprudence" and concluding sometime after he wrote his "Introduction to *Leviathan.*" If this is the case, then it is worth noticing, since it exhibits the idealist themes that I argue are solidly based in the absolute idealism he was abandoning in the decades following the thirties and Oakeshott chose not to publish it.[62] In any case, it is at least plausible to take this piece as indicative of his understanding of political philosophy in the thirties.

In exploring the concept of a philosophy of politics, Oakeshott adopts the same beginning strategy as he had in "The Authority of the State." He starts with the "ideas on this subject which I found in my head [which] were, I think the usual ideas," much like the common views earlier, and he commences to submit these to reflective examination.[63] The central attitude of most of these "usual ideas" is that a philosophy of politics is "the application of certain previously thought-out philosophical ideas, or of some previously thought-out philosophical doctrine, to political life and activity."[64] Such an application should then be able either to explain political life or give it a philosophical foundation. Whether one begins with a political practice and looks for a philosophical understanding of it, or begins with philosophy and turns to the activity of politics, a relationship between them is postulated. Reprising the refrain from *Experience and Its Modes,* Oakeshott immediately rejects this concept of political philosophy as being self-contradictory. To the extent that it remains focused upon what is given in politics, it is not entirely philosophical, and conversely, a philosophy of politics "which itself became genuinely philosophical would at once defeat its own end. It would return into the general philosophical theory from which it was, in fact, derived, and cease to have any connection with political life and activity."[65] This contradiction is made even more intransigent by what Oakeshott sees as the common insistence that a philosophy of politics "must, at all costs, conform to the 'facts of political life,'" which brings in the anomalous result that "a philosophy of politics [under this conception], therefore is likely to be unsound if it partakes too fully of a philosophical character."[66] In *Experience and Its Modes,* it was this self-contradictory character that led Oakeshott to dismiss political philosophy as pseudophilosophy. A philosophy of politics is neither of the world of practice itself, nor is it true to its own philosophical world of concrete experience. However, in "A Concept of a Philosophy of Politics" this contradiction is exhibited only in "the usual ideas" regarding a philosophy of politics. Here he offers something not conceived of in *Experience and Its Modes:* a noncontradictory philosophy of politics.[67]

The concept of a philosophy of politics that Oakeshott does offer is one that bears the character of philosophy that he developed in *Experience and Its Modes.* He maintains:

> A philosophy of politics I should describe in general terms, as—*an explanation or view of political life from the standpoint of the totality of experience.* It is the attempt, not to *separate* political life and activity from everything else in human experience and to treat them as if they were *sui generis* and belonged to a world of their own; but in the first place, to *distinguish* political life and activity within the totality of experience; and secondly, to *relate* them to the totality so that they are seen in their place in the totality.[68]

Oakeshott maintains the idealist elements of his conception of philosophy with just enough adjustment to allow for a philosophy of politics. Present here is the strong emphasis upon the notion of the totality of experience that only philosophy comprehends and enjoys. Oakeshott also reprises other familiar language from *Experience and Its Modes,* this being another section shared with "The Concept of a Philosophical Jurisprudence," explaining that this concept of a philosophy of politics relies on an understanding that "Philosophical knowledge is simply thought and knowledge *without reservation or presupposition.*"[69] However, while this definition is clearly closely allied to the earlier understanding of philosophy it is also an adjustment of it. It allows focus upon a limited aspect of experience—politics—and yet remains philosophical. A true philosophy of politics is able to accomplish this in a two-stage procedure. Oakeshott illustrates these steps with the example of the *"concepts of valuation."*[70] In the first step, not different from what one might find in the less satisfactory concept of a philosophy of politics, everyday "concepts such as 'government,' 'law,' 'sovereignty,'" are examined and transformed from what he calls "the standpoint of value."[71] However this is not the place to end in a true philosophy of politics; instead, a next step must be engaged, for "the standpoint of value" must itself be examined. "The criterion of value may be expressed in various ways," Oakeshott explains, "for example, in terms of 'good,' 'right,' or in the more general terms of 'ought.' But each of these expressions indicates a concept with a whole world of presuppositions behind it."[72] The second step is to move beyond "valuation" and "right"; as we might examine politics from the standpoint of value, we must then examine what is implied and presupposed by that standpoint itself. This second step "establishes the ultimate factual basis of right, or better, transforms the concepts of political life as conceived of in terms of right by relating the concept of right itself to the totality of experience."[73] This is of course almost exactly the assessment of political philosophy, as seen through the example of ethics, in *Experience and Its Modes*. In that book, a "pseudo-philosophy" would attend to some limited aspect of experience from the concrete world of ideas with the paradoxical result that the object of attention would evaporate under the intense light of philosophical scrutiny. The same process seems to be postulated here, but now Oakeshott chooses not to dwell upon the paradox. Rather, the second stage, that of "transformation," is viewed positively as the procedure that expands the context of political concepts, in a "task of continual redefinition of concepts until a comprehensively concrete result is achieved."[74] Again, the language Oakeshott uses reflects that of *Experience and Its Modes,* with the important exception that the pejorative consideration of this activity as "pseudo-philosophy" has changed. A philosophy of politics is now viewed as a true philosophy.

In "The Concept of a Philosophy of Politics," Oakeshott remains well within the absolute idealist tradition even if he does subtly adjust his attitude from *Experience and Its Modes.* The most important element remains the notion of the concrete world of ideas or totality of experience that philosophical experience comprehends and to which philosophy transforms the understandings of everyday life. A philosophy of politics performs exactly this function according to Oakeshott, although earlier he would have understood this as contradictory, because he considered such a transformation a destruction of the original concept. Oakeshott confronts this difficulty in the later essay, because he recognizes that it places him in a position similar to that for which earlier idealists had been criticized. When he suggests, "a philosophy of politics is an attempt to get away from what political life appears to be for commonsense . . . to a view of the character of political life from the concrete standpoint of the totality of experience," Oakeshott defends a position for which Hobhouse had abused Bosanquet.[75] Hobhouse, for instance, criticized the notion of the general will because it took for the real will something that is not actual. In this conception, an individual has a will that he or she might not know or understand, a dangerous idea to Hobhouse because of the power it gives to the person or institution that claims to be able to pronounce the general will. For Oakeshott, this criticism ties a philosophical concept too closely to the commonsense world from which it has been freed. While he does not comment directly on the validity of the idea of general will, Oakeshott alludes to Hobhouse's critique, arguing, "the notion of the general will may be something which never occurs to consciousness in political activity of any kind, but it may nevertheless be the ultimate definition of what is present in the consciousness, and certainly it must not be rejected as false merely because it cannot be shown to be present in the consciousness in political activity."[76] Here then, ten years or so after he first attempted to explore the idealist conception of the state, after a hiatus when he criticized the very notion of political philosophy, we find Oakeshott defending a thoroughly absolute idealist understanding of a philosophy of politics, even engaging questions about the expectations from such a philosophy that had been issues of contention twenty years earlier.

Everything that I have examined so far places the understanding of politics and political philosophy that Oakeshott held in the twenties and thirties squarely within the absolute idealist tradition. Also present has been a small portion of the skeptical idealism that played a part in Oakeshott's thought. This was seen most clearly in the first understanding of authority he offered, that which located authority in the judgment of those over whom authority is exercised. Little of this skepticism is seen in his notion of a philosophy of politics. For while Oakeshott is critical of the commonsense assumptions of politics, it is not from a skeptical position, but from the most confident of standpoints, the presumed concrete world of ideas that is the totality of experience—a most unskeptical idea. Oakeshott then moved from the actual consideration of politics in "The Authority of the State" to an examination of the undertaking of political philosophy. Throughout this change, however, absolute idealism holds the reins.

V

In Chapter Two I argued that after the thirties, Oakeshott quietly abandoned the absolute idealism that had typified his thinking, This abandonment can be seen in his understanding of political philosophy as well. While Oakeshott began to write much on politics in the later forties, he explicitly engages the idea of a philosophy of politics again in another previously unpublished essay simply titled "Political Philosophy." In this essay, Oakeshott has a different way of discussing the enterprise of philosophy than he had earlier. In a most arresting series of phrases he suggests, "a reflective enterprise which had the precise purpose of avoiding all . . . fixed points of reference, one designed to remain fluid, one for which no presupposition was sacred, would not improperly be called *radically subversive*. This, I believe, is the distinguishing characteristic of philosophical reflection."[77] Now philosophy is understood as "radically subversive." This reveals a characteristic that may be similar to the rejection of commonsense understandings in the earlier piece, but gone here is the presumption of the "con-

crete world of experience" to which philosophy ideally transforms commonsense concepts. This is a "fluid" and intrepid inquiry, not one directed
from and by a "whole world of ideas." The element of skepticism that
existed in the earlier work, to examine the limitations and false universal
claims of modes, is here too in this radically subversive, what I would also
call radically skeptical, enterprise.

Oakeshott's quitting of the absolute idealist notion of philosophy is also
clear in an image he uses to depict philosophical thought. In the image,
human reflection is likened to climbing a tower. Persons taken with different forms of reflection—like the modes—are content at various levels, but
not the philosopher. For the philosopher, "the essential difference is not in
the height attained, but in the pre-disposition of the climber. There is no
top to the tower, or at least the philosopher has no way of knowing
whether or not he has reached the top; for others there will be an optimum
level beyond which the 'things' to which this vision clings dissolve."[78] The
contrast with the earlier period is pronounced. The image of ascending a
tower does seem to imply stages or a hierarchy of experience. But more
importantly, this is undercut when he claims "there is no top to the tower."
In the earlier understanding of philosophy, of course there was a top to the
tower—the concrete world of ideas; of course the philosopher knew when
he attained it—if not, it was not philosophical experience that was
achieved.

Along with this change in the understanding of philosophy, the conception of specifically political philosophy has changed from the earlier
period as well. Gone is the task of redefining concepts in terms of the concrete world of ideas. Instead, Oakeshott suggests, "The only assured
achievement in political philosophy is the maintenance, in the face of innu-
merable temptations to abandon it, of this attitude of reflective radical subversiveness."[79] The character of political philosophy that he suggests here
contrasts sharply with that of the earlier essay. Earlier, in "The Concept of
a Philosophy of Politics," instead of understanding political philosophy as
the "maintenance" of an "attitude of reflective radical subversiveness,"
Oakeshott had held that "The business of a philosophy of politics is, rather,
the complete, or philosophical, *definition* of [political] concepts."[80] As seen
earlier in the discussions of *Experience and Its Modes,* this notion of philosophy has a goal, a "top to the tower," and in this case it is philosophical
"definition," by which he means something that is "complete" with reference to the totality of experience. Later, in "Political Philosophy," however,
Oakeshott identifies philosophy with a "pre-disposition" or "attitude," an
attitude radically subversive not only because it disrupts common ideas, but

also because it has abandoned the notion of the complete or unified world of ideas, the top of the tower. Political philosophy does not achieve complete definitions; the person who is a philosopher is so "not in respect to something he achieves at the end, but in respect of his predisposition towards the ascent."[81] This predisposition is that which typifies Oakeshott's skepticism.

There is, however, one important element of similarity between Oakeshott's understanding of political philosophy in the essay of that name and that of the earlier period: the relation of philosophy to practice. In *Experience and Its Modes,* Oakeshott made it clear that there was a complete separation between the modes and between each mode and philosophy. Oakeshott returns to this theme in "Political Philosophy." In this essay, the inability of philosophy to serve as a guide for political activity is found in its "radically subversive" character, the very fact that it does not achieve anything but questions everything. He maintains, "if we accept from political philosophy conclusions relevant to politics, the result will be either a political philosophy in which the reflective impulse is hindered and arrested by being made servile to politics, or a political activity in which the reflective impulse, disengaged from the necessary limits of politics, has lost its virtue."[82] Politics looks for answers to its questions, solutions to its problems, satisfaction of its desires. Philosophy, on the other hand, wants to question the questions of politics, examine the assumptions of the problems it identifies, subvert the desires it presumes. This is similar to but not the same as the earlier separation of philosophy from the practice of politics. In "The Concept of a Political Philosophy," the fact that philosophy achieved "complete . . . definitions," as opposed to the limited definitions held within politics, is what separated them. In "Political Philosophy," instead, it is its never-resting, skeptical, radically subversive attitude that prevents philosophy from contributing to politics.

The essay "Political Philosophy," written by Oakeshott in the late forties, provides a contrast with the way in he understood the philosophy of politics in the late twenties and thirties. In Chapters One and Two, I portrayed a change in Oakeshott's understanding of philosophy moving away from the absolute, idealist concentration in the early period. In his understanding of politics Oakeshott was greatly influenced by his idealist forebears, wholly taking over their conception of the state in his earlier works. He then left behind political philosophy, perhaps dissatisfied with the capacity to respond to all the criticisms of the idealist conception of state; but he did not yet abandon idealism. In 1935, Oakeshott still commented that the "Idealist theory of the State is the only theory which has paid thoroughgoing attention to the problems which must be considered by a theory of the State, and at the same time is a theory which has yet to receive a satisfactory statement."[83] Oakeshott however was never to supply this "satisfactory statement"; instead, he was about to relinquish the absolute idealism upon which it was based.

While it was an idealist theory of the state that informed "The Authority of the State," it was with Hobbes that Oakeshott concluded the essay. Hegel and Hobbes are the stars in Oakeshott's philosophical universe. It was in reference to a consideration of Hobbes that he introduced "The Concept of the Philosophy of Politics," and he ends that essay claiming "When we turn back to Hobbes, I think we can find there something of a genuine philosophy of politics in this sense. . . . And, I think, in spite of serious defects, there is also to be found in Hegel's *Philosophy of Politics* a genuine philosophy of politics."[84] But it is Hobbes's star that is rising as Hegel's is setting for Oakeshott; and following this it is Oakeshott's skepticism that waxes as the absolute idealism wanes. It is then to Oakeshott's interpretation of Hobbes's philosophy that I turn.

Chapter Four

Mister Oakeshott's Hobbes

I

"Hobbes is the political philosopher about whom Oakeshott has written the most; and it is upon his interpretation of Hobbes that Oakeshott's reputation still to a large extent rests," Paul Franco wrote a few years ago.[1] Patrick Riley goes so far as to suggest that one "could never doubt that [Oakeshott] was, from the Forties on, the supreme interpreter of Hobbes in this (or perhaps any) century."[2] What is surprising about these claims is that Oakeshott did not write very much about Thomas Hobbes. A few book reviews of others' interpretations of Hobbes, an introduction to an edition of *Leviathan,* one essay, and a radio talk make up the corpus of his interpretation. There is an interesting element, however, to Riley's comment that Oakeshott's reputation as an interpreter of Hobbes stems "from the Forties on," because Oakeshott's fame—such as it is—as a political thinker also really stems "from the Forties on." It is not with Hegel, Bradley, Bosenquet, and the idealist theory of the state that Oakeshott is most commonly associated, but with Hobbes and an especially English defense of tradition. It has been to defend a more complete and complex picture of Oakeshott than this that W. H. Greenleaf and Paul Franco have searched out the Oakeshott of the thirties, to reveal the idealism behind Oakeshott's philosophy and his earliest political philosophy. As is clear from my previous chapters, I agree that it is important to take seriously Oakeshott's early commitment to idealism, but I have also argued for reckoning with important changes to those commitments. One way to account for some of those alterations is to appreciate fully Oakeshott's relationship to Hobbes. It is possible to see from this not only a unique view of Hobbes, but also the effect that focusing upon Hobbes has upon Oakeshott's own political thought.[3]

One need not agree with Riley's enthusiastic endorsement to hope to learn much about Hobbes from Oakeshott, especially since he offers a reading less common and less popular than many. My primary interest here, however, is not in Hobbes but in Oakeshott. My inquiry asks: What can be learned about Oakeshott from his reading of Hobbes? My answer, at least in part, is that Oakeshott's interpretation of Hobbes reveals his own attraction to Hobbes's manner of working out political philosophy from a skeptical position similar to that which Oakeshott was moving toward. As Oakeshott abandoned the idealism on which he based his earliest political philosophy, Hobbes's thought offered an outlook which, while retaining the skepticism, fell prey neither to ideological sloganeering nor to pessimism or even nihilism. Oakeshott appreciated what he saw as Hobbes's ability to retain notions of authority and law, even while rejecting natural or absolute foundations for them. Oakeshott's affinity for Hobbes then begins with a similitude in their understanding of philosophical problems; their views on politics accompany this outlook. I do not suggest that Oakeshott shares everything in Hobbes's philosophy or his politics, but that his interest is founded in what Oakeshott might call a sympathy. Oakeshott's sympathy begins in an understanding of Hobbes's philosophy generally; it is only because of what he takes to be Hobbes's philosophical outlook that Oakeshott is attracted to Hobbes's thoughts on politics. In this chapter I examine Oakeshott's interpretation of Hobbes's philosophy, where he claims all discussion of Hobbes's political thought must be grounded, and then in the next chapter I consider Oakeshott's analysis of Hobbes's civil philosophy.

II

"The story of the fortunes of Hobbes and his writings is not remarkable. . . . It is a common, if slightly sordid history; and perhaps it is difficult to determine which part of it is more sordid, the death or exhumation."[4] So did Michael Oakeshott morbidly observe in 1935 while reviewing the seasons of fierce attention and forgetful indifference to Hobbes's works. The "exhumation" to which he refers was a recent revival of interest in Hobbes that was marked by "a flood of fresh literature [on Hobbes] and the foundation, in 1929 after an international congress in Oxford, of a Hobbes Society."[5] That Oakeshott was not sure if the recent "exhumation of

Hobbes" was more sordid than his death is an indication of his critical attitude toward the thirteen books and pamphlets that he takes under review
in his first writing about Hobbes.

Oakeshott was not distraught that theorists and historians exhibited a
renewed interest in Hobbes. Instead, he dismissed that which seemed to
motivate the renewed interest and the work that resulted from it: "the dis-
covery that Hobbes had a message for to-day."[6] That message, it was held,
was an explicitly political one. Oakeshott quotes one of the writers under
review as characteristic of this view: "Hobbes's philosophy possessed precisely that balance and commonsense that made him foresee the Great War,
and, furthermore, the subsequent striving for peace."[7] According to
Oakeshott—he of the thirties whom I presented in Chapter One—this
attitude reveals a fundamental mistake. "Every man, I suppose has his political opinions," he asserts, "but a political philosopher has something more,
and more significant, than political opinions: he has an analysis of political
activity, a comprehensive view of the nature of political life, and it is this . . .
which is profitable for a later and different age to study."[8] Hobbes, for
Oakeshott, is a philosopher. He comes to analyze politics as a philosopher,
and thus what is special that he has to offer is a political philosophy, not
something as time-bound as common sense. Furthermore, according to
Oakeshott, Hobbes must first be recognized as a philosopher in order to
understand his political philosophy—and also to recognize its greatness.
Oakeshott, with a wry observation, acknowledges that it may be easy to
neglect the philosophical character of Hobbes's work. However, he
entreats, "Hobbes, we have to remember, is, of English philosophers, the
one possessed of the greatest measure of philosophical imagination; and so
comparatively rare is this in English philosophical writing that we may
almost be forgiven for failing to appreciate it in Hobbes."[9] Because he does
so much appreciate it, I now turn to Hobbes's philosophy to find
Oakeshott's interest in his political thought.

On a traditional reading of Hobbes, his philosophy would not seem to
promise much to the Oakeshott who early in his career exhibited admi-
ration for nothing but philosophical idealism, since traditionally Hobbes
had been considered a materialist. W. H. Greenleaf explains this view. "The
traditional case, or orthodox interpretation of Hobbes, is that he is a materialist imbued with ideas of the 'new' natural science and that he method-
ically applies its themes and procedures (the laws governing bodies in
motion and their deductive elaboration) to the elucidation of civil and
ethical theory."[10] While some had argued that Hobbes had done a poor
job connecting materialism to his political thought, it was not the mate-

rialism that was doubted, but the working of it through.[11] Oakeshott establishes his interpretation of Hobbes by directly challenging the fundamental belief of Hobbes's materialism. "Two views," of Hobbes's philosophical system, writes Oakeshott in his "Introduction to *Leviathan*," "it appears, between them hold the field at the present time. The first is the view that Hobbes's philosophy is a doctrine of materialism. . . . A mechanistic-materialist politics is made to spring from a mechanistic-materialist universe."[12] The second view about his system, according to Oakeshott, maintains that while Hobbes intended such a materialist understanding of nature, and thus also of politics, he was not successful. That is, even though a coherent materialist or mechanistic philosophy was attempted, Hobbes did not pull it off. This second view, according to Oakeshott, maintains that "The joints of the system are ill-matched, and what should have been a continuous argument, based on a philosophy of materialism, collapses under it own weight."[13]

Each of these views misunderstands Hobbes's conception of philosophy, because for him, Oakeshott asserts, "to think philosophically is to reason; philosophy is reasoning."[14] Reasoning for Hobbes has a particular course, "cause and effect are its categories . . . [reason is] to determine the conditional causes of given effects, or to determine the conditional effects of given causes."[15] Because Hobbes expresses his understanding of reasoning in terms of the language of physical causes and effects, Oakeshott argues, he has been misconstrued as a materialist and mechanist. However, Oakeshott holds, Hobbes "does not say that the natural world is a machine; he says only that the rational world is like a machine."[16] I will explore more fully below Oakeshott's dismissal of the assertion that Hobbes was a materialist and how he thinks we should rather understand Hobbes. Yet first it is important to note that for Oakeshott, it is Hobbes's expression of his own philosophy that has mislead interpreters, because this relates to the second contention he addresses: that Hobbes attempts a materialist-mechanist view, but he fails in the endeavor. Oakeshott did understand Hobbes to have attempted a systematic philosophy, and also to have been successful. In fact, he had claimed,

> English philosophical writers are not, generally speaking, given to the construction of systems; and this abstinence is both the strength and the weakness of English philosophy. But Hobbes did construct a system, a complete and comprehensive view of the universe; and he conceived this system with such imaginative power that, in spite of its relatively simple character, it stands in comparison with even the grand and imposing creation of Hegel.[17]

Those who fault Hobbes for failing to achieve a coherent system, according to Oakeshott, have misunderstood what to expect from a philosophical system. "For what is expected here is that a philosophical system should
conform to an architectural analogue [however]. . . . The coherence of
[Hobbes's] philosophy, the system of it, lies not in an architectonic structure, but in a single 'passionate thought' that pervades its parts."[18] Oakeshott
claims Hobbes's civil philosophy is not an edifice built upon the philosophical doctrine of materialism; rather, it is connected to his system of
philosophy "because it is philosophical."[19] That is, it is built on the conception of reasoning he described above, for it is philosophy itself understood as reasoning that gives coherence to Hobbes's thought. Oakeshott
calls it "a guiding clue like the thread of Ariadne."[20] And it is this thread,
philosophy as reasoning, that ties Hobbes's philosophy into a system and
weaves his civil thought into the whole.

I return now to Oakeshott's rejection of the idea that Hobbes was a
materialist. This may be Oakeshott's unique contribution to debates about
Hobbes's philosophy. It is of interest here because such an interpretation
allows Oakeshott much greater affinity with Hobbes. If Oakeshott has
some partiality to Hobbes's political thought, as I will argue in Chapter
Five, then he must first discover a Hobbes with whose philosophy he can
be more comfortable—which means dismissing Hobbes's materialism.
Oakeshott discusses this through an analysis of Hobbes's relationship to
empirical science. It is not uncommon to claim that Hobbes was enamored
of science or attempted to bring the method of science into philosophy, or
that his political philosophy was scientific. Sheldon Wolin, for example, has
recently claimed, "Hobbes was one of the first, after Bacon, to interpret the
radical political and social implications of modern science and one of the
first moderns to undertake the role of mediator between science and society."[21] Oakeshott, however, dismisses any simple relationship between
Hobbes's philosophy and science, and especially Bacon's empirical and
inductive science. In the early review essay, Oakeshott noted appreciatively
that some recent studies of Hobbes had associated him more fully with "the
philosophy of . . . the Middle Ages"; hence, he suggests, "It is surprising now
to turn back to those older studies of Hobbes and see him coupled with
Bacon."[22] This gives some hint to the tradition with which Oakeshott
would identify Hobbes. He recognizes that Hobbes may have misled interpreters by his "polemics against schoolmen and his personal connexion
with Bacon," yet still Oakeshott will argue that he had much more in common with the former and rejected the latter outright.[23] Rather than acting
as a "mediator of between science and society," Oakeshott claims, "In an age

when philosophy was giving way at every point to science, Hobbes stood firm: he had probably less patience or sympathy for experimental science than for anything else in the world—not excluding the Pope."[24]

Oakeshott returns to this claim in the "Introduction." "In the writings of Hobbes, philosophy and science are not contrasted *eo nomine.* Such a contrast would have been impossible in the seventeenth century," and Oakeshott even goes on to grant that "Indeed, Hobbes normally uses the word science as a synonym for philosophy: rational knowledge is scientific knowledge."[25] This seems not a very promising start in the effort to establish a contrast. Still, Oakeshott maintains that a distinction does exist, albeit one that Hobbes had only "imperfectly achieved."[26] Hobbes's distinction between philosophy and science, according to Oakeshott, "is that between the knowledge of things as they appear and enquiry into the fact of their appearing, between a knowledge (with all the necessary assumptions) of a phenomenal world and a theory of knowledge itself."[27] The distinction, while one that Oakeshott recognizes is common to his contemporary readers, was only glimpsed in the intellectual ferment of the seventeenth century. For Oakeshott, that Hobbes's achievement was imperfect is less important than what he in fact achieved. Science relies upon observation and assumptions about the relations of the observer to the phenomenal world; philosophy, however, is reasoning that searches for the causes of the effects experienced as the phenomenal world. Once again, Oakeshott admits that the distinction was "imperfectly defined" by Hobbes. Still, he claims,

> But that philosophy meant for Hobbes something different from the enquiries of natural science is at once apparent when we consider the starting place of his thought and the character of the questions he thought it was necessary to ask. . . . And the question he asks himself is, what must the world be like for us to have the sensations we undoubtedly experience? His enquiry is into the cause of sensation, an enquiry to be conducted not by means of observation, but by means of reason.[28]

Where science undertakes its inquiry into cause and effect by relying on the assumption that the sensations we experience are reliable and transparent, philosophy instead relies solely upon reasoning to question even those sensations. Philosophy does indeed begin with sensations because those we "undoubtedly experience"; but philosophy is not satisfied with sensations.

Oakeshott recognizes that Hobbes's way of putting his argument does appear scientific, and perhaps increasingly so throughout his writings.

However, he claims that "Hobbes was never a scientist in any true sense, that is, his science is really conceived throughout through as an epistemology."[29] In the "Introduction," Oakeshott offers an explanation of a sort for why Hobbes puts the argument as he does; he suggests that Hobbes's answer to the question of the cause of sensation perhaps "owes something to the inspiration of the scientists," but this does not make his philosophy equivalent to science.[30] The difference is that "the scientists" actually took the world to be a machine, whereas Hobbes understood the world on the "analogy of a machine." A subtle distinction perhaps, but for Oakeshott it is fundamental. The scientist assumes the world acts in a mechanical way, takes it as a machine, and sets out to explore the running of the mechanism. Hobbes, however, regards the world on the analogy of a machine because his way of understanding how reason works made it convenient to do so; again, the analogy is a result of reason, not an assumption about the world. Oakeshott admits that because of this similarity of expression with the scientists, Hobbes "discovered some of the general ideas of the scientists could be turned to his own purposes. But these pardonable appropriations do nothing to approximate his enquiry to that of Galileo or Newton."[31] In the "Introduction" Oakeshott ends his discussion of the contrast between philosophy and science with an aside to Hobbes's political philosophy. Having sifted philosophy from science, Oakeshott makes the claim that it would be a mistake to see Hobbes's political writings as scientific; instead they are philosophical. Oakeshott maintains, "it is a false reading of [Hobbes's] intention and his achievement which finds in his civil philosophy the beginning of sociology or a science of politics."[32] Again, it is not science, but philosophy that Oakeshott claims is fundamental for Hobbes: "its source and authority lie, not in observation, but in reasoning."[33] For Oakeshott, this is no less true for Hobbes's political philosophy than for his philosophical outlook.

In rejecting the primacy of the alliance of Hobbes's philosophy with the beginnings of modern science, Oakeshott does substitute another association. I noted that Oakeshott saw Hobbes's rejection of the schoolmen as so much bluster, and that he appreciated that some of the recent work had a "surer grasp of the connexion between Hobbes and the philosophy . . . of the Middle Ages."[34] It is there, within a tradition of scholasticism, nominalism, and a brand of skepticism, that Oakeshott places Hobbes. Instead of understanding Hobbes as a revolutionary against this tradition, as Hobbes would sometimes have us believe, Oakeshott claims that he is its inheritor, as was his whole century. In arguing for a re-evaluation of the seventeenth century Oakeshott suggests "the revolution in politics, religion and philosophy which was believed to have taken place during the seventeenth century has (at any rate as regards its speed and comprehensiveness) been grossly exaggerated."[35] Oakeshott gives no more particulars here of what else would contribute to this reevaluation. But to connect Hobbes to the "philosophy of the Middle Ages" would seem quite difficult, especially given the raillery and rants against the schoolmen for which Hobbes is famous. Oakeshott admits as much, but maintains that Hobbes's philosophy was closely connected to scholasticism. "In detail [Hobbes] rejected the whole of the scholastic view, and he was among the first to subject that view to a thorough-going criticism."[36] This is certainly the view of Hobbes that seems most evident on the surface of his work. Oakeshott counters, however, "But [Hobbes's] conception of the nature of philosophy and of the philosophical argument was much more nearly related to that of Scholasticism than to the view of Bacon and his successors"; and Oakeshott cites with approval John Laird's observations that "however startling Hobbian novelties may be, they are nevertheless 'the moves of a master player who knew and kept to mediæval rules.'"[37]

In the review essay where these passages are found, Oakeshott does little to substantiate this view, relying primarily upon the claims of the works he is reviewing, but his one defense of this curious claim—that Hobbes's philosophy was related to his seeming nemeses, the scholastics—is curious in its own right. What of all the nasty words for the schoolmen? Oakeshott submits, "The expressions of hostility toward [scholasticism] which he allows himself arise, mainly, from an extraneous, non-philosophical interest and, if anything is to be neglected, must be neglected by a true interpretation of his work."[38] Unfortunately Oakeshott neither gives a clue as to what he thinks the "extraneous, non-philosophical interest" might be, nor does he provide much defense for this method of interpretation.[39] Regardless of the details of this curious interpretive strategy, it is notable that Oakeshott finds it important to put Hobbes in league with scholastics.

While Oakeshott does argue for the importance of seeing Hobbes in the tradition of the scholastics over that of the foundations of modern empirical science, he also recognizes some of the more contemporary associations of Hobbes's thought. It is in his thorough skepticism that Oakeshott sees Hobbes most as a child of his age. "An impulse for philosophy, may originate in faith (as with Erigina) or with curiosity (as with Locke)" Oakeshott maintained, "but with Hobbes the prime mover was doubt. Scepticism was, of course, in the air he breathed; but in an age of sceptics he was the most radical of them all."[40] What strikes Oakeshott about the skepticism of Hobbes is its "ferocity," as opposed to the "elegiac scepticism of Montaigne," or even "the methodological doubt of Descartes."[41] Yet even here, when placing Hobbes in context with contemporaries, Oakeshott describes Hobbes's skepticism as a "medieval passion . . . [by which] he sweeps aside into a common abyss of absurdity both the believer in eternal truth and the industrious seeker after truths; both faith and science"[42] What then is the relationship between scholasticism and skepticism, between the middle ages and the seventeenth century, both of which Oakeshott claims as Hobbes's heritage?[43]

Oakeshott always tries to balance the originality of Hobbes—and the originality that Hobbes claimed for himself—with his traditional aspects. In the "Introduction," Oakeshott seeks this balance, claiming "Perhaps the truth is Hobbes was as original as he thought he was, and to acknowledge his real indebtedness would have required to see (what he could not have expected to see) the link between scholasticism and modern philosophy which is only now becoming clear to us."[44] To return to the metaphor that Laird used, Oakeshott seems to be saying that Hobbes played "the moves of a master player who knew and kept to mediæval rules." because it was the only game he knew; and yet he recognized that the character and even rules of the game were changing. Oakeshott himself develops another metaphor: "[Hobbes's] philosophy is in the nature of a palimpsest. For its author what was important was what he wrote, and it is only to be expected that he should be indifferent to what is already there; but for us, both sets of writings are important."[45] Of course, Hobbes was not just indifferent, but often openly hostile to what was already there, scholasticism. Yet, an important part of what is "already there" sets in place the skepticism Oakeshott emphasized. It is a vital element that Oakeshott argues Hobbes inherited from medieval philosophy: nominalism. Oakeshott argues, "Hobbes inherited [the] tradition of nominalism, and more than any other writer passed it on to the modern world."[46] It is nominalism that connects the scholasticism and skepticism in Hobbes for Oakeshott. Having attempted to establish a contrast between "philosophy and science (reason and empiricism)" in Hobbes's thought, it is in a discussion of the contrast between "philosophy and experience (reason and sense)," that Oakeshott begins to reveal the centrality of the legacy of nominalism both given to and received from Hobbes.[47]

III

Oakeshott's contrast of "philosophy and experience" provides an insight into the type of skeptic that he interprets Hobbes to be, revealing it in the discussion of nominalism and Hobbes's thoughts on language. For Oakeshott, Hobbes's skepticism is, of course, based upon the doubt of any certainty about the world; and yet it can still accept the existence of universal truths. How can this be? Language, in Oakeshott's interpretation of Hobbes, is something both grand and mundane. It is the creation of meaning by humans, yet its reference is only internally to that construction, not a world external to it. The result is that the only guide for its use is its own consistency and coherence. A universal truth has that character within the universe of the users of language whose conventions recognize such as a truth, not in some "Universe" at large. This skepticism, which Oakeshott finds exhibited in Hobbes's thoughts on language, reflects the character of his own skepticism concerning the modes in *Experience and Its Modes,* and the voices in "The Voice of Poetry." It is an interpretation that brings Hobbes's and Oakeshott's skepticism close together.

Oakeshott discusses Hobbes's contrast of "reason and experience," claiming that for Hobbes, "In principle, experience . . . is something man shares with animals and has only in greater degree: memory and imagination are the unsought mechanical products of sensation."[48] Humans and animals each have sensations and thus each have, by definition, experience and the type of knowledge it allows. It is not clear here why humans have a "greater degree" of experience, but the fundamental point remains that the character of this type of knowledge is the same for humans and animals. However, Oakeshott claims that for Hobbes, in order to have rational knowledge more than sense is needed: "We require not only to have sensations, but to be conscious of them: we require the power of introspection."[49] Oakeshott maintains that for Hobbes introspection is not a function of the mind reflecting on the world (thought is not mimetic), but the product of language; language "is primarily the only means by which a man may communicate his own thoughts to himself, may become conscious of the content of his mind."[50] Oakeshott had earlier maintained that it was a mistake to see Hobbes simply as a materialist, and now he begins to intimate the alternative view that he offers. It is true that humans have sensations of a material world, but they are random and meaningless. It is only when humans can order those images, only when humans become conscious of what Oakeshott labels the "after-images of sensation," that humans can get beyond mechanical sensations to produce "the power of introspection" and reasoning.[51] Language, according to Oakeshott, allows for such introspection and ordering. But what is language? what does it communicate when it communicates thoughts?

Oakeshott recounts Hobbes's argument stating "The beginning of language is the giving of names to after-images of sensations."[52] Importantly, on Oakeshott's reading of Hobbes, words do not name things but thoughts or images. He quotes Hobbes's definition from *De Corpore,* "a name is a word taken at pleasure to serve as a mark that may raise in our minds a thought like some thought we had before."[53] It is the tenor of passages like these that appear to empower Oakeshott's argument that for Hobbes, "Language, the giving of names to images, is not itself reasonable, it is the arbitrary precondition of all reasoning."[54] Language is fundamental to reasoning; but language itself is based upon an arbitrary process of naming mental images. Thus, for Oakeshott, as powerful as reasoning may be for Hobbes, it is always limited by a prior arbitrary process in the human mind. Humans have sensations that leave "after-images," and language is founded on the process of an arbitrary "giving of names to [those] images."[55] On Oakeshott's reading there is no constant set of sensations or material objects that regulate the giving of images, and then names, and finally reasoning for Hobbes.

Two connected aspects of Hobbes's theory of language feature in Oakeshott's interpretation: 1) language is the giving of names to thoughts or images in the mind, not to things in the world; and 2) the naming process is not a reasoned procedure, but "the arbitrary precondition of all reasoning." Oakeshott's is a reading of Hobbes that Aloysius Martinich has labeled "the erroneous interpretation that Hobbes held an ideational theory of meaning, according to which the meaning of a word is what the word stands for, refers to, or *names* and what a word stands for, refers to, or *names* is some idea in the speaker's mind."[56] Erroneous or not, it is clear that for Oakeshott, what is in the mind is what language captures to allow "a man to communicate his thoughts to himself." This emphasis by Oakeshott doubles the arbitrary and conventional nature of Hobbes's notion of language. At the first stage, it is completely arbitrary what words we assign as names; the fact that we make particular sounds to act as these signifiers does not at all dictate which sounds are used. Secondly, we assign these names, on Oakeshott's reading of Hobbes, not to things in the world, but to images in our minds. Oakeshott claims that for Hobbes, "The achievement of language is to 'register our thoughts,' to fix what is essentially fleeting."[57] For this reason, Oakeshott argues that Hobbes held that "language . . . is not itself reasonable." For example, there can be no *a priori* reason to use the word "arbor" rather than "tree" for what I recognize as the leafy, tall, bark-enclosed affair outside my study window; and I only recognize these "fleeting images" because I have the word "tree" to secure and order them in my mind. That is to say, Hobbes's nominalism, on Oakeshott's reading, is most extreme. And this extreme nominalism is the philosophical basis of his skepticism.[58]

For Hobbes, according to Oakeshott, humans have the capacity to reason only because we have secured and ordered the unstable and random images of our minds through the arbitrary assignment of names to them. J. W. N. Watkins, writing after Oakeshott, also reflects this view of Hobbes's theory of language, labeling it "radical nominalism."[59] Watkins argued that "Hobbes held what may be called a Humpty-Dumpty theory of meaning," citing the following famous exchange from *Through the Looking Glass:*

> "When I use a word," Humpty-Dumpty said in a rather scornful tone, "it means just what I choose it to mean—neither more nor less."
> "The question is," said Alice, "whether you *can* make words mean so many different things."
> "The question is," said Humpty Dumpty, "which is to be Master—that's all."[60]

This snippet of dialogue captures the theory of language that Oakeshott attributes to Hobbes and also begins to show the political implications of such a theory.[61] As for language and meaning, Hobbes, according to Oakeshott, understood these to be entirely a human creation, but not a creation that reflects and expresses the world outside the mind. The mind is no *speculum mentis* and neither do the inventions of language and reason act as *specula*. They do not reflect the world, but rather create the world that humans inhabit. Language is not the reasonable assignation of names to consistent properties or accidents found in nature; language is instead "the arbitrary precondition of all reasoning." However, once names have been arbitrarily allotted it is possible to use them; becoming "conscious of the contents of his mind" through language, a human can explore through introspection those contents, and this is the precondition of reasoning.[62]

Oakeshott pronounces Hobbes's notion of language and meaning "at once a nominalist and profoundly sceptical doctrine."[63] In his interpretation, the nominalism and skepticism are not just fellow travelers for Hobbes; instead they are closely connected. Certain knowledge of an external world is not possible; instead, there is only the consistent and coherent accounting of names, the arbitrary assignment of signs to images of the mind. Philosophy, as reasoning (and science), can provide a type of certainty, but it is limited. "Reasoning," Oakeshott interprets Hobbes as saying, "is nothing but the addition and subtraction of names," and he goes on to quote Hobbes, "[reasoning] 'gives us conclusions not about the nature of things but about the names of things. That is to say, by means of reason we discover only whether the connections we have established between names are in accordance with the arbitrary convention we have established concerning their meanings.'"[64] Oakeshott's Hobbes is one for whom meaning is possible, but it is wholly arbitrary and conventional. This he makes explicit not only for meaning, but truth as well. Truth is possible, but is also limited to conventions concerning images in the mind. Oakeshott claims that for Hobbes, "Truth is of universals, but they are names . . . and a true proposition is not an assertion about the real world."[65] Again, the skepticism and nominalism are united.

The skepticism that Oakeshott claims for Hobbes bears similarity to what Richard Popkin calls "constructive or mitigated scepticism."[66] Popkin argues that the expressions of skepticism in the sixteenth and seventeenth centuries were primarily examples of "pyrrhonism," based on the rediscovery of Sextus Empiricus's *Hypotyposes (Outlines of Pyrrhonism).* "Pyrrhonism" in the ancient world "proposed to suspend judgement on all questions on which there seemed to be conflicting evidence, including the question whether or not something could be known."[67] In response to contemporary descendants of the pyrrhonists, Popkin suggests, a different form of skepticism was developed by the likes of Mersenne and Gassendi. It is these whom he labels "constructive or mitigated sceptics," and while he does not include Hobbes in their ranks, Oakeshott's interpretation would place him there. Like the pyrrhonists, these constructive skeptics rejected "a search for absolutely certain foundations for knowledge" but looked "for a way of living that could accept both the unanswerable doubts of the 'nouveaux pyrrhoniens' and the unquestioned discoveries of the intellectual new world of the seventeenth century."[68] The answer supplied by the constructive skeptics is also that of Hobbes: a philosophy established "through a realization that the doubts propounded by the pyrrhonists in no way affected *la verite des sciences,* provided that the sciences were interpreted as hypothetical systems about appearances, and not true descriptions of reality, . . . and not ultimate information about the true nature of things."[69] For Oakeshott this is "deeply skeptical," while for Popkin it is "mitigated skepticism," but seen in either way, Hobbes's philosophy ties nominalism to a skepticism in matters of both philosophy and science. Universal propositions can be true, but only hypothetical; "ultimate information about the true nature of things" is not available, but the "after-images" initiated through the senses can be ordered through language and reason.

Reviewing what Oakeshott has said concerning Hobbes's theory of language, we have seen him claim: 1) language is what makes conscious thought and thus reasoning and philosophy possible; 2) language is made up of words that are names of images in the mind or thoughts; 3) truth is not the reflection in propositions of the nature of an external real world and the nature of things in it, but exercise of reason to make connections between words while following arbitrary conventions of meaning. Oakeshott's emphasis upon this theory of language in order to understand Hobbes's philosophy is an interesting, perhaps questionable, interpretation of Hobbes; but more importantly, it reveals a sympathy between Oakeshott's and Hobbes's philosophy and his civil philosophy.

IV

In his singularly harsh "A Note on Professor Oakeshott's Introduction to *Leviathan*," J. M. Brown establishes the focus of his essay the following way: "This particular examination is confined to crucial passages of Professor Oakeshott's direct exposition of his author (pp. xxx-l) and some later pages that supplement these. For whatever else Professor Oakeshott says about Hobbes ought to be, and doubtless is, based on the understanding of Hobbism revealed in these pages."[70] J. M. Brown may confine his analysis as he will, but in this case the second sentence contains a tendentious claim. I have analyzed closely the sections of the "Introduction" preceding the one upon which Brown focuses (and earlier works) because Oakeshott makes it clear that it is his placement of Hobbes's civil philosophy (what I presume Brown means by Hobbism) in the context of his philosophical system that distinguishes his interpretation. This may or may not be a good strategy for interpreting Hobbes, but Oakeshott's choice to do so reveals his own relationship to Hobbes. Oakeshott's affinity for Hobbes begins where he says it does, in his appreciation of him as a philosopher. As Oakeshott interprets Hobbes, there are important similarities between his own understanding of philosophy and Hobbes's system of philosophy. Their philosophies are not the same and some of the differences are of great import; and yet between Oakeshott and Hobbes—or at least Oakeshott's Hobbes—there is a sympathy in matters philosophical that leads to a sympathy in matters political.

If one were simply to claim that there are philosophical affinities between Hobbes and Oakeshott, an initial difficulty would seem to present itself. Above, in Chapter One, I had introduced British idealism in part following W. H. Greenleaf's observation that this school had arisen from a dissatisfaction with two "contrasting traditions of philosophical speculation," one of which was "empirical nominalism."[71] Greenleaf suggested that this tradition "asserted that all we know is ultimately derived from organs of sense. It repudiated transcendental metaphysics as moonshine, arguing the so-called universal forms or essences were names."[72] Hobbes could fit comfortably into this tradition of empirical nominalism. Even as Oakeshott interpreted him, Hobbes held there were no "universals or essences" outside the mind, only names, and these were generated from the ordering of "after-images" of sense impressions. Greenleaf further suggested that "The characteristic procedure [of this tradition] was the classification of things in terms of the features selected because of their typical or prominent nature."[73] This is something like the traditional view of Hobbes that Greenleaf had suggested in his own discussion of him. If Hobbes is characterized as an empirical nominalist then it makes arguing for a philosophical sympathy between him and Oakeshott especially odd, since the idealism upon which Oakeshott's philosophy was based grew in part from a dissatisfaction with empirical nominalism.

While it may be possible to view Hobbes as an empirical nominalist, it should be clear from the preceding sections that Oakeshott did not do so. Hobbes, according to Oakeshott, held that the senses were opaque, not transparent and, further, "all we know" is *not* "ultimately derived from sense." The senses may provide or initiate the "fleeting images" around which certain knowledge can be formed, but knowledge based solely on sense is random and unreliable. Instead, the only truths we know are those "in accordance with the arbitrary convention we have established concerning their meanings." An interpretation emphasizing this also undermines applicability of the second tenet of "empirical nominalism" to Hobbes. For Oakeshott, Hobbes does not propose language to be "the classification of things" but rather "the giving of names to images." This understanding of the foundations of Hobbes's philosophy, what Martinich called an "ideational interpretation," leads Oakeshott to consider Hobbes's "a profoundly sceptical doctrine." It is also the connection to Oakeshott's own skepticism as it was growing out of idealism as the analysis of Oakeshott in Chapter One reveals. The central idealist contention that Oakeshott maintained in *Experience and Its Modes* was that "experience everywhere, not merely is inseparable from thought, but is itself a form of thought."[74] If Hobbes was a materialist, Oakeshott would have been opposed to Hobbes; however, instead of disputing Hobbes, Oakeshott set out to dismiss the materialist interpretation. In Oakeshott's interpretation, the central and primary contention regards the place of philosophy and reasoning; the mechanism and its attendant materialism, Oakeshott maintained, are derivative.

Here Oakeshott's emphasis upon Hobbes's nominalism becomes significant. Oakeshott stressed that for Hobbes language, and the words that make it, are essentially creations of the mind. But more than "words" simply being creations, what they name are elements of the mind as well: "Language [is] the giving of names to images." Oakeshott stresses that for Hobbes "The achievement of language is to 'register our thoughts,' to fix what is essentially fleeting." Language does not register or catalogue things in the world, but images in the mind. Here Oakeshott's contention about Hobbes's theory of language reflects his own idealist understanding of experience. Just as his interpretation of Hobbes did not countenance the idea that names reflect the real world, Oakeshott had maintained in *Experience and Its Modes* that "Facts are never merely observed, remembered, or combined; they are always made. We cannot 'take' facts, because there are none there until we have constructed them."[75] The world that humans understand themselves to inhabit, not only the knowledge they have of it, is located within their own minds for Oakeshott and for the Hobbes of Oakeshott's interpretation. Richard Flathman claims that "Thomas Hobbes is first and foremost a theorist of individual human beings as the *Makers* of themselves and their worlds."[76] Not only would Oakeshott agree with this as an interpretation of Hobbes, but it captures also Oakeshott's own ideas. Oakeshott's philosophy also differs from Hobbes's here. Oakeshott neither emphasizes that the contents of the mind are images that remain after sense impressions nor does he, in his own philosophy, emphasize the technicalities of a theory of language. But in his understanding of Hobbes, Oakeshott stresses the theory of language, and his interpretation of it reveals interesting resemblances to his own thought.

Oakeshott's consideration of Hobbes's nominalism discloses a common emphasis upon the central place of thought in the creation of the human world; this leads to another correspondence: the coherence theory of truth. Oakeshott had maintained in *Experience and Its Modes* that "a world of ideas is true when it is coherent and because it is coherent. Consequently there is no external means by which truth can be established."[77] His interpretation of Hobbes underscored the same notions. Oakeshott cited Hobbes's claim that "by means of reason we discover only whether names are in accordance with the arbitrary convention we have established concerning meanings." As Oakeshott reads Hobbes, truth is only a matter of whether names—having been randomly assigned—are used "in accordance with the arbitrary conventions." To put this in Oakeshott's terms, whether propositions cohere with the world of ideas established through the conventions of language determines their truth because there is no—at least no accessible—external standard.

Interestingly, this leads to another affinity between Oakeshott and Hobbes as he understood him. When Oakeshott had discussed modes and then voices, he claimed that they are able to express certainty, but such certainly only existed within, not between, modes and then voices. While I have argued Oakeshott altered his understanding of the relation of what he had called modes when he reconfigured them as voices, the conventional character of truth and certainty did not change. This is what he finds in Hobbes as well, and it has a similar affect upon how different conventions of certainty interact. Thus, for example, Oakeshott focuses upon the distinction between philosophy and science in Hobbes. He observed a distinction between the reasoning of philosophy and the empiricism of the sciences. On Oakeshott's reading, Hobbes understood philosophy to be concerned with what makes sensation possible, while science assumes the surety of the senses. However, this did not discount the sciences. Quite to the contrary, it secures their capacities even as it limits their scope and reveals their undisclosed assumptions. Another example of this attitude can be seen in Oakeshott's discussion of Hobbes's "contrast between philosophy and theology (reason and faith)."[78] Theology and faith, in considering "the universe as a whole, things infinite, things eternal, final causes and things known only by grace and revelation," do not admit of rationality because the human mind cannot comprehend the causes and effects of these things; thus these central notions of theology are not subjects for philosophy.[79] In Oakeshott's interpretation, Hobbes's understanding of conventions of philosophy, those of cause and effect, simply cannot grasp these things. However, Oakeshott claims that Hobbes "did not deny the existence of these things, but their rationality."[80] Now perhaps there is a pejorative in denying rationality to the concerns of theology, but as Oakeshott understands Hobbes, to hold otherwise is to commit a category error. Reason can only deal with cause and effect; those are its conventions. Conversely theology, as presented here, relies on "things known by grace and revelation." For Hobbes, according to Oakeshott, "philosophy and theology (reasoning and faith)" have different conventions for truth and certainty.[81]

Oakeshott's discussion of Hobbes reflects his own changing conception of philosophy as well. His early understanding of philosophical experience was experience "without presupposition, reservation, arrest, or modification."[82] Philosophy is experience that does not limit itself or rein itself; it boldly makes the "attempt to find what is completely satisfactory in experience."[83] In the essay "Thomas Hobbes," written after *Experience and Its Modes,* but before "The Concept of a Philosophical Jurisprudence," Oakeshott credits Hobbes's philosophical thinking as just such an attempt.

Radicalism, extravagance, the intrepid following out of a theory conceived
in the grand manner and the absence of any sign of dismay or compromise,
are not the qualities often to be found in English thinkers; but they flourish
in Hobbes almost unchecked. . . . Hobbes appears never to have been
tempted to make his conclusions more moderate than he found them; and
compromise and fear had no place in his intellectual character.[84]

Here it is clear that Oakeshott sees Hobbes as a genuine seeker of philosophical experience—his own conceptions of experience, not Hobbes's.
Hobbes shows no "dismay or compromise," but rather follows his philosophy "without reservation." The discussion of Hobbes's philosophy in the
"Introduction" alters from that above in a small but significant fashion,
again reflecting the alteration in Oakeshott's thought I discussed in Chapter Two. Of course, Oakeshott maintains that Hobbes is philosopher of a
system; yet he contends "that the system of Hobbes's philosophy lies in his
conception of philosophical knowledge, and not in any doctrine about the
world."[85] In the "Introduction," the conception of philosophy and its system is understood as a limited affair. Oakeshott argues that for Hobbes "We
can, then, surmount the limits of sense experience and achieve rational
knowledge; and it is this knowledge, with its own severe limitations, that is
the concern of philosophy."[86] Philosophy and rational knowledge are available but they suffer "severe limitations." Here it is more the skeptical nature
of Hobbes's thought that is featured, again reflecting the move toward
greater skepticism in Oakeshott's own career. Oakeshott emphasizes, and
appreciates, the limits he discerns in Hobbes's understanding of philosophy
as reasoning. "The lineage of Hobbes's rationalism lies not (like that of
Spinoza or even Descartes) in the great Platonic-Christian tradition, but in
the sceptical, late scholastic tradition. He does not normally speak of Reason, the divine illumination of the mind that united man with God; he
speaks of reasoning."[87] To Oakeshott this meant that for Hobbes "philosophical knowledge . . . is conditional, not absolute."[88] This shift in the characterization of philosophy and its endeavor may appear one of minor
importance, more of tone than substance. But given Oakeshott's own shift,
the change in his presentation of Hobbes's philosophy is significant.

V

Of course, it could be that all these sympathies I have identified between
Oakeshott's and Hobbes's philosophy exist only because Oakeshott understands him to be a philosopher; he might say the same about any philoso-

pher that he considered genuine. His comments about John Locke, however, should dispel this idea. In 1932, to commemorate the 300th anniversary of Locke's birth, Oakeshott wrote a short essay for *The Cambridge Review.* As with Hobbes, he begins by suggesting "In spite of his other titles to fame, John Locke must, I think, be remembered and considered first as a philosopher," and in the manner of his philosophical thinking, Oakeshott claims, "Locke shows himself to be a genuine, perhaps great philosopher."[89] There is no doubt then that Oakeshott considers Locke a philosopher, but what he has to say about his philosophy reveals by contrast just how much Oakeshott admired, and preferred, Hobbes.

Oakeshott manifests his antipathy for the philosopher Locke while discussing *The Essay Concerning Human Understanding.* He contends, "It springs, in the first place, not from any radical doubt, any purging scepticism, but from curiosity and a mild perplexity."[90] We can recall that Oakeshott had been most impressed with Hobbes's passionate skepticism—"the most radical of them all"—and here he seems almost distressed at Locke's mere "curiosity." However, the sting of his criticism of Locke is in the pointed adjective "mild." Locke was not radical or audacious or intrepid; instead he is inspired, if so it can be called, by a "mild perplexity." Oakeshott's characterization is so finely written that I quote it at length.

> Indeed, the view that it is equally unwarrantable either to doubt everything or to make extravagant claims on behalf of the human mind, which may be said to be the message of Locke's philosophy, was as much a prejudice and a compromise with which he began as a conclusion with which he finished. Locke is a cautious, patient thinker, not given to paradox and as little controversial as may be; there is nothing audacious about his speculations, and nothing dazzling or even brilliant about his writing. The *Essay* has perhaps less of the character of a *tour de force* than any other philosophical work ever published.[91]

Oakeshott's disdain for Locke is clear; and its source is precisely converse of the reason for his esteem for Hobbes. Hobbes was passionate and audacious and enjoyed controversy, and while drawn to this Oakeshott recognized that his passion for controversy sometimes distracted Hobbes, "For brilliance in controversy is a corrupting accomplishment. Always to play to win is to take one's standards from one's opponent, and local victory comes to displace every other consideration."[92] Yet, Oakeshott comes to view even this distracting passion positively, explaining that "Most readers will find Hobbes's disputatiousness excessive; but it is the defect of an exceptionally active mind."[93] Compared to this, Locke's cautious, compromising, patient approach must be the defect of an especially soporific mind. In what is another blow against Locke, Oakeshott claims, "The *Essay* is no system of philosophy, but a cautious attempt to determine the limits of our knowledge. . . . From its very plan, his work was destined to be inconclusive and to result in compromise. And it is the quality of compromise which is at once the distinction and weakness of this philosophy."[94] It is surprising that Oakeshott even counts this as philosophy since it is so filled with caution and compromise. The denial of system, while not terrible in its own right, looks especially harsh when we recall that what Oakeshott claims made Hobbes's philosophy a system "is the intention to be guided by reason and to reject all other guides." By contrast, Locke's cautious approach begins and ends with prejudice and compromise. Oakeshott does count Locke as a philosopher, yet Locke's approach is as far in character from Oakeshott's own conception of philosophy as Hobbes is near.

Oakeshott had claimed that it is necessary to understand the broader system of philosophy to which Hobbes connected his civil philosophy. I have taken him at his word and explored the contours of his understanding of Hobbes's philosophy as a prelude to discussing his interpretation of Hobbes's political philosophy. My interest in explicating what Oakeshott says about Hobbes has been to reveal his relationship to Hobbes as shown through his interpretation. Hobbes is a philosopher who moves from a philosophical position of skepticism to develop a political philosophy; as understood by Oakeshott, and using the language of Popkin, Hobbes was a constructive skeptic moving from a radically nominalist position to develop a civil philosophy. Sounding much like Oakeshott, Flathman suggests,

> The view that Hobbes's political philosophy is independent of the rest of his thinking is at odds with his own frequently reiterated understandings and intentions. Most important, by deflecting attention from his skepticism and in general his sense of the limitation on human capacities and powers, that view has been the chief source of misunderstandings and misappreciations of his most specifically political doctrines.[95]

While Oakeshott has perhaps suffered from many fewer "misunderstandings and misappreciations" than has Hobbes, Flathman's comments are appropriate to him as well. The problem for Oakeshott, however, has not been that attention has been deflected from his skepticism, but that his skepticism has been misunderstood. Oakeshott's skepticism, like Hobbes's, is philosophical; and Oakeshott's political theory, like Hobbes's, is connected to his philosophy.

I have ventured no further than to suggest that as Oakeshott interprets Hobbes there is an evident sympathy between his own philosophy and that of Hobbes. The relationship between the two within this sympathy is difficult to fathom. Did Oakeshott's initial inquiries into Hobbes's philosophy effect a more skeptical attitude in his own? Or, conversely, does Oakeshott turn to Hobbes because he finds in his philosophy an attractive and developed form of skepticism? These questions are compounded by the fact that Oakeshott seems drawn to Hobbes when he is giving increased consideration to political philosophy. Here, perhaps, is the central connection for Oakeshott; realizing the philosophical sympathies with Hobbes, Oakeshott seems drawn to his ability to construct a political philosophy while maintaining the skepticism. As I will discuss in the next chapter, Oakeshott comes to express his own political philosophy in the very terms that he characterizes Hobbes's. In fact, Oakeshott returns to the concept of his earliest political writings, authority, but now in a distinctly Hobbesian manner.

Chapter Five

Mister Hobbes's Oakeshott

I

"It may be said, then, that Hobbes is not an absolutist precisely because he is an authoritarian. His skepticism about the power of reasoning, which applied no less to the 'artificial reason' of the Sovereign than to the reason of the natural man, together with the rest of his individualism, separate him from the rationalist dictators of his or any age."[1] In this interestingly paradoxical passage, Oakeshott connects his emphasis upon Hobbes's skepticism with his interpretation of Hobbes's political thought. For Oakeshott, Hobbes was not an absolutist, because his skepticism served to undermine the certainty on which absolute claims—whether philosophical or political—could rest. In labeling Hobbes an "authoritarian," Oakeshott meant no pejorative; instead, he reveals authority as a central concept of his interpretation of Hobbes's political philosophy and, I will argue, of his own.

In Chapter Three, I examined Oakeshott's discussion of "The Authority of the State." Authority remains an important concept in his discussion of Hobbes, and I will begin to show in this chapter that Oakeshott's interpretation of the place of authority for Hobbes prefigures his own developing thoughts on authority. If there was a sympathy between Oakeshott's skepticism and his interpretation of Hobbes's philosophy, that sympathy doubles back in the way he understood Hobbes to offer authority in response to skepticism. Oakeshott reveals this connection not only in the themes of his discussion of Hobbes's ideas compared with his own, but in the very vocabulary that he uses in analyzing Hobbes. Most importantly, Oakeshott's preference for terms such as "recognition" and "acknowledgment" over "consent" and for *civitas* over commonwealth in his interpretation equip Hobbes with the very terms by which Oakeshott comes to express his own political thought. What is more, by tracing adjustments to Oakeshott's interpretation of Hobbes in a new version of his "Introduction to *Leviathan*," I highlight Oakeshott casting Hobbes as a theorist of civil association, perhaps the central concept of Oakeshott's own *On Human Conduct*.

The connection of skepticism and authority plays a central role in Oakeshott's interpretation of Hobbes. Having rejected a human capacity for certainty, the questions for Hobbes become whether there is any means whereby humans can know which claims—if any—oblige them, and whether there are any grounds on which the state can exercise power other than its ability and desire to do so. Beginning with the question of authority Oakeshott tightly weaves together the themes of law, duty, obligation, and morality in Hobbes's political philosophy. The tapestry that results is one that distinguishes Oakeshott's interpretation from others, and significantly reveals a pattern that will be re-inscribed in his own political theory. Focusing upon Oakeshott's interpretation of Hobbes also reveals a stage in interpretation that Paul Ricoeur holds as the most significant. "To understand is not to project oneself onto the text," Ricoeur claims, "but to expose oneself to it; it is to receive a self enlarged by the appropriation of the proposed worlds the text unfolds."[2] Oakeshott's interpretation of Hobbes contains both the moments of projection and exposure; it is an encounter that is reflected in his interpretation and in his own developing ideas so that we end up not only with Mister Oakeshott's Hobbes, but also Mister Hobbes's Oakeshott.

II

In the last chapter I explored the heavy emphasis that Oakeshott placed upon Hobbes's skepticism and nominalism. Oakeshott took Hobbes's philosophy to hold that reasoning is merely a hypothetical venture that can tell us nothing about a world external to language. In accord with this, Hobbes's conception of truth is not the character of statements that accurately reflect the world, but the coherent and consistent use of words, which are merely conventional signs used to secure fleeting images. Oakeshott had hinted at the implications of this understanding of his philosophy for Hobbes's political theory in his early essay "Thomas Hobbes." There he argued that "Hobbes's theory of law and government has, indeed, no ethical foundation, in the ordinary sense; but it is conceived throughout in purely naturalistic terms and begins in a theory of language."[3] The conventions of language secure the fleeting images of the mind, but there is no material foundation for them. So also there is no "ethical foundation" for government; instead conventional authority is needed to secure an anarchic world. As with truth in language, so also justice is a property internal to a system. Oakeshott only touched upon this in the early essay, but he develops it in full in his later works on Hobbes. There again his interpretation emphasizes the skeptical nature of Hobbes's philosophy. If humans can have no direct or unencumbered knowledge of nature, then there can be no grounding of authority in nature; similarly, if reasoning is merely conditional and hypothetical it can provide no categorical obligations upon humans. Hobbes's skepticism is too severe, according to Oakeshott, to allow for concepts such as natural authority or natural duty to serve as the basis of his political philosophy. Instead, authority, obligation, duty, law, and morality are human creations that regulate the seemingly haphazard and chaotic world they inhabit. Authority and law are artificial but no less important for being so. In fact, it is only because they are human creations, the artificial product of human wills, that authority, law, duty, obligation, and morality have meaning for humans and are binding upon them.

Briefly, Oakeshott's interpretation of Hobbes's political thought reads like this. Civil society is the only condition in which humans have obligations, the only situation in which concepts like justice and injustice have meaning, the only place where law binds them. Only in civil society can be found an authority that can create obligation, duty, and law. The sovereign power possesses this authority because it has been so authorized by those under its jurisdiction: it is the product of their wills, created and maintained to exercise authority. In civil society, subjects possess the duties they do and are bound by the laws they are because they acknowledge—Oakeshott's preferred term—the authority of the sovereign to so obligate them. The laws of nature are merely the prudential recommendations of reason; even when these are understood as God's law revealed in scripture, they obligate only within civil society once they are promulgated by the sovereign authority as binding.

Oakeshott says of his interpretation of Hobbes that "because it is an interpretation, [it] is not a substitute for the text."[4] This is, of course, no less true of my précis of his interpretation. Nonetheless, this outline of a skeleton lays bare the structure of Oakeshott's interpretation of Hobbes's political thought. For instance, based on his interpretation of Hobbes's nominalism and skepticism is Oakeshott's strong reading of Hobbes's contention that natural law—understood solely as the product of human rea-

son—is not binding as law until it is made so by a sovereign after the establishment of civil society. Until that time, the provisions of what might be
called the natural law are simply the precepts of right reason, and as such,
they are prudential recommendations only and thus impose no moral
obligations. For example, near the end of the first book of *Leviathan*
Hobbes writes: "These dictates of Reason, men used to call by the name of
Lawes; but improperly: for they are but Conclusions or Theorems concerning what conduceth to the conservation and defence of themselves;
whereas Law, properly is the word of him that by right hath command over
others."[5] Humans are not obligated by natural reason that discovers natural
law, but by the office that has the authority to create obligations. While
these words may lend support to Oakeshott's interpretation, even he recognizes that there are other places where Hobbes seems to be saying something quite different about the basis for validity of the natural law. However,
Oakeshott has put himself in a position to emphasize this theme with his
earlier stress upon Hobbes's skeptical philosophy, and from the particular
understanding of reasoning that he imputes to Hobbes. Oakeshott does not
deny—in fact, he insists—that reason is central to Hobbes's philosophical
system. However, he maintains, "From beginning to end there is no suggestion in Hobbes that philosophy [the product of reasoning] is anything
other than conditional knowledge, knowledge of hypothetical generations
and conclusions about the names of things, not about the nature of things"[6]
Given this understanding of Hobbes's view of reasoning, it is not surprising that Oakeshott would find that reason can neither provide humans
with obligations—for it can provide only "conditional knowledge"—nor
discern binding laws of nature—for it can provide only "conclusions about
the names of things, not about the nature of things."[7]

This starting place reveals a contrast between Oakeshott's view of
Hobbes's political thought and that of other interpreters. For example, in
"The Moral Life in the Writings of Thomas Hobbes," Oakeshott distinguishes himself first from Leo Strauss and then from Howard Warrender
and J. M. Brown, precisely on the issue of the source of obligation in
Hobbes. He imputes to Strauss the argument that because reason can determine that it is rational to "endeavor peace"—since it would serve the over-
riding goal of self-preservation—it must also be obligatory to follow this
precept and the others, all of which then can be seen as binding natural
laws. Oakeshott disagrees, noting that Hobbes "distinguished clearly
between merely rational conduct and obligatory conduct," and this is partially because "'reason' for Hobbes . . . has no moral force."[8] For Oakeshott's
Hobbes, reason, the provider only of "knowledge of hypothetical genera-

tions and conclusions about the names of things," is not capable of oblig-
ing conduct or establishing moral prescriptions.

Oakeshott also dismisses an interpretation that begins with a point similar to his own: that law is binding because it is the command of one who
has authority to make it so. In this interpretation of Hobbes, which
Oakeshott attributes to Warrender and Brown, "The Law of Nature, it is
contended, is law in the proper sense; it is binding upon all men in all circumstances because it is known to be the command of an Omnipotent
God."[9] Oakeshott has many difficulties with this interpretation, but central
is his rejection of the idea that in Hobbes's view, reason could provide
humans with the knowledge of God that would allow recognition of him
as the sovereign authority of the universe, who has established duties for
humans in nature. For Hobbes, on Oakeshott's reading, the most that reason can provide humans is the hypothetical notion of a "First Mover" or
"First Cause," but this is in no sense an understanding of a God who can
impose moral duties and rule over the earth.[10] To have an understanding of
this sort of God, reason would have to be supplemented by scripture. But
scripture offers no real solution. First, it would require that God actually be
recognized as the author of the miscellaneous set of writings known as
scripture. Second, even if these writings were so recognized, there is so
much variance in understanding and accepting the scripture that an
authoritative interpretation would still be required. Each of these problems
reveals a dependence upon some other, earlier form of the acceptance of
authority, one prior to the acceptance of the laws of nature seen as God's
law. The dependence upon scripture requires the acceptance of the authority of those writings and their interpretation; both of these needs of scripture can only be fulfilled after the establishment of civil society.[11] For
Oakeshott, viewing the laws of nature as binding because they are God's
laws would require that reason be able to demonstrate that the two are the
same; and reason cannot accomplish this. This criticism comes back to
Oakeshott's understanding of Hobbes's skeptical view of reason. He maintained "The lineage of Hobbes's rationalism lies not . . . in the great Platonic-Christian tradition, but in the skeptical, late scholastic tradition. He
does not normally speak of Reason, the divine illumination of the mind
that unites God with man, but with reasoning."[12] Since reason cannot give
an understanding of God other than as the hypothetical first cause,
Oakeshott thinks it would be absurd to hold that for Hobbes reason can
provide a link between that hypothetical entity and reason's prudential recommendations that could make them morally binding laws of nature.[13] But
if moral and political laws are not authoritative because of their relation-

ship to reason—or God via reason— why do they have authority? Hobbes's answer, according to Oakeshott, is simply that they are the product of an office that has been authorized to make such rules.

At first glance, this merely displaces the question about the source of the authority of laws to a second question about the source of the authority of the office that produces them. Oakeshott, however, does provide a substantive answer to this second question. It is an answer that reveals that, in Oakeshott's view, Hobbes's discussion of moral and political obligation is in terms of law, and his understanding of law is purely formal. Thus, the question "How do I know if I have an obligation in this matter?" is answered by a reply to the question "Is there a law which covers the matter?" And to answer the question "How do I know whether I need obey this law?" does not involve examining something like the law's natural justice or its relationship to God's law, the law of nature, or even the principles of right reason; and it does not matter whether I approve of the conditions it imposes, or that it contributes to a common good or is reflective of a general will. I need only be concerned "with whether or not the command is law in the proper sense, that is, whether or not it has been made by one who has authority to make it."[14] The substance of the law matters only in the consideration of how to apply it to circumstances, not in the judgment of a duty to obey it or not.[15]

But if the only question appropriate to ask is whether a law has been made by one who has authority, what is the source of the authority of the office that makes these laws? Oakeshott has claimed that it is not from reason or nature that an individual or group has the authority to enforce moral and political obligations (i.e. to make laws). Instead, he holds, "a lawmaker in the proper sense is one who has acquired this antecedent authority to be obeyed by being given it, or by being acknowledged to have it."[16] Here Oakeshott cites Hobbes's claim that "there being no obligation on any man which ariseth not from some act of his own," suggesting that the mere exercise of reason cannot qualify as the act of giving or acknowledgment that obligates.[17] Reason, however, can point to the "act" from which obligation "ariseth": the authorization of the sovereign. Establishing authority takes an act of creation, of authorization, by those authors who will be under the command of the instituted office of authority. In the "Introduction" Oakeshott cites in full the covenanting oath from Chapter Seventeen of *Leviathan* to reveal the nature of the institution of what he calls the "office of authority."[18] With the institution of the office of the sovereign comes also the establishment of the *civitas,* the civil society or civil association that is nothing other than the acceptance of the rule of the authorized sovereign.

The sovereign office is an artifice, as then also are obligation, law, moral-ity, and justice, which it creates and maintains. Oakeshott has emphasized that language and reason and philosophy are all artifice. None of these is any less important or efficacious for being so. Each, instead, works to mod-ify and condition otherwise chaotic and fleeting human experience: lan-guage works to "fix what is essentially fleeting" and civil society works to "abate" somewhat "the unconditional competition with . . . others" that is the human plight.[19] The effect of Oakeshott's emphasis upon Hobbes's skeptical philosophy is to free Hobbes's political thought from an "ethical foundation" by denying such foundations. Law and obligation are human conventions, as is language. This, however, only makes more difficult and important the question of authority. If one denies that universal dictates of reason or promulgations of God can act as an "ethical foundation" of law and government, then a thorough investigation of the "artifice" that can create authority is required. Hobbes, of course, takes recourse to a hypo-thetical founding contract to explain this artifice. Oakeshott, however, as I discussed in Chapter Three, had long displayed an aversion to consent the-ories of authority; he comes then to diminish the importance of contract even while emphasizing the human artifice of authority. In so doing, Oakeshott produces a Hobbes who reflects his own skeptical concerns and whose political thought exhibits many of Oakeshott's own developing political ideas.

III

In this brief overview of the central features of Oakeshott's interpretation of Hobbes's political philosophy, I have given my attention to the elements that connect his emphasis upon Hobbes's skeptical philosophy with the particular character of his political philosophy. In doing so I have focused primarily upon Oakeshott's "Introduction to *Leviathan*" and his essay "The Moral Life in the Writings of Thomas Hobbes." While a coherent inter-pretation of Hobbes can be taken from these works, there are actually many changes in Oakeshott's interpretation both between those two essays, and, interestingly, also between the "Introduction" as it was published with the Blackwell's Political Texts edition of *Leviathan* in 1946 and the version that Oakeshott published some thirty years later in his 1975 collection *Hobbes on Civil Association*.[20] Some of the changes of interpretation are relatively minor and some are substantive, some are clarifications of earlier problems identi-fied by critics, and some appear to be merely matters of expression and word choice. Oakeshott's interpretation of Hobbes's philosophy has already produced a Hobbes congenial to the skeptical position Oakeshott was moving toward. The effect of exploring these changes in his interpretation, however, is to reveal how his reconstructions of Hobbes's political thought increasingly reflect and perhaps prepare the way for the developed positions of Oakeshott's own political philosophy.

It is not surprising, perhaps, that over thirty years one might change an interpretation, yet Oakeshott would lead us to believe that these alterations in his studies of Hobbes are relatively minor. For instance, in his "Preface" to *Hobbes on Civil Association,* he provides only a few remarks on the "Introduction, 1975," claiming that what "I wrote for it has also been overtaken by the tide of recent writing on the subject"; and as for the new version, he merely states, "I have removed some of its more obvious blemishes."[21] It sounds as if Oakeshott is merely referring to the correction of a few minor but conspicuous corrigenda, when arguably there are noteworthy alterations. The impact of these changes does not go to core of his interpretation of Hobbes; there are almost no changes, for instance, in the first four parts of the "Introduction, 1975" where he examines Hobbes's context and philosophical system. However, especially in section "Five: The Argument of *Leviathan,*" significant changes do appear. These changes reveal the increasingly close association between Oakeshott's own political thought and that of Hobbes.[22]

An example of the changes over the years in his analysis of Hobbes is Oakeshott's alteration of his view of the relationship of moral and rational obligation. This change can begin to be glimpsed in his discussion of Strauss's interpretation of Hobbes in "The Moral Life in the Writings of Thomas Hobbes"; there Oakeshott rejected Strauss's view that "dutiful conduct is rational conduct . . . and that it is dutiful because it is rational."[23] Disagreeing, as I noted above, Oakeshott argued that Hobbes always "distinguished clearly between rational conduct and obligatory conduct"; yet in the "Introduction, 1946," Oakeshott himself had introduced the concept of "rational obligation" as a way to help understand Hobbes. He suggested there that Hobbes claims "the conclusions or theorems of reasoning are said to 'forbid' a man, to 'oblige' him, and even to create a 'duty.' . . . While they are still are only theorems, they are said to oblige on account of their rationality."[24] Now Oakeshott does claim here that this type of obligation is distinct from moral obligation, "an entirely different kind of obligation"; nonetheless it is a form of obligation that he does not entertain at all in "The Moral Life."[25] The impact of this change can be seen especially in the "Introduction, 1975," where he completely omits the discussion of "rational obligation."[26] Did Oakeshott think that the idea of "rational obligation" was merely an "obvious blemish" to be eliminated? Perhaps, but it appears less than obvious. After all, he himself felt the need to highlight it and argue against the idea in "The Moral Life."[27] Nor has this idea of the connection of the conclusions of right reason to obligatory conduct, as a form of natural law, been "overtaken by recent writing"; instead it remains an issue in contemporary Hobbes scholarship.[28]

There are other interesting deletions in the "Introduction, 1975" that seem to be more than mere removal of "blemishes," with that term's implied superficial and cosmetic quality. For instance, in "Introduction, 1946" Oakeshott included a section dedicated to discussing the "rights of the sovereign authority . . . what it *may* do; [and] its duties [which] are what it *must* do."[29] Interestingly, however, in "Introduction, 1975" the section contains no mention of duties of the sovereign—only the rights of the office. The question of whether the sovereign has duties or not is of course a contentious issue, but Oakeshott tacitly removes himself from the fray. Another deletion involves a relatively famous passage. In the "Introduction, 1946," in his closing section, Oakeshott had claimed,

> For politics, we know, is a second-rate form of human activity, neither an art nor a science, at once corrupting to the soul and fatiguing to the mind, the activity of either those who cannot live without the illusion of affairs or those so fearful of being ruled by others that they will pay their lives away to prevent it. And a political philosophy which represented the gift of politics to mankind as the gift of salvation itself would at once be suspect if not already convicted of exaggeration and error.[30]

Oakeshott himself could never stand convicted of this exaggeration and error, but perhaps he came to reconsider the statute of conviction; this whole passage is dropped from the later edition. Oakeshott's diminution of politics—and the criticism he received for it—is nothing new; the possibility that he quietly retreated from it may be.

There are, however, not only "blemishes" removed from the "Introduction," but additions made as well. In the "Introduction, 1946," Oakeshott claimed his exposition of the "artifact" of the civil body created through the act of authorization "may be done most conveniently under three heads: (1) the constitution of the sovereign authority, (2) the rights and duties of the sovereign authority, (3) the rights and obligations of the subject."[31] Besides deleting the discussion of "duties" in section (1) and altering "rights" to "liberties" in section (2) of the revised "Introduction, 1975," he adds a fourth head "(4) the civil condition," a section that is longer than the first section he lists.[32] Somewhat oddly, Oakeshott spends more time in this section on the place of public religion in the civil association than on the civil condition itself, making the argument that "In a *civitas* the *pax dei* is an integral part of the *pax civilis.*"[33] Nonetheless, the significance here is that Oakeshott does add, not just remove, elements of the "Introduction," and, as will become more clear below, his attention is focused more on the "civil" elements of Hobbes's political theory.

These changes and others do not necessarily add together to indicate a fundamental change in Oakeshott's view of Hobbes, yet I think the issues they discuss, even taken independently, count for more than mere "obvious blemishes" to be removed.[34] They entail adjustments or reconsiderations of contested matters of interpretation both when he wrote and when he revised. However, even if these were the minor adjustments that Oakeshott considers them, there is another type of change that does indicate a more significant alteration: the restyling of the central terms with which he discusses Hobbes. This terminological change does not so much transform Oakeshott's interpretation of Hobbes as clarify the increasing affinity of Oakeshott's political thought to that of Hobbes.

Oakeshott entitled his collection of essays on Hobbes's political philosophy *Hobbes on Civil Association,* and this title reveals the primary terminological change in Oakeshott's interpretation of Hobbes. "Civil association" is not a term that Oakeshott used in any of the essays collected in the volume in their original form. However, in the "Introduction, 1975," Oakeshott introduces this term (which is not Hobbes's) and often uses the term *civitas,* and in so doing he develops a more clearly articulated concept than existed for the various terms for which they substitute. Moreover, Oakeshott does not simply refine his analysis, reading "civil association" back onto Hobbes and also into his early writing on him. Instead, he discloses the proximity of his own political philosophy to that of Hobbes, since "civil association" is a term that Oakeshott himself, by the time of the "Introduction, 1975," had begun to use as one of the two ideal forms of human association, and in particular the one that he judged as the more appropriate model of the state. In the "Introduction, 1946" Oakeshott most often used the term "civil society" for the organized situation of human relationships that contrasts with the natural state. In the "Introduction, 1975" almost every place where Oakeshott had used "civil society" he substitutes "civil association." An example comes from the place where he is making a transition from his discussion of Hobbes's philosophy to his "civil philosophy." In the "Introduction, 1946," he wrote, "Civil philosophy, the subject of *Leviathan,* is precisely the application of this conception of philosophy to civil society. It is not the last chapter in a philosophy of materialism, but the reflection of civil society in the mirror of a rationalistic phi-losophy."[35] In the new version, "Introduction, 1975," he writes, "Civil phi-losophy, the subject of *Leviathan,* is precisely the application of this conception of philosophy to civil association. It is not the last chapter in a philosophy of materialism, but the reflection of civil association in the mir-ror of a rationalistic philosophy."[36] And so the substitution goes throughout the "Introduction."

By "The Moral Life in the Writings of Thomas Hobbes," Oakeshott had already ceased using "civil society," preferring to use the Latinate *civitas,* a term that Hobbes himself uses to describe his reconstruction of civil soci-ety. In the "Introduction, 1975," Oakeshott uses *civitas* (a term he did not use in the original) as a synonym for "civil association," also substituting it in places for "civil society." But in his use of the interchangeable terms, his substitution expands. For instance, in an earlier section of the "Introduc-tion," in both versions, Oakeshott holds that "the nature of political philos-ophy . . . [is to] establish the connections . . . between politics and eternity."[37] When he returned to this theme, near the close of the "Intro-duction, 1946," he claimed, "Political philosophy, I have suggested, is the consideration of the relation of politics and eternity. The end in politics is conceived to be the deliverance of a man observed to stand in need of deliverance."[38] In the "Introduction, 1975," however, Oakeshott states, "Political philosophy, I have suggested, is the consideration of the relation between **civil association** and eternity. The *civitas* is conceived as the deliverance of man observed to stand in need of deliverance."[39] There is an odd residue of the earlier idealism in both of these claims, where eternity (the whole, absolute world of ideas?) is the marker of what philosophy can accomplish. Notable for my interest here is that in the later "Introduction" Oakeshott has soaked up politics, an activity, into civil association, a condi-tional form of collective human association. I have already noted Oakeshott's removal of the disparaging comments about politics as a sec-ond-rate activity in the second version; a partial explanation for this may be that he has removed politics entirely from his account.

Civitas is an interesting choice of terms for Oakeshott. As I noted, he does not use *civitas* in the "Introduction, 1946," but he does use it often in "The Moral Life" and some in the "Introduction, 1975." Hobbes, in fact, does use *civitas* in *Leviathan,* but what makes this a significant choice by Oakeshott is his neglect of the term Hobbes uses most often in place of *civ-itas:* "commonwealth." Hobbes uses the term *civitas* three times in the whole of *Leviathan*—not at all in *De Cive*—and each time merely as an appositive of "commonwealth." For instance in his own introduction,

Hobbes claims "For by Art is created that great Leviathan called a Common-wealth or State (in latine Civitas) which is but an Artificial Man."[40] "Commonwealth" is Hobbes's term of preference for the civil creation. "Of the Common-wealth" and "Of A Christian Common-wealth" are the titles of two of the four parts of *Leviathan,* and it is also a term in four chapter titles. Beyond its titular significance, Hobbes simply uses the term often. On the other hand, Oakeshott uses it seldom, primarily in passages quoted directly from Hobbes; instead he almost always prefers *civitas* or "civil association." Below I will develop the argument that Oakeshott chooses this in order to avoid the ancillary usages of "commonwealth" that are closer to enterprise than civil association, but first I will detail more terminological changes that situate this choice.

One more interesting alteration is Oakeshott's use of the concept of "office." I noted earlier that a distinctive feature of Oakeshott's understanding of Hobbes's theory of authority is that obligations emanate from an established institution. In his sole use of the term "office" in the "Introduction, 1946" Oakeshott claimed, "The covenant then institutes an office, which may be held by one man or an assembly of men, but which is distinct from the natural person of the holder."[41] In the "Introduction, 1975," however, Oakeshott uses the term in the upper case as the title of the sovereign authority. For example he claims, "What is created and authorized in this covenant is an Office . . . this Office may be occupied by one or many. . . . But if the Office is occupied by an assembly of men. . . ."[42] In the first introduction "office" is only a common noun used once as synonym for the sovereign institution or authority. In the new version it becomes a proper noun, a title representing the sovereign authority. Now Hobbes does use the term "office," employing it as Oakeshott does in both "Introductions" as a way to speak of the institution of authority as opposed to the person or persons holding it. For instance, he entitles Chapter 30 of *Leviathan,* "Of the Office of the Sovereign Representative."[43] So for Oakeshott, we have the question, why the change of emphasis between the two introductions? Why draw out "office" and feature it as "Office"?

Now it might be suggested that the substitution, in the later version, of "civil association" and *civitas* for "civil society" and "politics" does not change the interpretation from the original. Or it may be argued that the elevation of the term "Office" in the new version is meant merely to clarify for the reader what exists under many terms in the original. My point, however, is not to suggest that these radically alter Oakeshott's interpretation of Hobbes, but rather that attending to the changes reveals the proximity of Oakeshott's own political philosophy to his understanding of

Hobbes. His own way of expressing his political philosophy, while not identical to Hobbes, begins close to Hobbes and becomes only closer. This begins in the intermediate essay "The Moral Life" and strengthens in the new version of the "Introduction." It even shows itself in other comments about Hobbes in later writings. In the previous chapter, I suggested that Oakeshott's affinity for Hobbes is based in a common skeptical philosophy. I now want to suggest that Oakeshott also presents Hobbes's philosophy in a fashion that is increasingly congenial to his own; or put differently, as Oakeshott turned his attention to political philosophy, his understanding of Hobbes played a strong role in the development of the themes and expression of that political philosophy.

IV

I have illustrated how Oakeshott imports civil association into his discussion of Hobbes as it becomes a central concept in his own political thought. It is in the discussion of the authority of civil association and the character of the rule of law in it that Oakeshott displays another significant relationship between his own political thought and his account of Hobbes. That is, in the "Introduction, 1975," Oakeshott uses "acknowledgement" and introduces "recognition" to substitute for "consent" in his account of Hobbes, using them in the same way and for the same purposes in his own discussion of civil association, authority, and the rule of law. In discussing Oakeshott's account of Hobbes's theory of obligation, I focused upon the claim that duties are imposed by rules that have authority (i.e., "law in the proper sense"). Law has authority because it is the product of an institution with authority to make it, the office of the sovereign. Oakeshott also emphasizes Hobbes's insistence that there is "no obligation on any man which ariseth not from some act of his own." So Hobbes's theory of obligation, according to Oakeshott, must reconcile an office with authority to make law with the idea that one is only bound by an act of one's own. Obligation must combine both an institution with authority and a voluntary act. One way of bringing these together—Hobbes's way, it would seem—is with the idea of the hypothetical generation of the sovereign through the authorizing covenant. Making a contract or joining a covenant would be an act of one's own that could create obligation, and it would authorize an institution that would then have the authority to impose obligations. This seems a tidy answer, but it presumes a positive answer to a thorny question: can a *hypothetical* covenant or contract count as the sort of "act of one's own" that can create obligation?

It may be that Hobbes uses the hypothetical contract as an illustrative model for the type of authorization, that would maintain the authority of the sovereign institution. The sovereign office gained its authority from some original act of authorization, and it retains it by the logical connection of those under its jurisdiction to that original act of institution by way of their continual consent. In *Leviathan,* Hobbes claims, "For it is evident, and has already been sufficiently in this Treatise demonstrated, that the right of all Sovereigns, is derived originally from the consent of every one of those that are to bee governed."[44] It is consent that originally and continually makes authority. A significant problem, however, with Hobbes's formulation of this has been identified by Richard Flathman:

> [Hobbes] regularly construes concepts such as "voluntary" and "assent," "consent" and "agreement" in ways that permit him to say that, despite what most of us would regard as substantial evidence to the contrary, these voluntarist conditions have been satisfied by an agent's actions and hence that obligation has become binding upon her. Most important, his latitudinarian criteria for the "consenting" or "covenanting" necessary to commonwealth . . . makes it all but impossible for anyone in the claimed jurisdiction to show that she *hasn't* given her consent to its authority.[45]

Flathman's argument is that Hobbes bleeds away most of the *voluntas* with his account of the actual voluntary actions that create obligation. While Hobbes emphasizes the importance of creating an obligation through an act of "consent" or "covenant," Flathman contends that Hobbes undermines the importance of this by assuming consent in almost all circumstances: it remains hypothetical, not actual consent. In this case, the connection of the authoritative office and an act of one's own that creates obligation is weak to the point of nonexistence. This seems to be an especially significant problem for Oakeshott's interpretation, since it turns on claiming that Hobbes's account of authority and obligation is unique because he understood "that moral authority derives solely from an act of will of him who is obliged."[46]

In this discussion I have begun to use the term, "consent." Its introduction is worth drawing attention to because it is a concept used by Hobbes that Oakeshott studiously avoids. In either version of the "Introduction" and in "The Moral Life" Oakeshott's only reference to "consent" appears in a footnote in the "Introduction, 1946": one that he deletes in the newer version. Oakeshott claimed "Hobbes sometimes uses 'consent' in this connection [of creating obligation]. And his theory has some claim to be regarded as the only one sufficiently individualistic to make 'consent' something more than hyperbole."[47] In Chapter Three, I demonstrated that early in his career Oakeshott was a critic of an understanding of authority that relied on the notion of consent. Here, Oakeshott seems to have made an interpretive choice that is reflective of his own dislike of the idea of consent; Oakeshott elects not to saddle Hobbes with what he considers a spurious concept on which to ground authority. Yet consent does play a role in Hobbes's thought. Oakeshott claims that Hobbes "sometimes uses 'consent,'" and while Hobbes does not use it as frequently as "covenant," it is a term that he uses in passages that manifest central features of his thought, even putting it in the upper case on occasion.

It may be that Oakeshott avoids the term "consent" because he is sensitive to exactly the sort of concern that Flathman would later identify as slipping into reliance upon "the obnoxious notion of tacit consent."[48] Oakeshott, like Flathman, does emphasize the voluntarist notions in Hobbes's account, but he also offers two different terms to connect the hypothetical founding contract with the need of a voluntary "act" from which obligation can arise. One of these terms is Hobbes's: "acknowledgement"; the other is not: "recognition." Oakeshott's use of these terms is well demonstrated in a passage from "The Moral Life." In explaining his understanding of Hobbes's theory of obligation, Oakeshott claims his interpretation "entails understanding [Hobbes's] expression 'whose command is addressed to one formerly obliged to obey him' (used by Hobbes to define the law-giver in the proper sense) to signify 'one who has already covenanted to set him up, or who has otherwise **recognized** him, or **acknowledged** him as a sovereign law-maker.'"[49]

Oakeshott's gloss on Hobbes's passage reveals him wrestling with the same issue that Flathman pointed to above by providing another way in which a voluntary act other than the original founding act can still maintain authority. Flathman is concerned that while Hobbes uses a term like "consent," he stretches its meaning for use in many instances where he insists obligation does and must exist, and yet few would see anything like consent. Oakeshott, instead, looks to different terms, "acknowledgement" and "recognition," that are provisionally voluntary but that do not require the same sort of explicit action that "consent" implies. Oakeshott understands that this may attenuate the strength of obligation as a product of an act of will. He glosses his own gloss, "This, I believe, in spite of the weakening of the word 'obliged' that it involves, is the most plausible reading of this expression."[50] Indeed, "in spite of the weakening" Oakeshott uses especially "acknowledge" regularly to describe the source of obligation, simply pairing it with "covenant." For instance, he claims that for Hobbes natural laws are not obligatory "except where they appear as the commands of a law-giver *who owes his authority to a covenant or an acknowledgement.*"[51] This leads to two questions: Are "acknowledgement" and "recognition" fair terms to use in place of "covenant" and "consent" for Hobbes? And why does Oakeshott prefer the former terms?

Hobbes, in fact, does use the term "acknowledge," although in a variety of contexts, not simply in the matter of the authority of the sovereign. He is perhaps more famous for using the term when speaking of how we may or may not admit certain qualities in others. For example, a requirement of the principles of right reason that lead to the covenant and peace states that "If Nature therefore have made men equall, that equalitie must be acknowledged."[52] Hobbes does also use it as Oakeshott suggests. For instance, in the central passages concerning the original, authorizing covenant, Hobbes says, "The only way to erect such a Common Power . . . [is] to appoint one man or Assembly of men, to beare their Person; and everyone to own and acknowledge himself to be the Author of whatsoever he that so beareth their Person shall Act."[53] So Oakeshott is not mischaracterizing Hobbes by using "acknowledge." Yet most of the places where Hobbes uses "acknowledge" are not in the generation of the commonwealth, but in speaking of the authority of God over his chosen human subjects. In the "Introduction, 1975" (wherein he uses "acknowledge" more than in the earlier version) Oakeshott does discuss acknowledgment in terms of an obligation understood as God's law. What is peculiar about this case is that unlike the generation of a *civitas,* humans neither create God nor his office as sovereign of the universe. Instead,

> In a voluntary act of acknowledgement they would have submitted themselves to the rule of divine commands. They have not authorized God to make rules for their guidance and they have not endowed him with power to enforce these rules, but they know he exists, that he is a law-giver and omnipotent, and they have acknowledged themselves to be his subjects.[54]

Thus knowledge of God, his capacity as law-giver, and his omnipotence are closely connected with acknowledgment of submission to him—to his authority. It is in this same discussion that Oakeshott also introduces the term "recognize" to get at the same idea. He says, for instance, "the theorems of natural reason about prudential conduct" would be obligatory for a people if they "were to be recognized as the *laws* of God, and further if this God were to be recognized as their God and they to lie within the jurisdiction of these rules."[55] Here again, if something further is known about the theorems of natural reason, that is, that they are the laws of God, then they are understood as obligatory. "Recognize," however, unlike "acknowledge," is not a term Hobbes uses in this context; it is Oakeshott's way of casting the argument. While in these works Oakeshott uses "recognize" only in this connection with God's laws—unlike "acknowledge"— he later uses "recognize," like "acknowledge," in a political context. Oakeshott claims in his essay "The Rule of Law" that in Hobbes's argument, "obligation to observe the conditions of *lex* . . . lies solely in the recognition of the authenticity of *lex*."[56] "Recognition" and "acknowledgement" serve as synonyms for the voluntary act that creates obligation in Oakeshott's interpretation of Hobbes: one, however, is taken primarily from Hobbes's discussion of God's authority and the other is grafted on.

What can we determine about "acknowledgement" and "recognition" and how they are used? Both have roots that have to do with knowledge, and in particular knowledge about something that already exists. "Acknowledge" has an English lineage in which the base of "knowledge" is evident, but also implied in its etymology is the meaning to admit something as true. "Recognize" is an English derivative from a Latin base, *recognoscire*, to know or know again.[57] Oakeshott's use of these terms in this context is especially interesting. According to Hobbes, God exists and is powerful and rules over the world as its creator. What makes his rulership unique, first for Jews, and then for Christians, is their recognition of this power. They do not create God's authority—he is not their artifice—rather they acknowledge his already existing authority for themselves. God's power and authority precede them, but a unique relationship develops though the "voluntary act of acknowledgement" by which they "have submitted themselves to the rule of divine commands."[58] Somehow an act of knowing and an act of will combine together in this sort of acknowledgment.

Now Oakeshott's claim that a "weakening of the word 'obliged'" exists when using "recognition" and "acknowledgement" is perhaps more clear. If one covenants to create an institution that has the authority to impose obligations, it is explicitly an act of will that obligates. If one merely acknowledges or recognizes that such an institution already exists, is this also "a voluntary act" of submission? Oakeshott seems willing to concede it is, although admittedly in an attenuated form. "To recognize" and "to acknowledge" each carry with them at least two senses. One the one hand, they connote the idea of knowing something; each implies that a person, who either doubted or did not understand something, now sees the truth or fact of something. A student needs, for instance, to recognize that the earth, though seeming flat, is round. But there is another sense in which each of these also implies validation. Practitioners in a field of medicine may come to recognize the benefits of using a certain technique and integrate it into their repertoire or they may acknowledge that an older practice no longer is effective and discontinue its use. Each of these goes beyond having knowledge to allowing that knowledge to effect a change in activity. The medical practitioner may accept as valid the decision of a medical board about the appropriateness of certain techniques, acknowledging its authority in these matters and recognizing its validity. In drawing out "acknowledgement"—and using "recognition"—Oakeshott chooses a term that calls up each of these meanings. When one recognizes the authority of God, one both accepts as true that God is omnipotent and accepts as valid that God has authority over the universe and oneself. With the knowledge comes the acknowledgment.

For Oakeshott, one advantage of using these terms is that it admits of the fact that while few—perhaps none—either contract to create a sovereign institution or partake of an explicit act of consent, the office can be maintained through an acknowledgement or recognition of its authority. As with God, a civil association most likely is a pre-existing condition for most of its members. Similarly, the civil association into which one is born most likely exerts power over an individual, as does God over the world. And as the rules of right reason become obligatory only when God is recognized as their author, when one recognizes oneself as being under God's jurisdiction, so also the rules of civil association are dependent upon being recognized as the commands of a sovereign institution with the authority to make them obligatory. To turn this equation around, if one asks "which rules obligate me?" just as Christians can answer "the laws of God," so also *cives* answer "those rules which are promulgated as laws by the Sovereign office."

We still find ourselves back asking why Oakeshott would prefer these terms, avoiding the more common term "consent" in characterizing Hobbes's theory of obligation and authority. This problem is compounded by the fact that Hobbes had available the concept of recognition, with the meaning Oakeshott ascribes to it, and did not use it. The benefit to Oakeshott in using "recognition" and "acknowledgement" seems to be that they retain aspects of voluntarism but also reduce the expectation of what counts as a voluntary act. This usage avoids the sort of criticism made by Flathman that by lowering the threshold from an explicit act Hobbes relies on tacit consent; thus, in using these terms, Oakeshott perhaps weakens without undermining the voluntarism central to his interpretation. Not by an act of consent, but through a more complex, although perhaps less voluntary, acknowledgment or recognition a sovereign institution's authority is maintained. Flathman criticized the abuse of the idea of consent as Hobbes chose to use it; Oakeshott, on the other hand, uses the terms "acknowledgement" and "recognition," accepting a weakening of the notion of obligation that they support.

Another effect of substituting "acknowledgement" or "recognition" for "consent" is that it diminishes the rationalist element of the maintenance of authority. Hobbes has shown that "the theorems of natural reason" point to the "prudent conduct" of the ending of the state of war through the institution of the sovereign with exclusive authority and power. This approach trades on the fear of the effects of the imprudent action and the seemingly simple and rational avenue to security. Yet perhaps for Oakeshott this still relied too heavily on reason. He has claimed that while Hobbes does not maintain a Platonic conception of reason, he is still a rationalist. Hobbes's approach seems at times to rely on the unreality of each subject going through the reconstructive, reasoning exercise that he has mapped out, in order to arrive at a clearer view of authority. This approach also discounts other considerations in accepting authority; it is understood wholly as a rational decision.

Oakeshott's interpretation addresses each of these concerns, again maneuvering around the idea of consent. In answer to the first concern, Oakeshott suggests that the reason why there is so much talk about the obligatory laws of nature in *Leviathan* is that for most subjects, all they need to know is that the laws of nature are the same as the laws of God, whose authority they already acknowledge.[59] Thus each subject need not go through the hypothetical-reasoning exercise in order to understand his or her obligations. For most, it is a matter of seeing more clearly the commands of God's law, an authority they already recognize. As for the second concern, Oakeshott explores the idea that Hobbes sees another reason that we might acknowledge the authority of the sovereign: it might not be from rational fear that one would consent; rather one might acknowledge authority out of pride. Oakeshott draws out of Hobbes a figure "whose disposition is to overcome fear not by reason (that is, by seeking a secure condition of external human circumstances) but by his own courage."[60] Thus it is not rationally determined consent, but a willingness to acknowledge authority "that springs from a 'contempt' of injustice."[61] Oakeshott recognizes that Hobbes does not and cannot rely exclusively on this pride, but it is one way around rational consent as the product of fear.

There is one more reason why Oakeshott might possibly choose to diminish the place of "consent" in his interpretation of Hobbes. The etymologies of "acknowledge" and "recognize" revealed the place of knowing in each of these and the connection between knowing and admitting or accepting something as valid. "Consent," like "recognize," is another Latin derivative, but with a quite different meaning. Here the root is *consentire*, which means to be in harmony or unison of opinion, or to be of the same mind, or to form a common plan of action.[62] The lingering overtones of these earlier Latin meanings may have been too strong for Oakeshott. While he does admit to the language of covenant, he does not at all impress upon Hobbes the idea that the agreement between covenantors concerns anything other than the establishment of the office of the sovereign. In discussing the *civitas,* Oakeshott claims, "There is in this association no concord of wills, no common will, no common good; its unity lies solely in the singleness of the Representative."[63] Earlier, authority did not have a natural basis; and here it is not founded in a "common will" or "common good." No harmony of purpose or unison of will exists in the *civitas;* in *civitas* there is *recognoscere* but not *consentire.*

His rejection of concord, common will or common good, may also provide some insight to Oakeshott's choice to avoid the term "commonwealth" in either "Introduction." "Commonwealth" connotes that there is a common weal or welfare around which the association is constructed, an idea that Oakeshott here wants to disassociate from Hobbes. The civil association is instituted to allow for the pursuit, although no longer unconditional, of the private weal, individually chosen by each associate. This, in effect, returns me to where I started this chapter: Oakeshott's denial that Hobbes is an absolutist. In Oakeshott's interpretation, Hobbes's individualism remains at the forefront, and this individualism is a direct result of nominalism and the attendant skepticism.[64] The product of the agreement among covenantors is strong, but the agreement itself is limited. On Oakeshott's reading, Hobbes is not an absolutist primarily because he does not envision the provenance of the sovereign to include the provision or promotion of a "common good" or "common will" even though the sovereign is commonly authorized. "To authorize a representative to make a choice for me does not destroy or compromise my individuality," Oakeshott maintains "There is no confusion of wills, so long as it is understood that my will is in the authorization of the representative and that the choice he makes is not mine, but his on my behalf."[65] Thus, even though Hobbes uses the term "Common-wealth" repeatedly, Oakeshott's interpretation likely leads him to avoid the term with its implications of a common good.

V

"Hobbes is not an absolutist precisely because he is an authoritarian," Oakeshott claimed. This is a meaningful distinction for Oakeshott because of the way in which he interprets Hobbes's concept of authority. Oakeshott also reveals his attraction to Hobbes as authoritarian; for him, however, the label is not pejorative, because the artifice of authority is an appropriate strategy to moderate the haphazard world that emits no meaning or justice of itself. For Oakeshott, Hobbes is an authoritarian because his system is based on the recognition that in a chaotic world, political and "moral authority derives solely from an act of him who is obliged."[66] Human artifice to abate chaos is a consistent feature of Oakeshott's interpretation of Hobbes's thought. In philosophy, meaning and truth are created by human convention to fix the fleeting images within humans' minds; they are not features of an external world that the mind discovers and conveys in language. In regard to politics, obligation and justice do not derive from a source outside of human association, determined by upper-case Reason or established by Natural Law; instead obligation and justice generate from humanly created authority, established by the institution of the office of the sovereign.

This act of institution, however, neither emanates from a common will nor generates a common good that sanctions authority. Instead, Oakeshott claims that Hobbes's skepticism and nominalism reveal such a strong strain of individualism that no common will or common good could be considered. Authority does not require the unanimity of a common good or will, for again, the *civitas's* "unity lies solely in the singleness of the Representative." Thus, according Oakeshott, Hobbes can have the unity necessary to maintain the authority of the *civitas,* but retain a firm place for the individual. Oakeshott wrote in his earliest consideration of Hobbes that "what is remarkable in Hobbes's doctrine of authority . . . [is] that it finds no place whatsoever for authority except in the control of men's actions."[67] Here is the real reason that Oakeshott does not consider Hobbes an absolutist: he contends that while Hobbes understood the need for authority to regulate actions, he did not advocate for control of thoughts and feelings. It is for this reason that Oakeshott argues later, "it is Reason, not Authority, that is destructive of individuality."[68] Reason expects conformity of the mind to its processes and to its results; authority expects only the conformity of actions to the rules its commands.

Oakeshott's emphasis here, upon the control of action, not mind, reveals the peculiarity of his interpretation. In developing his authoritarian

Hobbes, he ignores passages of *Leviathan* where Hobbes suggests that the sovereign authority may, perhaps must, control both. For instance, in describing the right of the sovereign to "Judge of what Doctrines are fit to be taught," Hobbes claims "For the actions of men proceed from their Opinions; and in the wel governing of opinions consists the well governing of mens Action."[69] Hobbes does limit this to those matters that affect peace, but again, the sovereign is sole judge of which those are. Oakeshott argues on behalf of Hobbes that "law as the command of the sovereign holds within itself a freedom absent from law as Reason or custom."[70] In doing so, he disregards Hobbes's empowerment of the sovereign to determine custom. Nonetheless, for Oakeshott, Hobbes's understanding of authority is one that does not position authority and liberty at odds; rather it places them in a close relationship. An example of this relationship of authority and liberty is found in Oakeshott's discussion of Hobbes's understanding of religion in the civil association. On the one hand, Oakeshott maintains that for Hobbes the civil association "must display [its] unity in the worship of God. He is to be recognized and honored in a public *cultus* and in utterances and gestures determined by the civil Sovereign. In a *civitas* the *pax dei* is an integral part of the *pax civilis*."[71] Here Hobbes recognizes the right of the sovereign to dictate public worship. Yet this is not based on a belief that the sovereign knows or can know either the certain truth of religion or what the subjects believe, for on the other hand, Oakeshott also holds that "the freedom of the Christian subject is the silence of the law with regard to his thoughts and beliefs; for if it be the right of the sovereign to suppress controversy, he has no right to interfere with what he in fact cannot control."[72] Authority here is expressed in the control of the acts of public worship and the public professions of faith; this is one more contribution to the arbitrary regulation of a chaotic world. But Oakeshott contends that Hobbes sees the limits of this authority and preserves liberty by recognizing that human thoughts are beyond the control of the sovereign, and thus beyond its authority. Oakeshott comments "It is a darkly sceptical doctrine upon which Hobbes grounds toleration."[73] The skepticism is one that holds that humans cannot know the thoughts and feeling of others, but can only engage with their actions.[74]

Authority is the central concept in Oakeshott's interpretation of Hobbes. Before leaving that interpretation, however, it is worth noting a significant lacuna: power. Oakeshott hardly mentions power in his interpretation of Hobbes. He speaks of the various rights of the sovereign office, and of course its authority, and earlier even of its duties. However, Oakeshott's only significant comment on power is when he notes that the founding institution "is a covenant not merely to transfer a right . . . but to be continuously active in supplying the power required to exercise it—for the Office can have no resources of its own."[75] Over and over again in *Leviathan* Hobbes maintains that it is power that ensures that promises are kept, contracts are maintained, and covenants are valid. A famous example from the opening page of Part II "Of the Common-Wealth" illustrates the importance of power to Hobbes. "For the Lawes of Nature," Hobbes declares, "of themselves, without the terrour of some Power, to cause them to be observed, are contrary to the naturall Passions. . . . And Covenants without the Sword, are but Words, and of no strength to secure a man at all."[76] For Oakeshott's purposes, however, the importance of *Leviathan* is not that it is a consideration of power, but that it is a reflection upon what exercises of power by whom are authoritative. In any event, while Hobbes writes often not only of the authority of the sovereign, but also of the significance of its power, Oakeshott passes by this latter dimension of Hobbes's argument.

In the previous chapter I detailed Oakeshott's interpretation of Hobbes's philosophy, in particular the version of skepticism with which he associated Hobbes. This chapter follows by detailing the effect that emphasis has upon Oakeshott's version of Hobbes's political thought and drawing attention to those elements that reveal just how close Oakeshott's interpretation of Hobbes is to his own political thought. The changes in terminology reflect the development of Oakeshott's own conceptual framework, particularly as it would come to be expressed in *On Human Conduct*. My point is neither to claim that Oakeshott simply models his understanding of civil association after Hobbes's, nor to make the unexceptional observation that there is an imprint of the interpreter upon the interpretation. Instead, it seems that Oakeshott finds in Hobbes a philosopher whose version of skepticism reflects his own developing philosophical tendencies. Beyond this, Oakeshott also seems attracted to a skeptic who instead of landing in nihilism and resignation, developed a political theory of authority that can serve to abate the dangerously random existence his skepticism tells him is his plight.

I have now spent two chapters exploring features of Oakeshott's interpretation of Hobbes, and it seems important to reflect explicitly upon why these features are of significance. I suggested in the beginning of Chapter Four that while we might learn something about Hobbes from Oakeshott, it is the latter who is my concern, and I have explored his writing on Hobbes because of the view of Oakeshott and his political thought that such an endeavor provides. In Chapter One, I examined Oakeshott's early idealism, and then in Chapter Three the political theory, in particular the idealist theory of the state, that he developed in accordance with it. In Chapter Two, I argued for significant alterations in Oakeshott's conception of philosophy from one of idealism to one primarily of skepticism. To trace out the implication of this alteration for Oakeshott's political thought I have chosen to focus on his interpretation of Hobbes, because his attention to that earlier English skeptic reveals the shape of the questions about politics that Oakeshott himself begins to ask—and some of the solutions he offers. It is a preparation for a particular reading of *On Human Conduct* and his idea of civil association that, I will suggest in ensuing chapters, allows me to position Oakeshott's work with contemporary questions about democracy, where only a few have placed him.

My strategy is one that highlights a different development of Oakeshott's thought from those that, instead of emphasizing the Hobbesian strain of Oakeshott's later political thought, emphasize the Hegelian elements. Most importantly, Franco suggests that "Hegel's notion of *Sittlichkeit* . . . must be kept in mind as we try to grasp the meaning of civil association."[77] Further, after observing that some "commentators have made . . . points about the un-Hegelian character of *On Human Conduct,*" Franco goes on to assert the unique character of his reading: "It should be clear that my interpretation of *On Human Conduct* goes in quite a different direction."[78] And that direction, of course, is a Hegelian one. I do not doubt that it is interesting and insightful to pose aspects of Oakeshott's understanding of the civil condition through Hegel as Franco suggests. I do, however, want to suggest some advantages to perceiving Oakeshott's political thinking in *On Human Conduct* and other later works through his reading of Hobbes.

One advantage is the existence of Oakeshott's readings of Hobbes, interpretations that are written and published during the periods of Oakeshott's most explicit attention to political philosophy. Conversely, Oakeshott produced relatively little explicit commentary on Hegel; he did, of course, write the clearly idealist "Authority of the State," and "Concept of a Philosophical Jurisprudence," but as I argued in Chapter Three, these stem from a distinctive and limited period of idealism. This is not to say that Hegelian elements do not survive; certainly they do, just as there was already interest and adaptation of Hobbes in his work in the thirties. I merely mean to point out the advantage of having access to his writings on Hobbes, because as I began to argue in this chapter, the interpretation— both in its construction and its expression—reflects so closely Oakeshott's own developing political thought.

There is one other advantage that I can only allude to here but will develop more fully in Chapter Seven. Oakeshott's interpretation of Hobbes emphasizes the significance of nominalism, with its commitment to radical individualism and deep skepticism. I have already argued that Oakeshott's philosophical commitments are moving toward similar positions, but what of his political commitments? Oakeshott's famed conservatism, perhaps best understood as a disposition about politics, change and governance, reflects a skepticism and radical individualism similar to what he has observed in Hobbes. Near the end of "On Being Conservative" he writes, "What I hope to have made clear is that it is not at all inconsistent to be conservative in respect of government and radical in respect of almost every other activity. And in my opinion, there is more to be learnt about this disposition from Montaigne, Pascal, Hobbes and Hume than from Burke or Bentham." But Oakeshott has not shown that a conservative disposition is a necessary result of such a skeptical position, only that it is one appropriate and not-inconsistent response to it. "Scepticism," Oakeshott had commented, "was, of course, in the air [Hobbes] breathed."[79] Again, at the other end of the trajectory of modernity from Hobbes, we find ourselves breathing the air of skepticism, even while many consider it a noxious vapor. Now, however, it is those who wish to be radical in respect to government as well as to almost every other activity who are its advocates. So, I argue, a final advantage to this Hobbesian Oakeshott is that with his emphases and themes, he is better prepared to breathe in this skeptical atmosphere, to engage with contemporary nominalists and skeptics than a Hegelian Oakeshott. "In an age of sceptics," Oakeshott also claimed, Hobbes "was the most radical of them all."[80] Can the same be said of Oakeshott? Probably not, for in the end the disposition he mentions above restrains his skepticism; yet by explicitly highlighting those restraints he points the way to what an even more radical skepticism might entail.

Chapter Six

Civil Association, Politics, and Authority

I

"It is no exaggeration to call Oakeshott's ideal of civil association the heavenly city of a skeptic and unbeliever"; or so claimed Sheldon Wolin in a consideration of Oakeshott's *On Human Conduct*.[1] Wolin's ironic title of the heavenly city for the unbeliever characterizes the relationship of Oakeshott as skeptic and his concept of civil association. Civil association is Oakeshott's attempt to fashion a conception of association through which to understand the modern state, to describe the character of politics that sustain and endanger it, and to accomplish all this from his own position of skepticism. This direction of Oakeshott's work was first revealed in his reading of Hobbes; he viewed that earlier skeptic as developing an understanding of sovereignty and authority that he came to call civil association. In examining this interpretation of Hobbes, Paul Franco asks of Oakeshott "What does Hobbes's skeptical doctrine about the nature and role of reason mean for his understanding of politics?"[2] In the past two chapters I have supplied one answer to this question: the authority of the sovereign is based not on natural law or right, not on a notion of the common good or common will, but rather upon the recognition or acknowledgment of those subject to that authority. Franco, emphasizing the place of the will in Oakeshott's interpretation, suggests that for Oakeshott "the rejection of the rationalism of the 'Platonic-Christian' tradition entails the replacement of reason by will. Hypothetical reasoning is incapable of imposing duties or obligations. Legitimate authority can only derive from an act of will on the part of the person who is obligated."[3] I do not disagree with the point of this observation, yet I have noted that Oakeshott diminishes the place of explicit acts of will such as consent and contract in the substance of authority, relying instead upon recognition and acknowledgment. Still, Franco has expressed his interpretation in terms of the same concept that I suggested above is central to Oakeshott's interpretation of Hobbes: authority. As Franco asked of the interpretation of Hobbes, I now ask directly of Oakeshott: What does his skepticism mean for his understanding of civil association and the place of politics within it? More specifically, given his rejection of rationalism, natural law, natural right, acts of will such as consent and contract, the common will, and the common good, is it possible for the state modeled as civil association to have authority, and if so how? As I began to show in the previous chapter, a good share of Oakeshott's answer can be seen in his interpretation of Hobbes, but there is more as well.

I have tracked two different trends in Oakeshott's thought. One is his movement from a strict form of absolute idealist philosophy to a skepticism directed toward philosophy as well as other modes of human experience. The other, which follows upon this first movement, is an attention to Hobbes such that much of Oakeshott's expression of Hobbes's thought and that of his own coincide. The second of these two trends acts something like a culmination of the first, as Oakeshott comes to question whether any understanding of the state can accompany, indeed withstand, the skepticism he had adopted; or as I put it above, if we are skeptical of the various claims of natural law, natural right, consent, contract, common will, or common good, on what basis—if any—can the state exercise its power with authority? It is authority, its proper constitution and office, that concerns Oakeshott. I have already shown how authority was a primary idea in his earliest philosophical considerations of politics, and how, differently understood, it is central to his interpretation of Hobbes. Now I want to examine its place in his later political philosophy, especially, though not exclusively, in *On Human Conduct*.

II

In the previous chapters, I have reviewed how Oakeshott understands Hobbes to offer an image of what he calls civil society and later civil association. It is civil association that Oakeshott himself also offers as a model for understanding the authority of the modern state, again reproducing a good share of what he understood Hobbes to claim for civil association. His later work expands and develops this concept by contrasting it with what he calls enterprise association. Oakeshott understands each of these types of association to be candidates for the appropriate model for the state and the generation and maintenance of its authority. From the beginning, Oakeshott accepts both of these types of association as appropriate forms of human association, but for him, civil association is the more suitable model for the constitution and office of the state. What distinguishes them as models for the state is something that Oakeshott's interpreters have paid little attention to and about which he himself had little to say. However, central to Oakeshott's distinction between the two forms of human association and his preference of civil association for the state is the place of power.

Before I begin my discussion of civil and enterprise associations it is important to point out a series of terms that Oakeshott uses that carry with them similar but not exactly the same meanings. The central theoretical distinction in Oakeshott's *On Human Conduct* is between civil association and enterprise association. Yet he uses a series of Latin terms to explore this distinction. For instance, in discussing civil association, Oakeshott uses "*civitas* for this ideal condition . . . and *respublica* for the comprehensive conditions of association."[4] This becomes a bit more confusing when in the third essay of *On Human Conduct* Oakeshott introduces the term *societas* for the historical expression of civil association and *universitas* for historical expression of enterprise association. Finally, Oakeshott uses the concept of "The Rule of Law," in his essay by that name, to describe and substitute for civil association. Thus Oakeshott has on the one side: civil association, *civitas, respublica, societas,* and rule of law; and on the other: enterprise association and *universitas.* I will favor using civil and enterprise association in my discussion, but in following Oakeshott's various discussions will need recourse to the other terms as well.[5]

The distinction between civil and enterprise associations and Oakeshott's arguments in preference of the former over the latter as a model for the state center on one central theoretical claim posed as a self-evident, empirical observation: "a state on any reading of its character, is a comprehensive, exclusive, and compulsory association."[6] Citizens in modern states do not, except under extraordinary circumstances, choose the state in which they live. Of course, there are the possibilities of immigration and naturalization, but in maintaining the medieval principle of *ne exeunt regno,* modern states determine and enforce rules regarding these options. The "compulsory" character he observed in the modern European state has great significance currently because he also claims "the 'power' now at the disposal of governments . . . reflects the vast increase in modern times of the ability to control men and things."[7] Oakeshott is ambiguous about what he means by "the ability to control men and things." Assuming a fairly traditional account of power, Oakeshott claims, "the current governments of Europe may be said to be 'powerful' in virtue of being able to formulate their designs clearly and to make them known in utterances which reach and are readily understood by all those concerned, to enlist continuous support or to compel continuous acquiescence, to act rapidly, economically, and with the likelihood of achieving the wished for outcome."[8] However, as David Mapel has pointed out, because of Oakeshott's emphasis upon "the apparatus of control and surveillance" available to the modern state, its power as conceived by Oakeshott has "surprising affinities with the work of theorists like Foucault."[9] For instance, Oakeshott reveals an intriguing ambivalence about the state's power to create "literate subjects upon whom the duty of reading notices and filling in forms may be imposed with some confidence, among whom utterances . . . may be freely disseminated, each of whom may be required to carry *documenti* and may be identified with certainty by means of names, signatures, photographs, fingerprints, etc."[10] Oakeshott, however, is less concerned about detailing a theory of power than considering a set of questions that generate from the initial recognition of the state as "a comprehensive, exclusive, and compulsory association." Given this complete and coercive character of the state, and a relatively greater power to coerce in modern times, is it still possible for the state to recognize and incorporate human freedom? Is there a model of the state that, while not rejecting compulsion (which would reject the state), still admits human freedom? To pose and answer these questions means relying also upon a conception of human freedom. Only when that has been established will the possibilities for a state to incorporate freedom become more clear. This can be seen as the course of the argument given in *On Human Conduct:* first, Oakeshott details an argument about human freedom, next he explores how this freedom is reflected in different forms of human association, and finally he offers an historical investigation of the exhibition of these associations in the development of the modern European state.

Oakeshott's conception of human agency and conduct, and the concept of freedom that accompanies it, is complex, and I will not explore all of its dimensions here.[11] There is, however, one essential element that is central to the various ways he conceives of freedom. Oakeshott claims,

> The 'freedom' intrinsic to agency is, then, the independence enjoyed by the
> agent in respect of being a reflective consciousness composed of acquired

feelings, emotions, sentiments, affections, understandings, beliefs, convictions, aspirations, ambitions, etc., recognitions of himself and of the world of *pragmata* of the world he inhabits, which he has turned into wishes, and wishes he has specified in choices of actions.[12]

There are a number of interesting observations to be made about these claims for the "'freedom' intrinsic to agency." First, it should be clear from this long passage that Oakeshott does not hold an understanding of a unified, a-historical subject. An "agent" is a composition of acquisitions. No essential set of characteristics make up what it is to be a human agent. For Oakeshott, "An agent has a 'history', but not 'nature'; he is what he becomes"; and there is no teleological prescription for what he will become.[13] This attitude is certainly in keeping with the skepticism in Oakeshott's thought that I have earlier emphasized. To claim that "An agent has a 'history', but not a 'nature'" is to reject the idea of a universal essence to all agents; instead agency is only the contingent association of a unique set of "feelings, emotions, sentiments, affections, understandings, beliefs, convictions, aspirations, ambitions, etc." Still, there does remain a certain essential feature to agency that is significant for the distinction of civil and enterprise associations as model associations for the state. Oakeshott maintains that this understanding of freedom considers "the independence enjoyed by the agent in respect of being a reflective consciousness." Even if this "reflective consciousness" is moderated by the understanding that it is a composition of all that follows in the passage above, the two sides of the last conjunction of the quotation reveal that for Oakeshott, human agency is broken into understandings of the world and choices about the actions appropriate to take in response to those understandings. Agency is not only a reflective consciousness of the congeries listed above, but also a connection of those turned into wishes and choices. Later he extends these elements by claiming that the freedom associated with this conception of agency is related to acting upon those choices, suggesting that there is a "link between belief and conduct which constitutes 'free' agency."[14] These aspects of the state and human agency together again produce this central question for Oakeshott: Given this exclusive and coercive character of the modern state, is it still possible for it to recognize and incorporate human freedom? The conceptions of civil and enterprise associations are in some ways candidates for models of the state that might answer this question.

Human agents exhibit their freedom in pursuing their own choices. When agents choose to pursue their choices in common with others, a relationship or association is established. This is what Oakeshott calls enterprise association. An enterprise association is a mode of human association that is "relationship in terms of the pursuit of some common purpose, some substantive condition of things to be jointly pursued, or some common interest to be continuously satisfied. It is association not merely concerned with satisfying substantive wants, but in terms of substantive actions and utterances."[15] Oakeshott accepts enterprise association as a wholly appropriate mode of human association, and he gives many examples of such. For example, human agents so associated "may be believers in a common faith . . . they may be partners in a productive undertaking (a bassoon factory); they may be comrades, or allies in the promotion of cause, colleagues, expeditionaries, accomplices or conspirators; they may comprise an army, a 'village community,' a sect, a fellowship."[16] In an enterprise association the terms of contract and consent, which Oakeshott had been critical of as an understanding of associates' relationship to the state, have a home because they reflect the character of agreements that join those engaged in a common purpose. One might agree with others that Jesus of Nazareth was (is?) the Saviour and so mutually choose with others to commit or refrain from certain acts, and perhaps even join with others to save souls; or one might contract with others to invest in a "bassoon factory" with the desire to make bassoons or at least make a profit. Both of these, however, imply the capacity either to lose one's faith and abandon the mission or disagree with the management of the corporation and sell one's shares.[17] The freedom of agency is represented both in the reflective consciousness choosing a goal and in the choice of joining with others in association to pursue that goal. Importantly, however, in order for such an associate to retain her freedom she must also be able to change her choices, readjust her goals; to remain free she must reserve the capacity to withdraw from the association if her understanding of her place in the world and the goals she seeks change, or if she comes to judge the association as ineffective or even destructive of the sought-for goal. If such an agent could not rescind membership, then it would not be a choice based on her understanding of the world about her; membership would neither express nor retain the freedom of human agency.

It is, perhaps, clear now that Oakeshott will have difficulties with the choice of enterprise association as a model for the state. If the freedom of human agency entails that one can choose to join with others to achieve a common substantive good, it also requires that one must be able to rescind one's membership. However, a state, as "a comprehensive, exclusive, and compulsory association," cannot admit of this freedom. Understood as an enterprise association, the state disrupts the freedom of human agency.

Oakeshott explains: "For [an agent] to be associated in the performance of joint actions contingently related to a common purpose and not to have chosen his situation for himself and to be unable to extricate himself from it by revoking his choice, would be to have severed the link between belief and conduct which constitutes moral agency."[18] The state understood as enterprise association chooses substantive ends and directs actions for its associates, and in doing so it inhibits the associates' capacity to choose their own actions to pursue their own ends. As appropriate as an enterprise association may be for any number of less comprehensive relationships, it cannot serve as the model for the state because of the recognition that the latter is comprehensive and compulsory.[19] A state as such would dissolve "the link between belief and conduct which constitutes 'free' agency."[20]

In different ways and in different places Oakeshott has criticized the image of the state that is modeled on enterprise association. In his famous commentary from the forties in "Rationalism in Politics" and similar essays, Oakeshott develops a critique of the understanding that politics is about managing the activities of citizens toward the direction of some substantive good to be shared by all. In a recently published, but previously unknown manuscript, we see that in the fifties Oakeshott developed a critique of the tendency to the "politics of faith" that takes up the salvation of the subjects (from sin, want, or insecurity) as the central goal of politics.[21] Later in the fifties and early sixties Oakeshott construes this critique in terms of the morality and political theory of "collectivism" and of the "mass man" to whom these attend.[22] In the historical essay of *On Human Conduct*, Oakeshott recalls the medieval *universitas* to focus his criticism of the model of state that bases itself on the goal of directing subjects toward a substantive good or in developing the virtue of its citizens. In each of these critiques, Oakeshott makes many observations and analyses concerning his difficulties with this model for the state; it is, however, the connection between his argument about "the 'freedom' intrinsic to agency" and his claim that "a state on any reading of its character, is a comprehensive, exclusive, and compulsory association" that provides the theoretical impetus to his rejection of the enterprise association paradigm for the state.

III

Oakeshott examines the ideal of enterprise association as one model available for understanding the character of the state. For Oakeshott, this model fails because the compulsory nature of the state is destructive of the very type of freedom enterprise association promises. But for Oakeshott there is another model available that he develops initially in his interpretation of Hobbes: civil association. How does civil association stand in the matter of freedom's relation to the power of the state? According to Oakeshott, it stands quite well. This is because Oakeshott maintains that civil association does not expect its associates to share common beliefs about the proper set of substantive ends, purposes, or goods. Instead, it requires of associates only that they modify or qualify their actions according to rules while pursuing their own self-chosen ends. As in his interpretation of Hobbes, it is in the recognition of those rules as having authority that Oakeshott maintains civil association is found.

According to Oakeshott, the rules of civil association are not to be understood as demanding associates to take certain actions in order to achieve a particular, substantive, common purpose. Instead, such rules are to be understood as formal considerations to be subscribed to in pursuing one's own ends. The central feature of Oakeshott's understanding of civil association is that "*cives* . . . are related solely in terms of their common recognition of rules which constitute a practice of civility."[23] Oakeshott often takes recourse to language as an analogy to describe this type of relationship, suggesting that the rules of civil association adverbially modify actions; as a practice of civility, the rules of civil association are simply understood as "the *adverbial* conditions of a procedure."[24] The rules in civil association are like the rules of language or, he also suggests, like the rules of a game. As he understands them, "rules do not enjoin, prohibit, or warrant substantive actions or utterances; they cannot tell agents what to do or say. They prescribe norms of conduct."[25] Here, even proscriptions against particular types of actions can be understood as mere requirements to modify how one acts: "A criminal law, which may be thought to come nearest to forbidding actions does not forbid killing or lighting a fire, it forbids killing 'murderously' or lighting a fire 'arsonically.'"[26] Again, rules are formal considerations an agent must take into account when pursuing her own set of actions; just as the rules of syntax do not tell an agent what to say, but how to speak grammatically, so also the rules of civil association do not tell associates what to do, but how to act civilly (i.e. as a *civis* or civil associate). This seems, perhaps, to be a rather simple view of language and agency in which a subject begins with wants and desires fully formed and then chooses words or actions to express or achieve those desires. Yet while it may have aspects of such a model, Oakeshott does not present it simply so. For instance, in describing agency he claims, "Human conduct is not first having unconditional wants (individual or communal) and then allowing prudential reason and moral sensibility to indicate or determine the choice of actions in which their satisfaction is sought; it is wanting intelligently (that is in recognition of prudential and moral consideration)."[27] Here the rules are not applied to actions or choices but are understood as part of them.

The analogy to language or a game may be of interest for understanding Oakeshott's idea of a civil association, but when thinking of civil association as a model for the state the analogies have some important limitations. Oakeshott noticed that when civil association is understood as a state and rules are understood as laws, or "*lex*" as he calls them when discussing the ideal of *respublica,* that other, earlier consideration must be added: the observation that unlike language or a game, "a state on any reading of its character, is a comprehensive, exclusive, and compulsory association."[28] The state responds with force to those who fail to accommodate themselves to these rules or laws in their actions. This brings us back again to the question, can freedom be aligned within the coercive state? How is being forced to obey a law understood as a rule in a civil association different from being forced to follow a law dedicated to the common good of the enterprise association? According to Oakeshott, the state as civil association differs in the matter in two ways. First, civil association does not expect common action or allegiance toward a common substantive good; rather it allows associates to pursue self-chosen actions and to choose differing substantive goods. Second, civil association does not expect approval of its rules, but instead only demands the recognition of their authority.

The first of these two claims is simply true according to how Oakeshott defines civil association. He has claimed that a rule of civil association does not tell an associate what to do, but prescribes "norms of conduct" that act as formal considerations in choosing and acting. Thus to look again at Oakeshott's rather odd example from above, if one chooses to light fires one is free do so, with the stipulation that one not do it "arsonically." There are perhaps some important limitations with this understanding of freedom. To be able to redefine a prohibition against arson as an adverbial, formal consideration to be accounted for in action shows that just about any action could be so redefined; or, conversely, variant types of actions can all be brought under adverbial and formal consideration. Thus the substantive choices that Oakeshott wants to protect can simply be recast as adverbial considerations.[29] For example, a rule against acting recklessly could be applied to any number of self-chosen actions and could be interpreted to confine so narrowly the place of choice in action so as to make it meaningless. Or the substantive command that one ought not blaspheme God can also be construed as a rule that one ought not speak blasphemously. John Liddington makes a similar observation directed exactly at the char-

acter of Oakeshott's usual concerns by asking, "If a law prohibiting fire-rais-
ing may be said to qualify rather than determine the performance of fire-
lighting, why may not a law prohibiting say 'bourgeois' education be said
to qualify rather than determine the performance of learning and teach-
ing?"[30] In other words, formal considerations can be understood as substantive considerations and vise versa. The point for Oakeshott, however, is
not simply that one's choices are affected by such rules. Of course, they are;
if not they would be meaningless. Instead, the important consideration is
that these rules do not exchange those choices for others dictated by the
regulative and substantive ideal of the common good or common will. In
an enterprise association model of the state, this exchange would take place
for all those who did not initially choose the common good.

Richard Flathman provides another view upon Oakeshott's "adverbial"
understanding of this character of the rule of law found in civil association.
The advantage of Flathman's view is that it does not rely exclusively upon
the theoretical strength of the distinction of rules understood as either
enjoining substantive actions or formal considerations. Instead, he draws
attention to the affect upon agents to which rules apply. "The distinguishing
features of this vision (of civil association), however, are not its institutions or
practices in what we might call their material, rule governed form, but rather
the understandings its *personae* have of themselves, of their relationships with
one another, and of the arrangements to which they mutually subscribe."[31]
To Liddington's and my own concern that substantive commands can merely
be rephrased adverbial qualifications, Flathman might propose that we not
place too much emphasis on the "merely." That is, even if the theoretical distinction may not be purely maintained, there is a practical political effect in
favor of the freedom of agents when as *cives* they must qualify their actions
in such a way, and law must be promulgated in such an adverbial fashion.
Oakeshott, in fact, suggests that one course of politics in civil association is
the transformation of substantive considerations into formal concerns. He
describes this as a necessary procedure for those *cives* who wish to appropriately pursue substantive wants or interests according to the rules civil association. "What it means is that a proposal which may begin in a want, a wish
for a benefit, or a plea for a removal of a disadvantage must lose this character and acquire another (a political character) in being understood, advanced
and considered as a proposal for amendment of the *respublica* of civil association."[32] Recognizing the difficulty of such translations highlights its benefits,
and Flathman recalls that for Oakeshott, "life in a rule of law association
requires no less than a 'disciplined imagination.'"[33] Yet, following Oakeshott,
he also maintains "The demands [civil association] makes, severe as they are,

would be as little burdensome for the human beings it postulates and pro-
motes as life in a political organized rule association can be."[34]

Liddington's and Flathman's considerations, however, do not get at the
whole issue of the "'freedom' intrinsic to human agency." One of the ways in
which an enterprise association incorporates freedom is to allow disassociation. If one no longer accepts the goals of an enterprise one can walk away,
quit the scene, terminate membership. This was a central reason why
Oakeshott rejected it as a model for the state: "a comprehensive, exclusive, and
compulsory association" does not allow such disassociation, or does so only on
its terms. A state modeled on enterprise association expects all associates to
choose the common good, to approve of the goals of that comprehensive association; here disapproval of the common good or purpose is seen as treason or
heresy. However, a civil association, since it does not require agreement upon
a common purpose, can maintain a different appreciation for disagreement
concerning the conditions it prescribes and thus addresses the second claim
regarding the freedom of human agency. Civil association is not dependent
upon consensus concerning a common good, where the choice of different
ends must be disallowed as disruptive of that end. Instead, Oakeshott claims:

> There is, then, in civil association nothing to threaten the link between belief
> and conduct which constitutes 'free' agency, and in acknowledging civil
> authority *cives* have given no hostages to a future in which their approvals
> and choices no longer being what they were, they can remain free only in
> an act of disassociation. Civil freedom is not tied to a choice to be and to
> remain associated in terms of a common purpose; it is neither more nor less
> than the absence of such an approval or choice.[35]

Understood as civil association, then, the compulsory association of the
state is not abusive of freedom, because it only asks that its rules be recognized as having authority; it is based on acknowledgment of the authority
of the rules of association understood as laws, not their approval. Civil freedom is tied to the common recognition of rules in self-chosen actions, not
"to a choice to be and to remain associated in terms of a common purpose." For Oakeshott, the recognition of authority indicates "a formal, not
a substantial relationship; that is, association in respect of a common language and not in respect of having the same beliefs, purposes, interests, etc.,
or in making the same utterances."[36] In enterprise association, one could
exhibit her freedom in possessing different goals from the enterprise only
by choosing to disassociate, but this is not allowed by the state. In civil association, approval of the rules is not asked for—instead, only recognition of

their authority. In civil association, Oakeshott maintains, "Civil freedom is . . . neither more nor less than the absence of such an approval or choice." Civil association does not ask for the soul, it does not require associates to be patriots, it does not expected associates to accept their fate for the roles they play in a common purpose; civil association asks only that those rules, with which one may disagree, be recognized as authoritative and acknowledged in conduct.[37] David Mapel points to this as the distinctive benefit of Oakeshott's view of authority: civil association does not "encourage approval or disapproval of the conditions it prescribes. Strictly speaking, this indifference opens up the maximum amount of space for criticism."[38] Below I will examine these advantages and the still existing limitations Oakeshott has in place.

I began this chapter with a question about the relationship between Oakeshott's skepticism and his understanding of politics. It his understanding of human freedom and skepticism about a common substantive goal around which a state could be constructed that has allowed him to suggest the ideal of civil association as a model for the state. Civil association, for Oakeshott, incorporates this skepticism first by rejecting the idea that the authority for the state is generated outside of the state itself in universal or natural principles and next in rejecting the idea that it is founded on the substantive idea of commonly held beliefs about the proper end or good of society. This skepticism about the basis of the authority of the state allows the development of a model that can incorporate its coercive elements and yet also his conception of human freedom. Human agents are understood as different histories expressing different beliefs and purposes, yet sharing an enforceable, formal, civil relationship. However, as much as Oakeshott wants to have done away with the need for consensus, clearly it is still present: it exists in the consensus required for the recognition of associates of the authority of the state. Authority is the central concept for civil association, for it is in the acknowledgment of the authority of its rules that civil association exists, not in consensus regarding a good for which the state is organized. But where is this authority and of what consists the judgment that leads to acknowledgment and recognition of it? What is the relationship of recognition and approval of the rules of civil association? What sort of consensus about authority is required to uphold civil association?

IV

In Chapter Three, I discussed Oakeshott's early essay "The Authority of the State." There I suggested that the examination of Oakeshott's considerations of the authority of the state was interesting not only because it was his first published work on political philosophy, but also because it revealed skeptical and idealist elements similar to his philosophy as a whole. I argued that aspects of his considerations in "The Authority of the State" would remain but be transformed when Oakeshott discarded the idealist elements of his thought to the further development of the skeptical. The tour through Oakeshott's interpretation of Hobbes can now give insight into the understanding of authority as part of his own skeptical thought turned toward questions of politics. Authority was a central feature of that interpretation and now returns in his own understanding of politics.

Very early in his career, in "The Authority of the State," Oakeshott had argued that authority is not something external, but rather something that is based upon the judgment of the person over whom authority is exercised. He had, however, also maintained that "an authority is always its own sanction. That which is . . . absolute and unlimited. . . . The real authority of all belief and action is that which can show itself to be absolute, irresponsible, self-supporting, and inescapable."[39] To the discussion of civil association above, this latter aspect of his earlier ideas of authority seems entirely foreign. Nothing in Oakeshott's later thought could allow for something that is "absolute, irresponsible, self-supporting, and inescapable," and he sacrificed this aspect of his conception of authority when he also abandoned the idealist "whole world of ideas" upon which it was based. What this leaves is the basis of authority in judgment, though Oakeshott does not use the language of judgment in his later discussions of authority but rather, as in his interpretation of Hobbes, that of acknowledgment and recognition. There are, perhaps, some significant differences between his early conception of judgment, on the one hand, and recognition or acknowledgment on the other, but there is a common thread that links them. In his various discussions, Oakeshott locates the source of authority within those over whom authority is exercised.

In the rejection of enterprise association as a model for the authority of the state, Oakeshott—like his Hobbes—rejects the idea that any sort of common good or common will is what gives authority to the state. To discuss the authority of the civil association as a model for the state, Oakeshott uses two alliterative phrases, which will also sound familiar after the earlier discussion of Hobbes: the recognition of rules and the acknowledgment of authority. The central feature of Oakeshott's understanding of civil association is that "*cives* . . . are related solely in terms of their common recognition of rules which constitute a practice of civility."[40] For Hobbes, a central question revolved around determining who or what office had the authority to create and enforce such rules. Oakeshott will eventually engage this discussion as well. First, however, he explores the conditions of being associated according to the recognition of rules and what this model offers as a conception of the state.

For Oakeshott, members of a civil association, *cives,* are free precisely because they are only associated in terms of "their common recognition of rules." Agents may be associated in any number of ways; as Oakeshott noted above, they "may be believers in a common faith . . . they may be partners in a productive undertaking (a bassoon factory); they may be comrades, or allies in the promotion of cause, colleagues, expeditionaries, accomplices or conspirators; they may comprise an army, a 'village community,' a sect, a fellowship" etc. Each of these, of course, has its own goal, or good, or purpose, but as I emphasized above, and as Oakeshott emphasized in his interpretation of Hobbes, they share no common goal or good. Yet if all the members of the different and various associations listed above are also members of the same state, understood as civil association, they are related in a comprehensive association that is based exclusively on what he calls the recognition of rules. A member of an atheist society and a member of a Christian church may have not only different but conflicting goals; however, this is irrelevant to their common persona as *cives,* associates of the civil association. As *cives,* they all recognize a common "practice of civility," that is, civil association, by which they must qualify the pursuit of those goals. The maintenance of a "practice of civility" may appear to be another such common goal or good. But unlike these others, civil association is not based upon the pursuit or achievement of substantive good, but is a set of formal considerations: the recognition of rules. It is recognition, a term Oakeshott used in the same manner in his interpretation of Hobbes, that he understands to support the authority of the civil association.

> The recognition of *respublica* which constitutes civil association is neither approval of the conditions it prescribes nor expectations about the enforcement of these conditions; it is recognizing it as a system of laws. What relates *cives* to one another and constitutes civil association is the acknowledgement of the authority of *respublica* and the recognition of the subscription to its conditions as an obligation.[41]

This passage establishes, although it does not yet make clear, the distinction of approval of conditions and recognition of them; it also introduces the other phrase that Oakeshott uses to characterize the basis of civil association: the acknowledgment of authority. This phrase, woven together with the recognition of rules, provides the primary way in which Oakeshott discusses authority.

Civil association is a "relationship in terms of the recognition of rules as rules"; and when rules are acknowledged to have authority, they are recognized as law.[42] But what is the substance of this acknowledgment or recognition? Why would a *civis* acknowledge one institution as having authority and another as not, or how might a *civis* come to recognize a rule? As is often the case, Oakeshott clarifies his meaning by listing what does not allow for such a recognition or acknowledgment in civil association. *Respublica,* Oakeshott maintains,

> cannot be acknowledged to have authority on account of its being recognized to have some other valuable quality or attribute. . . . Thus, it cannot be alleged to have authority on account of being identified with a 'will' of any sort, that of a ruler, a majority of *cives,* or a so-called 'general' will. Nor can the authority of *respublica* lie in the identification of its prescriptions with a current 'social purpose,' with approved moral ideals, with a common good or general interest. . . . Civil association has no such common purpose, and the attribution of authority does not postulate approval of the conditions it prescribes.[43]

This is a long list and Oakeshott has many more additions to it. What unifies many of these is that looking to them as the basis of authority would confuse civil association with enterprise association. For those whose relationship is unified by a common purpose, Oakeshott maintains, enterprise association is appropriate, but it cannot be this that gives authority to the state or that characterizes civil association. Again, this would take unity that can only be generated by rescindable choice and place it in a context of compulsion.

If none of this long list, then what does allow *cives* to recognize or acknowledge the authority of *respublica?* Oakeshott replies simply "the answer is that authority is the only conceivable attribute it could be indisputably acknowledged to have."[44] For Oakeshott it is a matter of definition; and here again a connection to Hobbes is evident. For Oakeshott, the civil condition is that condition in which rules are commonly acknowledged to have authority, just as for Oakeshott's Hobbes the common-wealth is where rules, which were previously simply prudential recommendation of reason, are recognized as binding because they are promulgated from the authorized office of the sovereign. And Oakeshott, like his Hobbes, both strengthens and limits this authority. The authority of *respublica* is "indisputable," but it also is its "only conceivable attribute." It may have power, but that is not what maintains *respublica;* a common good may result from the civil condition, but this is not what it pursues; it may incorporate moral ideals, but without these it would not sacrifice being a *respublica*. So how do we understand this recognition? Oakeshott claims, "The recognition of rules is one of our most familiar experiences."[45] Perhaps this so, but he provides very little guidance in locating it in our "familiar experiences," which is an especially strange omission given the centrality of this idea to civil association. This problem grows when he relies upon an almost mystical claim about the "self-authenticating property of *respublica,*" which seems to return to his earliest idealist claims about the authority of the state.[46] If he means by a "self-authenticating property" that *respublica* does not rely upon an external source for its authority, that would certainly be consistent with skeptical dismissal of such. *Respublica* could have no other authority than the recognition of the selves who maintain it through their association. If, however, this means that the authority of *respublica* resides anywhere but in the recognition or acknowledgment of *cives*—in some property of the rules themselves—then it would undermine these claims made elsewhere. Again, he says so little about what constitutes recognition or acknowledgment that this remains an obstacle to understanding this conception of authority.

There is some insight, perhaps, in the contrasts he laid out above. As Mapel emphasizes, Oakeshott wants to allow for a wide range of what he understands to be freedom by not associating the authority of civil association with an assumption about the desirability or "approval of the conditions it prescribes" or with any dependence upon "approved moral ideals, with a common good or general interest." By doing so he hopes to have disavowed the need for consensus and the disruption it causes in "the link between belief and conduct which constitutes 'free' agency." There is a difficulty here, however, because civil association still requires consensus about what ought to be recognized or acknowledged as authoritative. Oakeshott has merely moved the place of required consensus regarding a substantive purpose, good or end, to a consensus regarding authority. In doing so he makes no argument for why this requirement for consensus—that which underlies the recognition of the associates of civil association of its authority—does not threaten the "link" central to his conception of human freedom.[47] It is in his discussion of the activity of politics that Oakeshott provides a deeper view into this requirement for consensus regarding authority.

Oakeshott never denies that there are disagreements about the desirability of the conditions of *respublica*. Instead he wants to retain a place for these disagreements by removing from them the issue of authority. Politics is what Oakeshott understands to be the forum for deliberation and disagreement concerning the desirability of conditions. The activity of politics is the deliberation of differing ideals to be incorporated in *respublica*. He claims, "In considering the engagement to deliberate the conditions prescribed in *respublica* in terms, not of their authority but of their desirability, to imagine them different from what they are and to undertake or to resist their alteration, we are concerned with politics properly speaking."[48] Politics then is an activity of deliberation about the particular conditions that constitute *respublica*. In civil association, there is no expectation, of course, that this process of deliberation will result in a common good or general will, but rather that it will consider the alteration or maintenance of current conditions. I will discuss below some of Oakeshott's thoughts about what ought to be included in this deliberation, but I want to highlight here how what he excludes from politics reveals the fundamental need for consensus about authority. The requirement for consensus of belief about what ought to be acknowledged to have authority is seen in Oakeshott's claim that politics concerns the deliberation of conditions, but "not of their authority." That is, politics can only take place if the *lex* of *respublica,* the rules of civil association, are already recognized as possessing authority; and he completely excludes from politics any discussion concerning whether those rules, or the institutions and procedures through which they are created and interpreted, are authoritative. "Political engagement," Oakeshott claims, "then, is an exploration of *respublica* in terms of the desirability of the conditions it prescribes, and this entails a relationship to *respublica* which is at once acquiescent and critical. The acquiescence is assent to its authority. Without this there can be no politics."[49] Where Oakeshott has assumed consensus is not in terms of the desirability of the *conditions* of *respublica,* but in the recognition of its authority. There he can countenance no disagreement and assumes a unanimity of shared belief that supports the acknowledgment of authority.

Here Oakeshott's allegiance to Thomas Hobbes again becomes clear. "Dissent from the authority of *respublica* is giving notice of a resolve to terminate civil association, and genuine dissentients are either secessionists who design to place their investment in civil discourse elsewhere, or they are disposed to destroy the civil condition in civil war."[50] A rejection of the obligation to recognize the authority of civil association is an inducement to civil war.[51] For Hobbes, however, this logical step was easier to conceive since the denial of authority was notionally the termination of a contract or covenant, terms that Oakeshott avoids because of their overtones of enterprise association. Hobbes, with his detailed rendering of the founding covenant, offers the simple option that the rejection of authority entails a return to "a war of everyman against everyman," a condition where no civility exists as all. However, when Oakeshott claims that politics in *respublica* requires acquiescence, and "the acquiescence is assent to its authority," he reveals that in civil association itself there is something "to threaten the link between belief and conduct which constitutes 'free' agency." If one does not believe that a rule, or the institution that produced it, possesses authority, and yet must still follow that rule, then one is in no better condition than in a state as enterprise association where one does not believe in the goal. Claims to authority can simply mask the exercise of power that is as much abusive of free agency as is the common good in an enterprise association.

In *On Human Conduct,* Oakeshott provides little insight into the character of the beliefs that allow for the recognition or acknowledgment of authority, and so there is no reason to think that these beliefs, which lead to choices concerning acquiescence and assent to authority, are any different from those that lead to the sorts of choices that support enterprise associations. In each case, consensus is required; and while Oakeshott provides reasons for why the consensus required for enterprise raises grave difficulties for it as a model for the state, he does not in the case of the consensus required to support authority in a state conceived as a civil association. In the necessity for acquiescent assent to authority, I argue, "*cives* have given . . . hostages to a future in which their approvals and choices no longer being what they were, they can remain free only in an act of disassociation." The "approvals and choices" need not only be those concerning particular rules, but also those beliefs about what institutions ought to be recognized as authoritative. If beliefs about authority change, but the institutions of adjudication, legislation, and rulership do not recognize this change, and politics is restricted from addressing this issue, then "hostages" have been given. I am not pointing to the approval or disapproval, desirability or undesirability of the conditions prescribed by *respublica,* because Oakeshott defines his conception of politics around deliberation of such desirabilities. Instead, I am concerned with deliberation that would critically engage the question of whether the institutions that create and maintain such laws reflect beliefs about authority. Even more, I want to be able to question whether, in fact, there is a common set of beliefs or consensus regarding what ought to be acknowledged or recognized as authoritative. Instead, it would seem that the skepticism about such common attitudes that sours Oakeshott on the enterprise model ought to be directed here as well.

V

I have focused upon Oakeshott's development of the concept of authority and politics as found in *On Human Conduct,* and I have suggested that his insistence upon consensus in the practice of civility is inconsistent and excessively restrictive. However, readers familiar with some of Oakeshott's other works might suggest that he does examine the ground for that consensus more fully elsewhere. In essays such as "Rationalism in Politics" and "Political Education," Oakeshott provided elegant explorations of the concept of tradition that may perhaps compose that common set of beliefs I searched for above.[52] He wrote famously in the latter essay, "Politics is the activity of attending to the general arrangements of a collection of people who, in respect of their common recognition of a manner of attending to its arrangements, compose a single community. To suppose a collection of people without recognized traditions of behaviour . . . is to suppose a people incapable of politics."[53] Here again politics takes place within a community, which is a community precisely because it shares a tradition that allows it to recognize a manner of attending to its arrangements. Yet he is also ambivalent about the relationship of the activity of politics with the arrangements it addresses, because the arrangements are also what makes politics possible at all—and these are also open to question and change. In *On Human Conduct,* Oakeshott sees no place for questions about authority in the politics of civil society, because consensus about authority allows a real but appropriately limited form of politics. However, back in "Political Education," he continues, "The arrangements which constitute a society capable of political activity, whether they are customs or institutions or laws or diplomatic decisions are at once coherent and incoherent; they compose a pattern and at the same time they intimate a sympathy for what does not fully appear. Political activity is the exploration of that sympathy."[54] Of course, much has been written about this passage, but I point to two aspects of it for present purposes.

The first is Oakeshott's claim that these "arrangements which constitute a society capable of political activity . . . are at once coherent and incoherent." Expressed differently, it is that incoherence that I have drawn attention to. Here Oakeshott suggests that at any given time those arrangements do not hold together completely; they may be more or less coherent, but never completely so. I have tried to suggest a few forms of that incoherence: the activity of some supposedly authorized agent or institution which does not cohere with the commonly recognized arrangements and which then needs to be open to political critique and, more importantly, arrangements that at once cohere with some, perhaps most, *cives'* beliefs about authority, and yet are also incoherent for others. The second aspect is that Oakeshott not only acknowledges some level of incoherence here—as opposed to assuming or requiring consensus—but he explicitly understands politics to be about addressing this incoherence. The irony, of course, is that this form of political activity is never complete. Even a successful attempt to address an incoherence, for instance, through the alteration of some institution or procedure, will create another incoherence. Oakeshott even wistfully appreciates this irony, conceding that some will label his a "depressing doctrine," yet he goes on to suggest, "in the main, this depression springs from the exclusion of hopes that were false."[55] While Oakeshott gets along without such false hopes in the essay "Political Education," and even chides there those who cannot as having "lost their nerve," later, in *On Human Conduct*, that hope is seen in the assumption and requirement for consensus in the matter of authority in *respublica*.[56]

In the period in which Oakeshott wrote most of the essays in *Rationalism in Politics*, there were other places where he considered these matters as well. From some of these sources, I want to draw out a conception of politics that can get along without the requirement for consensus that Oakeshott maintains in his discussion of *respublica*. In a series of lectures given at Harvard University in 1958, Oakeshott developed a number of ideas that would eventually find their way into the third essay of *On Human Conduct*. There Oakeshott defines politics in the following manner:

> Politics is an activity, not of governing, but of determining the manner and matter of government, and where those are predetermined and are regarded as immune from choice or change, there is no place for 'politics.' Thus political activity, the activity in which the composition and conduct of authority is considered, discussed, determined, criticized, and modified, may be said to be an invention of Western Europe which has spread about the world from this center.[57]

Here he includes in political activity a role for critical discussion of "the composition and conduct of authority." Later, in *On Human Conduct*, Oakeshott only allowed politics to include critical discussion about the conduct of authority: that is, what ought to be the rules that have authority, what he calls the "engagement" or "office of government" in the earlier lectures.[58] But in the Harvard lectures, instead of demanding acquiescence in the issue of the authority of government, he understands politics as only able to exist when critical deliberation "of the manner and matter of government" also exists. Importantly, this discussion of manner and matter that he calls politics here includes "thoughts and expectations about the constitution, composition, and authorization of the governing authority."[59]

This distinction between the thoughts about the office of government and its constitution also exists in *On Human Conduct,* but there Oakeshott does not include discussion of the former as part of politics. He does, however, reveal that in order for authority to be recognized or acknowledged there must be beliefs that allow for that recognition. In the lectures, he was concerned that discussion of the authorization of government and the office of government not be confused, yet he recognized each as part of politics. In the later work he also comments on what he sees as confusion of the two "which is apt to be concealed from us because the important words we use to denote beliefs about the constitutions of government (and hence their tenure or authority) have become ambiguous by being used also to denote beliefs about the engagements and achievements of government."[60] The important difference between these two similar observations—that there are considerations of both the constitution and the office of government—is that the earlier expression allows both to be part of politics, while the latter allows only the discussion of the engagements and achievements of government. Oakeshott is clear on the point that authority does rest upon belief, but later he takes out of politics the place of differing beliefs about the appropriate tenure or authority of government.

It is important to note here that in fact Oakeshott recognizes that there are beliefs that support authority even though he writes at times as if beliefs and values were only about substantive goods and thus inappropriate within civil association. But again, while holding that there are beliefs about the tenure or authority of government, Oakeshott does not consistently recognize the possibility that *cives* might differ in their beliefs about authority, or that even common beliefs that do exist and allow for the acknowledgment of authority might change. Politics in civil association would require a procedure both for acknowledging differences and deliberating how to accommodate or incorporate changes into institutions to reflect alterations within prevailing beliefs. Oakeshott seems to allow for such when in *On Human Conduct,* he claims that

any change of circumstance or belief may generate [situations calling for politics] or push them to the surface, and a lively political imagination may recognize them before they are half over the moral horizon. And, of course, every adjustment of *respublica,* is a disturbance of the tensions which hold it together and is liable to bring thitherto concealed discrepancies to the surface.[61]

While Oakeshott wants to restrict discussion to desirability of conditions, he appears perilously close here to admitting of discussions of authority as well. The tensions he describes must include the beliefs that allow for the recognition of its authority, for otherwise, they would not be what "hold it together." Even in the mere expression of his claim that the concern of political activity includes "that the *respublica* shall, so far as possible, adequately reflect what is currently held to be civilly desirable" allows some place for deliberation of authority.[62] It would seem that "what is currently held" must mean something like what people believe or value as "civilly desirable." The modifier civilly is important because it brings into play the requirement that the institutions and offices and rules of civil association reflect what agents would acknowledge to be authoritative. So *On Human Conduct* does, in fact, imply some critical reflection on authority in politics even as Oakeshott denies it.

Oakeshott returns to these topics in one of the last new essays he published during his lifetime, "The Rule of Law."[63] There he seems to be somewhat more concerned with the relationship between the activities of politics and the understanding of the authority of the rule a law. In this essay, Oakeshott examines the understanding of rules to judge if they have the character of law, and he does so in terms of both their authenticity—their authority—and desirability.[64] To have called something a law is to have rendered a judgment in favor of its authenticity; and Oakeshott again uses the term *lex* to identify such an authentic rule (i.e. one which has authority). To broaden the discussion of desirability, however, and thus the activity of politics, Oakeshott also employs another Latin term, the concept of *jus*. *Jus* is what he uses to identify "a rule understood in terms of the 'rightness' or 'justice' of the what it prescribes."[65] Here then Oakeshott allows into the vocabulary of politics ideas about "rightness" and "justice" as a means to consider the desirability of conditions.

This separation of the concept of authenticity and desirability primarily develops a similar separation seen in *On Human Conduct*. Oakeshott continues to maintain that what gives authenticity or authority to the rule of law is not "the common recognition of the desirability of the conditions prescribed in all or any of the laws, or some quality of 'rightness' or justice or 'reasonableness' they may be deemed to posses."[66] Thus the recognition of authority, as he had described it earlier in terms of civil association, has nothing to do with either the desirability or the justice of the conditions prescribed. In "The Rule of Law," Oakeshott does allow into politics the discussion of rightness, or justice of law, with the introduction of the concept of *jus*. He details the character of the requirements for discussions of politics, arguing that what the rule of law "requires for determining the *jus* of a law is not a set of abstract criteria but an appropriately argumentative form of discourse in which to deliberate the matter"; this seems to reintroduce the critical element of politics discussed above.[67] Oakeshott again limits the character of this element of deliberation, developing a list of things that ought not be considered in such deliberation. He suggests, for instance, that it should be "insulated from the spurious claims of conscientious objection, [and] of minorities for exceptional treatment;" and he also rejects the place for "a so-called Bill of Rights," because these falsely claim to be "unconditional principles of *jus*."[68] Yet even with these limitations, introducing *jus* at least helps to fill out the meager form of politics that Oakeshott suggested in *On Human Conduct,* one that is so severely limited that Richard Flathman wryly concludes, "It is therefore something of an understatement that engagement in this 'politics entails a disciplined imagination' as Oakeshott had called for."[69] By introducing *jus,* Oakeshott has conceptualized somewhat more fully and clearly what it is that he considers appropriate to deliberate about in politics.[70]

Importantly, however, Oakeshott here does not think that such deliberation affects the authenticity or authority of *lex*. Here now Oakeshott separates himself from Hobbes, claiming that "the *jus* of *lex* cannot be identified simply with its faithfulness to the formal character of law."[71] Such a consideration would be about its authenticity, not its *jus*. Instead, "To deliberate the *jus* of *lex* is to invoke a particular kind of moral consideration: . . . the negative and limited consideration that the prescriptions of the law should not conflict with the prevailing moral sensibility."[72] This is an amendment to his truncated and Hobbesian discussion of justification in *On Human Conduct,* where he claims an action is just "only in respect of its relationship to a moral practice understood as a composition of rules."[73] Oakeshott here wants to make it clear that it is possible to judge a law to be *injus,* or unjust, and yet still recognize that it is a law with authority. He does not, however, consider if there is a limit to the number or enormity of *injus* laws that can be tolerated before they come to reflect upon the authority of the law. He says nothing of the character of "prevailing moral sensibility," or how much conflict it can exhibit or accept.

However, Oakeshott's discussion of the rule of law in the 1983 essay also reveals another aspect of politics and its relationship with authority. There he claims that the authenticity connected with the rule of law has to do with its creation—that is, with what he calls the "legislative office."[74] A rule or command is only authentic if it is understood to have been created by an office recognized to be endowed with the authority to do so. I have suggested that some sort of beliefs or values would have to be represented in institutions in order for them to be recognized as authoritative, even though Oakeshott seems ambivalent about that claim. In examining the distinction between *jus* and *lex,* he provides some insight into the sort of beliefs that support the recognition of authority. Oakeshott claims, "To favor a so-called 'democratically elected' legislature is to express a belief that its authority will be more confidently acknowledgeable than that of a legislature assembled or constituted in any other manner; it forecasts nothing whatever about the *jus* or *injus* of its enactments."[75] Thus Oakeshott again dismisses the idea that it is this authenticity that will secure the *jus* of a law produced in such an authentic procedure. But in claiming that something that has been the product of a democratically elected legislature does not guarantee that it will have the quality of justice, he reinforces the idea that there are beliefs and values that support authority and reveals something about the character of those beliefs.

In the first matter, once more, it is important to have established that the recognition of rules or acknowledgment of authority rests upon beliefs about authority because of Oakeshott's reason for preferring civil to enterprise association. Enterprise association threatened the link between belief and conduct because it demanded consensus of belief concerning common substantive ends. However, I have argued that while Oakeshott seems to mask it in places, civil association demands a similar consensus in the matter of belief about authority. This is the acquiescence required in *On Human Conduct.* However, considering the passage about democratically elected legislatures, it seems quite possible that one might not confidently acknowledge, or might not acknowledge at all, the product of a procedure that one did not recognize as authentic—for instance as authentically and thus authoritatively democratic. Thus while Oakeshott wants to restrict politics to the discussion of *jus* and desirability, it seems necessary to include critical deliberation concerning the authenticity of the various procedures and offices from which *lex,* or rule, generates.

Secondly, it is of interest that among the values or beliefs that can be used to assess the authenticity of law, and the one that Oakeshott chooses, is that of the place of a democratically elected legislature. I cited above a passage in which Oakeshott suggested that a "common confusion" regards words that properly denote authority to discuss the engagements of government. The example he uses to illustrate this muddle is that of democracy. Oakeshott complains,

the word democracy, which properly speaking signifies a manner of constituting a government and of authorizing it to rule, is also used to characterize particular acts or policies of a government. . . . This is often a piece of
political subterfuge: . . . this confidence trick is an emblem of ambiguity
which has infected the vocabulary of all political discourse, and an 'authority' word escapes corruption only when it is safely laid to rest.[76]

Now again, Oakeshott wants to preclude from politics any discussions concerning authority. But there he gives no reason given why such discussion
can confidently be "laid to rest." In fact, earlier in the discussion of the historical development of the state, Oakeshott suggests that "a constitutional
change may be recognized as the expression of a tentative belief about
authority."[77] Yet when it comes to discussing politics, he disavows the need
for such constitutional adjustment to reflect changes in belief about authority. In "The Rule of Law," Oakeshott also recommends that the term
democracy—or democratic—ought not be used to modify particular proposals or acts of a government or legislature. Democracy is a concept
appropriate for understanding the type of constitution and the beliefs it
must embody in order to be recognized as authoritative. However, when
Oakeshott claims that "to favor a so-called 'democratically elected' legislature is to express a belief that its authority will be more confidently
acknowledgeable than that of a legislature assembled or constituted in any
other manner," he leaves himself open to the extension of his idea of
politics from the deliberation of what is desirable in terms of *jus* to the
critical deliberation of what is more and what is less confidently
acknowledgeable.

   This reading of Oakeshott recognizes that for him authority is a constitutional matter in which the existence of a certain form of constitutionally
based legislation and governance offers a presumption of recognition on
the part of those under its jurisdiction. But there is nothing in Oakeshott's
usage that suggests that if a certain constitution with a particular set of
offices for making *lex* exists, then it must therefore necessarily be acknowledgeable. In *On Human Conduct,* Oakeshott was explicit about this prescription for acquiescence. Here, however, he merely wants to make clear
that recognition of the authenticity of *lex* is not equivalent to the granting
of the *jus* of *lex*—and conversely, denying *jus* does not affect *lex*. Justice may
be an important consideration in critically examining a law to deliberate its
desirability, but deciding that a law is unjust does not, for Oakeshott, undermine its authority. Yet just as Oakeshott envisions an argumentative discourse about *jus* in which different ideas about justice can be engaged, and

as in *On Human Conduct,* the assessment of the desirability of rules reveals disagreement and change, it is quite likely that the prevailing ideas about authenticity are subject to disagreement and change. As Oakeshott accepts deliberation about *jus* and the desirability of rules as part of politics, so also subject to deliberation and change of politics must be the institutions, offices, and procedures that are to embody such beliefs.

The importance of this becomes even more evident when one reviews the rest of the passage in *On Human Conduct,* where Oakeshott claims that "a constitutional change may be may be recognized as the expression of a tentative belief about authority." There Oakeshott also reverses the direction of this procedure, suggesting that "with every change in a constitution this task of acquiring authority had to begin afresh."[78] His observation shows that not only ought constitutions reflect beliefs about authority, but in fact sometimes the governments established by constitutions take up the task of acquiring authority.[79] Unfortunately, Oakeshott gives little insight into what this procedure entails, although it leaves the impression that governments work to develop the beliefs that would allow for their own recognition. Given that such a government already has power, Oakeshott might want to have considered the possibility that such an activity might "threaten the link of belief and conduct." The procedure that would be more in line with his concern about authority, power, and freedom would be his earlier formulation from the Harvard lectures, where "politics is an activity, not of governing, but of determining the manner and matter of government, and where those are pre-determined and regarded as immune from choice or change, there is no place for 'politics'"; and in which changes in a "tentative belief about authority" are reflected in political activities that bring into question the current constitutional procedures and institutions. This reasoning suggests that politics must include these critical deliberations of the offices and procedures that claim the authority to make and interpret *lex*. Such a critical deliberation would make explicit the relationship between the various beliefs about authority and the institutions that assert this authority. While in *On Human Conduct* he disavows such deliberations as part of politics, Oakeshott himself has acknowledged the contingent and volatile relationship between beliefs about authority and the constitutions and legislative offices and procedures that claim to embody them.[80] By including deliberation about authority within politics, I merely mean to acknowledge the change and volatility in beliefs about authority that a call for "acquiescence" cannot address.

Is civil association the heavenly city of the skeptic as Wolin suggested? Oakeshott has attempted to fashion it as such. Certainly, he has removed from this model of the state, and the politics that take place within it, much that would seem offensive to his skeptical disposition. He rejects the idea of universal rights, the common good, natural law, etc. as either the foundation of the authority of the state or the basis upon which claims can be pressed in politics. The authority of the state is based on nothing but the recognition of its rules as being authoritative, and he restricts politics to only the critical discourse regarding the desirability of the particular rules of association, eventually allowing consideration of their justice as well.

But I have suggested that the skeptic might not yet have found a heavenly home. In warding off from politics any critical examination of the basis of authority, any consideration of disagreements about beliefs about the authoritative, any deliberation concerning whether current legal or constitutional arrangements reflect changing beliefs about authority, Oakeshott reintroduces some of the types of considerations that he had set out to dispense. Nonetheless, Oakeshott lays much of the ground work of that skeptic's city. In my concluding chapter, I will consider attempts to appropriate Oakeshott's skeptical starting point and much of its analysis to argue for a distinctly democratic style of politics. I will close with a discussion of some examples of the type of critical democratic politics about authority that Oakeshott might not allow for, but that I argue can be drawn from his considerations nonetheless.

Chapter Seven

Oakeshott, Dissent, and Democracy

I

In one of the more famous passages of one of Oakeshott's more famous essays he contends:

> Politics is the activity of attending to general arrangements of a collection of people who, in respect of their common recognition of a manner of attending to its arrangements, compose a single community. . . . And the form it takes, because it can take no other, is the amendment of existing arrangements by exploring and pursuing what is intimated in them.[1]

Much of Oakeshott's later conception of politics, which I discussed in the previous chapter, are suggested in this passage from Oakeshott's Inaugural Lecture at the London School of Economics given in 1951. Politics here is an important but limited activity. It is an image that requires those engaged in politics to have enough imagination to receive intimations to pursue and enough energy to pursue them. Oakeshott also understands politics to take place in a single community, one that already commonly recognizes how one ought to attend to its arrangements. As I discussed in the previous chapter, this presentation of politics does not distinguish between amending particular rules because they are more or less desirable and questioning their authority; rather, politics includes both. It is true that a "common recognition" is what makes a people, but nothing prevents altering the "manner of attending to its arrangements." Instead, Oakeshott reveals the close connection in politics of both the manner (authoritative procedures and institutions) and matter (desirable or undesirable arrangements) of amendment through an intriguing example: the enfranchisement of women. In demonstrating what he means by "the amendment of existing arrangements by exploring and pursuing what is intimated in them" and the limited character of the activity of politics it entails, Oakeshott explains

> For example, the legal status of women in our society was for a long time (and perhaps still is) in comparative confusion, because the rights and duties which composed it intimated rights and duties which were nevertheless not recognized. And on the view of things I am suggesting, the only cogent reason to be advanced for the technical "enfranchisement" of women was that in all or most other important respects they had already been enfranchised.[2]

Perhaps Oakeshott chose this example to tweak the noses of the advocates of women's rights, implying, yes women deserved to be enfranchised, but not for the reasons you think, for he continues, "Arguments drawn from abstract natural right, from 'justice,' or some general concept of human personality must be regarded as either irrelevant or as unfortunately disguised versions of the one valid argument; namely that there was incoherence in the arrangements of society which pressed convincingly for remedy."[3] However, from the perspective of my discussions of politics and authority in the previous chapter, there is much of interest in this particular example.

In Oakeshott's conception of politics from "Political Education," the restrictions to women's legal and political rights, and arguments for and against them, entail deliberation about authority. When Oakeshott claims that an incoherence had developed, he seems to mean that the laws that restricted women in legal and political matters simply no longer reflected beliefs and practices that were necessary to sustain their authority. Glenn Worthington, in explaining—and defending—this passage to those who complain that Oakeshott's argument for enfranchisement could just as well be used for continued disenfranchisement, suggests, "Simply to have denied that women were educated, that they played an economically significant role in the community and were capable of exercising political responsibility would have made for an intolerable situation."[4] The issue of enfranchisement was not simply a matter of what some desired and others did not, but of recognizing what could no longer be acknowledged as bearing authority. And in particular, laws restricting women from participating by "attending to . . . arrangements" (that is, from politics) were incoherent with "the common recognition of the manner"; the authority of those existing arrangements was challenged.

There is a further ambiguity in this early conception of politics that

Oakeshott provided: where exactly in this example was the politics? The laws restricting enfranchisement did not simply present themselves as an "incoherence in the arrangements of society which pressed convincingly for remedy"; some agents needed to identify them as such, and then persuade others to that view through political action and deliberation. Was politics in the persuasion by some of others that enfranchisement was now needed? in the political protests staged by the suffragettes that brought attention to this incoherence? in the debates in Parliament about whether women should be enfranchised? in the development of the particular legal format for how enfranchisement would be incorporated? Oakeshott gives no clue as to which is appropriately part of politics and which not, although it is at least worth noting here that the "incoherence . . . which convincingly pressed for remedy" was propelled by a variety of forms of political action—including civil disobedience—that questioned not only the desirability of women's enfranchisement, but the authority of its continuing denial.

In "Political Education," Oakeshott does not distinguish deliberation of the authority from the desirability of law, but he would seven years later, in the Harvard lectures collected in *Morality and Politics in Modern Europe,* where he differentiated within politics the deliberation of both the manner and matter of government. Yet again, in those lectures, he included both styles of consideration in his conception of politics. In both cases, politics is understood as the deliberation required for the adjustment of institutions to changing shared beliefs. Later, in *On Human Conduct,* Oakeshott describes this as the critical element of deliberation in politics. "The ingredient of criticism, of questioning, and of non-acceptance is concerned with approval or disapproval and with desirabilities."[5] But it is only there, while keeping the general character of the earlier conceptions, that Oakeshott limits politics significantly by removing questions of the authority of the common arrangements from politics; thus, the element of critique in politics eventually regards only the approval or not of arrangements, but not their authority. I suggested in Chapter Six that Oakeshott's assumption of shared beliefs about authority and his requirement for acquiescence about what sort of institutions or procedures would be recognized as bearing authority is a significant and problematic limitation. When civil association demands such acquiescence, then it also "threaten[s] the link between belief and conduct that constitutes 'free' agency," as Oakeshott put it in his criticism of the enterprise association as a model for the state.[6] In the same fashion that there are differences in belief about ends and goals to be pursued, so also there must be differences regarding what sort of institution or procedure ought to or can bear authority—and which does not or cannot. Still, it seems possible and even appropriate to reintegrate into his conception of politics the critical deliberation about the authority of governmental institutions and arrangements that he himself included in the Harvard lectures. This incorporation is both more fully in keeping with Oakeshott's skepticism and in line with the concern about the freedom in human agency for which he expresses concern in *On Human Conduct*.

Oakeshott's concern in these matters begins in the recognition of the modern state as a comprehensive and compulsory institution. When not comprehensive and compulsory, enterprise association is a fine model for associations and institutions, because associates choose to pursue common goals, and if they desire they can rescind membership; the freedom of human agency is reflected in the joining, pursuing, and rescinding. However, he rejected this model for the state, because as a state (comprehensive and compulsory), enterprise association cannot respect these elements of freedom; whatever ends it, or even a majority of its members, chooses would be abusive to any of the conflicting, self-chosen ends of its subjects or citizens. I now want to extend Oakeshott's criticism of the enterprise model of the state to the issue he thinks escapes it, authority in civil association. Oakeshott is skeptical of the assumption of consensus about common ends and thus rejects enterprise association as a model for politics. He hopes the advantage of civil association is that it neither expects consensus about the desirability of its institution, nor views disapproval as a sign of bad faith or a mark of a bad citizen. In fact, it allows for difference and critical engagement about the particular rules of the civil association, or *lex* of the *respublica*. However, the state doubtlessly does exercise power over those who not only desire another rule, but also those who do not recognize its authority—or at least the authority of certain of its offices and agents.

Building from much of what Oakeshott has written, I propose: first, his skepticism needs to be directed at the beliefs that allow the recognition of authority; second, the critical posture and deliberation he describes regarding the approval or disapproval of laws and institutions be directed to the matter of their authority as well; and finally, democratic politics should be construed to encompass both types of critical deliberation. I recommend such a democratic politics in the matter of authority not because it is more likely to generate the shared beliefs about authority that allow certain institutions to be acknowledged as authoritative, although that might occur. Instead, in keeping with a skeptical incredulity toward such shared understandings, I suggest democratic politics makes more likely the recognition of the disagreement in beliefs about the authority of the state. However, it might be objected, does not even democratic politics need consensus about something for the polity to exist at all? Does not its authority need to based upon something, perhaps an allegiance to democratic or liberal principles, to accomplish anything or at least to establish a plain upon which all other political battles will ensue? My response here is to turn the question around: discussions do ensue and they are concluded—at least temporarily—policies are made, laws are enforced, procedures are established, used, and attended to for doing these things. To skeptically deny that consensus exists for the authority of such actions cannot and will not prevent citizens and agents of the state from doing these and other things. To the contrary, those so acting often do claim authority and presume a consensus based upon principles like the rule of the majority, minority rights, civil discourse, the rule of law not of men, *et al.* Indeed, sometimes what they do and how they do it may reflect a greater or lesser amount of such recognition. Yet, the skeptical lesson from Oakeshott is to be suspicious of the claims of unanimity and consensus. In a democratic age, it may be necessary for those who wish to maintain or alter political arrangements to claim that they act only upon such a consensus and that such consensus is a reflection of the willing allegiance and recognition of the citizens. But therein lies a danger. To those who are not part of that consensus, it is only power by which such arrangements are enforced, maintained, and perhaps even altered; what is recognition by some is mere resignation and compliance by others.

Perhaps the desire for consensus is founded in a hope to replace power with complete or unanimous recognition of authority and willing allegiance to procedure, if not policies. But this is one of the false hopes that Oakeshott referred to in "Political Education." Oakeshott closes the version of that essay included in *Rationalism in Politics* by claiming, "The view that I have expressed in this essay may be taken to represent . . . a stage reached when neither 'principle' . . . nor any general theory about the character and direction of social change seem to supply an adequate reference for explanation or for practical conduct."[7] The demand—or fearful hope—for consensus about authority seems to retreat back to a reliance upon "principle" or "general theory." *Rationalism in Politics* and *On Human Conduct* point to the dangers to human agency and freedom posed by politics oriented around a rational plan or the implementation of policies that serve a supposed common good. Conversely, Oakeshott asserts that civil association is uniquely posed to reconcile agency with the power of the state through authority. However, I contend that civil association cannot in "principle" or "general theory" offer this unique position. Just as there are those who are unfree because they do not choose the ends of the state in its "enterprise" moments, so also there are those unfree because they do not recognize its authority in its "civil" moments. I am not debating the potential practical benefits of civil association pointed to by Flathman. I am merely redirecting Oakeshott's skeptical caution regarding enterprise association to his own theoretical position concerning the consensus he presumes necessary for authority. Oakeshott was wary of the enterprise association model for the state because it exchanged self-chosen ends with those of the state; but I contend we must be wary also with a civil association model, for while some see the exercise of power by the state as an expression of their beliefs about authority, to others it is mere coercion. A democratic politics not only can acknowledge the dangers of the former, but can interrupt the bifurcated options Oakeshott allows in the matter of authority. For him there is only either acquiescence in the matter of authority or civil war (or secession). However, we may scale back our assumptions regarding consensus to accept that there are overlapping, cobbled-together, differing beliefs about authority that land us between "acquiescence" and "civil war." Political possibilities exist whereby the exercise of power by the state is questioned both to consider on what authority it undertakes its engagement and to bring to light those who disagree with such a claim to authority. Does this make authority weaker? Most likely. Does it destroy authority? No. Though it does heighten caution about the exercise of power and acknowledges that the state acts in ways that some subject to its power do not recognize as authoritative.

II

Curiously, cautious attraction to Oakeshott by advocates of democracy and radicalism are not new. In an early review of *Rationalism in Politics* in the *New Left Review,* Colin Falck suggested "Oakeshott is very close here to the foundation of any serious socialist thinking. Emphasizing the concrete and historical, he is opposed to the politics of the slogan and the empty framework of liberal (or any other) values; and his claim that we can only know where to go next on the basis of a thorough understanding of where we have come from is a profoundly Marxist idea."[8] Yet Falck warned against this tempting affiliation because Oakeshott's "actual account of this understanding is . . . a deliberately romantic and untheoretical conception."[9] In the years since Falck, there has continued to be a handful of those committed to democratic and even radical politics—and theory—who have been tempted by opportunities in Oakeshott's work. Now, given that there is a broad menagerie of democratic and radical theorists to draw upon, why would, for instance, Chantal Mouffe, an avowed advocate of "a radicalization of democracy," look to Oakeshott? or why would David Mapel bother to suggest "participatory democrats should therefore recognize [Oakeshott's] view of authority as their own"?[10] This, after all, is Michael Oakeshott, whom admirers praise for his "distinctly contemporary contribution to conservative thought," and detractors, such as Perry Anderson, happily agreeing, have placed among the members of the "The Intransigent Right."[11] Perhaps these overtures are mere rhetorical flourishes to suggest that an idea or commitment is not just from the radical left, but instead, even Oakeshott the conservative holds similar views. But the attraction is not just rhetorical, for each of these, among others, finds theoretical potential in Oakeshott's work. While many who are primarily interpreters of Oakeshott have dismissed such claims, I argue that Oakeshott's account does offer the view of authority that Mapel says it does and Oakeshott's conception of civil association does possess the opportunities that Mouffe claims for it. However, as is clear from above, I also suggest that there are some significant limits to Oakeshott's thought for those interested in democracy, and Oakeshott is not only aware of these limits, he explicitly advocates for them. Yet, ironically, in doing so, he helpfully reveals a boundary, sometimes explicit, sometimes implicit, of liberal democratic theory and practice that must be crossed if a more full—if more unruly—democracy is desired.

To get an idea of the character of the opportunity afforded by Oakeshott to democratic theorists, I consider Mouffe's appropriation. Primarily, Mouffe is attracted to Oakeshott's elaboration of civil association as a rejection of an enterprise model, with its regulative conception of a substantive, common good. Likewise, she appreciates Oakeshott's understanding of political community based on the common recognition of rules. Mouffe differs from Oakeshott in the elaboration of the particular conditions of a practice of civility, but it is this image of the character of political community that appeals to her. For Mouffe, the opportunity for those interested in radical democratic citizenship comes in the elaboration of the "conditions specifying [the] common or 'public concern.'" She claims, "To be associated in terms of the recognition of liberal democratic principles, this is the meaning of citizenship I want to put forward." Political association is a moral community because associates recognize common principles by which they condition or qualify their actions and "what links them is the common recognition of the authority" of these principles.[12] According to Mouffe, these principles can be, although they are not necessarily,

understood to be "liberal, democratic principles." Such principles, understood in terms of civil association, have the authority of common recognition and yet, in keeping with the ideal of *societas,* do not require allegiance
to a common good or purpose.

Mouffe acknowledges what she calls the "conservative use [Oakeshott]
makes of *societas* and *universitas,*" but she claims this use is only because he
suggests a different "content" or set of conditions for *societas,* not a necessary requirement of this style of association.[13] On Oakeshott's terms,
Mouffe is not restricted from advancing a different set of rules for the *societas,* so long as it is done in keeping with the formal character of civil association; a *civis* in a civil association would be free to disagree with the
prevailing content and to offer what she considered to be a more desirable
content if she wished. Mouffe then develops her claims, suggesting, "I do
not believe that the distinction between *universitas* and *societas* necessarily
commits us to reject state intervention as being inherently linked to a conception of a state as a purposive common enterprise. One can perfectly justify state intervention on the basis of a certain interpretation of the
respublica."[14] Mouffe, unfortunately, does not reveal what this "certain interpretation" would be, but she makes clear that she considers the "content"
of civil association to include state intervention and yet retain its formal
character.[15] However, Mouffe does directly criticize what she calls
Oakeshott's "flawed idea of politics"; she claims "What is completely missing from Oakeshott is division and antagonism."[16] She recognizes that the
set of rules and considerations that make up *respublica* require a consensus
in the same way that the idea of a substantive common good does for *universitas.* However, any requirement for consensus also needs to acknowledge
and account for antagonism, because "Forms of agreement can be reached
but they are always partial and provisional since consensus is of necessity
based on acts of exclusion."[17] Political community understood as *societas*
may require consensus in a different fashion than *universitas,* but it seems to
require it nonetheless; Mouffe faults Oakeshott for neglecting the antagonism that consensus even about rules necessarily entails.

In criticizing Oakeshott's conception of politics, Mouffe claims, "To
introduce conflict and antagonism into Oakeshott's model, it is necessary
to recognize that the *respublica* is the product of given hegemony, the
expression of power relations, and that it can be challenged."[18] Conversely,
this is exactly where David Mapel finds the advantages of Oakeshott's conception of authority. He points out that "even a completely egalitarian, participatory democracy must face the objection that it rests on a structure of
domination," and the benefit of Oakeshott's view of authority is that it does

not "encourage approval or disapproval of the conditions it prescribes. Strictly speaking, this indifference opens up the maximum amount of space for criticism"[19] Similarly to Mapel, I contend that Oakeshott understands himself to have allowed for considerable conflict and antagonism in his discussion of politics, and in particular in terms of the principles by which *societas* is structured. However, I go beyond Mouffe and Mapel in suggesting that what Oakeshott does not allow is conflict and antagonism concerning "the recognition of the authority of the conditions specifying their common or 'public' concern." Oakeshott excludes from politics questions about the authority of the institutions and conditions of political association. Oakeshott's skepticism about the common good of community is arrested in the matter of authority. Yet in detailing the sort of questions about which politics cannot allow conflict—questions of authority— Oakeshott ironically exposes one more element for the skeptical politics of democratic, critical deliberation. Following Mouffe's usage, if "conflict and antagonism" can be registered not simply with the desirability of institutions and arrangements—where Oakeshott's theory can accept it—but also in the matter of the shared beliefs about authority, from which he precludes it, then improbable as it might seem, Oakeshott's ideas can lend themselves to the cause of plural and even radical democracy. This democratic politics, instead of acquiescing in the face of authority, would acknowledge fundamental and irredeemable "conflict and antagonism." This radical, plural democratic politics, founded in skepticism about common ends and about authority, manifests the limitations of shared beliefs and discloses who does not share those beliefs. The state will still exercise power with whatever authority it can cobble together, relying on the beliefs about authority that it can accommodate with some coherence.

III

I began this chapter with Oakeshott's assertion that "Politics is the activity of attending to general arrangements of a collection of people who, in respect of their common recognition of a manner of attending to its arrangements, compose a single community." But I have just suggested that politics, at least democratic politics, must also allow critical deliberation of the character of that recognition, the authority of the procedures of attending to arrangements, and the arrangements that actually result. Perhaps a good share of politics in modern states that share in the characteristics of civil association turn out to be exactly what Oakeshott proposes in *On Human Conduct:* critical deliberation about the desirability of altering or maintaining existing arrangements. Yet as I hope to have shown, this alone cannot account for those who do not recognize their beliefs about authority in the institutions and agents of the state who claim authority. A more fully democratic politics needs to incorporate a variety of opportunities for this type of dissent. Of course, without such a place for dissent about authority in politics, it is possible that a citizen would choose to recognize the authority of the state for the simple self-interest in the security offered by the rule of law—the Hobbesian explanation. This is not recognition based on belief but fear, although it may not be fear of the exercise of power by the state but rather of the consequences of destroying that power. A constitutional democracy with amending procedures to its fundamental law already allows for some politics regarding the alteration of arrangements whose authority can be challenged. In this case, a political response is open to those who cannot acknowledge the authority of some arrangements by strategically employing existing decision-making structures— even if some agent, office or institution is acting in an "unrecognizable" fashion—and to use official deliberative procedures to adjust either the institution or values.

Yet a thoroughly democratic politics must also recognize the position of those citizens who may still not accept the values and may even risk putting into question the authority of the offices or institutions; these citizens might find that there is no way for them to acknowledge the authority of a rule or institution and in this case take on a type of action that explicitly rejects the law or office. One expression of this activity may be through passive resistance to state power exercised as authoritative. In an act of civil disobedience such as this, those rejecting the authority of the law or office may attempt to reveal that it does not cohere with the shared and common beliefs of the society. This is one way to view the strategy Rev. Martin Luther King Jr. described in "The Letter from Birmingham Jail." There he not only defends his actions in terms of a long tradition of resistance but also develops his critique of Jim Crow and voting restrictions by arguing that these were not in keeping with the ideals of the American tradition of democracy. There are many ways to read King's essay, but in "The Letter from Birmingham Jail," he discusses a variety of understandings of "just law." While he calls upon Saint Thomas, claiming that "A just law is a man made code that squares with the moral law or the law of God," King also suggests, "A law is unjust if it is inflicted on a minority that, as a result of being denied the right to vote, had no part in enacting or devising the law."[20] This claim is not simply about the desirability or approval of a law, but about what sort of procedure can claim to be recognized as authoritative. Thus it seems that at least one way to view his "Letter" is as a strategy to call upon a variety of beliefs about both of what Oakeshott calls *jus* and *lex* in order to highlight how current legal and political institutions do not reflect them.[21]

In this case of civil disobedience, one acknowledges the authority of the rule of law generally, accepting arrest and detention, but refuses to acknowledge the authority of particular laws or institutions. The distance traveled from Oakeshott here is clear. Civil disobedience, for him, would be an oxymoron; the disobedient must misunderstand the character of civil obligation. But again, this is because Oakeshott can accept only two options: the recognition of rules as having authority or civil war; from his perspective, the activities of civil rights protestors who are civilly disobedient cannot be seen as political. However, this insistence, I have argued, ignores both the possibility that some elements or agents of institutions of governance do not reflect beliefs about authority or that there are differences in belief that support recognition of authority. From a democratic perspective that is skeptical of the notion of completely shared beliefs about authority, the civilly disobedient citizen attempts to highlight at least the first of these and possibly the second as well.[22]

Stephen Carter has attempted a similar analysis, emphasizing the significance of dissent. In *The Dissent of the Governed,* he argues for a place in politics for dissent regarding claims to authority made by the state that is distinct from what he calls disallegiance. In a creative rereading of the Declaration of Independence, he emphasizes not the consent of the governed, but the complaints in it that the British crown and Parliament had ignored the grievances of the colonists. "It is not the failure of consent but the failure of dissent that . . . thus provided the impetus, and still more the justification, for the separation of the American colonies. True, it is the consent of the governed that delivers the initial legitimacy . . . to the government. But it is the rebuffing of the 'repeated petitions' that dissolves that legitimacy."[23] Dissent and how governments treat dissenters then is the center of Carter's formal theory of democracy. His substantive consideration is the public place of religion; he claims for instance "Mainstream politics, with its arrogant rejection of religious argument and traditional religious values, has alienated tens of millions of voters . . . there is a widely shared perception that institutions of government, far from reinforcing the values many people want their children to learn, actively frustrate them."[24] Carter struggles for an understanding of democratic governance that instead of "alienating tens of millions of voters" acknowledges their dissent.

I say Carter struggles because in the end it is unclear whether he wants to preserve dissent or have the conditions that create it ameliorated. Carter seems to maintain the ideal that a government, by listening more carefully to the petitions of those aggrieved and adjusting its institutions to those concerns, will progress to increasing legitimacy. He suggests that we judge a government by how it treats its dissenters, but the implicit goal is a government that has no dissenters. I would follow David Mapel's suggestion above that "even a completely egalitarian, participatory democracy must face the objection that it rests on a structure of domination." This dissent cannot be done away with, and we ought not contemplate doing so. Yet even while I disagree with Carter's final claims about dissent, his example of how citizens of certain religious traditions in the United States feel alienated from the state and its institutions, agents, and the values upon which they claim authority illustrates the problem with Oakeshott's requirement for acquiescence in the face of authority. Carter's regard for dissent also aligns with the aspect of democracy I mean to emphasize.

Finally, however, some who refuse to recognize the authority of the state may simply choose to withdraw or to work actively to destroy the institutions claiming authority. This is the strategy of secession or civil war (and that Carter calls disallegiance) that Oakeshott saw as the only posture relative to authority other than acquiescence. Here even radical citizenship has ended, because the *civitas* is rejected *in toto,* there being such conflict among the institutions claiming authority, ideas about what is required to recognize authority, and the values and beliefs of some group. Depending upon the size of this breakdown, it may mean the end of civil association. The radical, democratic citizen here turns into the revolutionary. This is the farthest extreme of the criticism and rejection of authority, but again it is the only option that Oakeshott acknowledges other than acquiescence. Perhaps in fear that any infringement or criticism of authority leads inextricably to civil war, more and more like Hobbes, Oakeshott shields it from critical deliberation. Yet the skepticism concerning common purposes and will that allows Oakeshott to reject the enterprise association needs to be focused on these common recognitions of authority as well.

Critical deliberation about both the desirability of governing institutions and also their authority may in the end weaken authority. Yet it may also strengthen those institutions that can be readjusted or at least highlight the coercion of those institutions when they exercise power against those who do not recognize their authority. Following the passage with which I began this chapter, Oakeshott famously continues, "The arrangements which constitute a society capable of political activity, whether they are customs or institutions or laws or diplomatic decisions are at once coher-

ent and incoherent; they compose a pattern and at the same time they intimate a sympathy for what does not fully appear. Political activity is the
exploration of that sympathy."[25] He has been criticized for the mystical and
darkly conservative connotations of politics understood as the pursuit of
intimations. But as I highlighted in Chapter Six, a more radical element of
this passage is evident here as well, and it is an appropriate reminder to the
later Oakeshott. Incoherence is an inescapable feature of politics; coherence
may be greater or less, but it will not be complete. The problem of rationalism, as Oakeshott saw it, was not that it could do away with incoherence, but that it attempts to do so; the problem with Oakeshott's
conception of civil association is that it attempts to do away with incoherence in beliefs about authority. A more appropriately democratic state association will acknowledge such incoherence, accept politics that draws
attention to problems with authority, and more cautiously exercise its
power, recognizing that to some, such actions are mere coercion, not those
of authority.

Notes

Notes for Introduction

1. Michael J. Oakeshott, "On Being Conservative," in *Rationalism in Politics and Other Essays* (London: Methuen and Company, 1962, reprinted with additions and edited by Timothy Fuller by Liberty Press, 1991), p. 434.

2. Michael A. Mosher, "The Skeptic's Burke: *Reflections on the Revolution in France,* 1790–1990," *Political Theory* 19 (August), p. 394.

3. Ibid., p. 395.

4. Oakeshott, "Political Education," in *Rationalism in Politics,* pp. 56-7, see also pp. 66-9.

5. Perry Anderson, "The Intransigent Right at the End of the Century," *London Review of Books* 14 (September 24, 1992): 7-11.

6. Robert Devigne, *Recasting Conservatism: Oakeshott, Strauss, and the Response to Postmodernism* (New Haven: Yale University Press, 1994).

7. Paul Franco, *The Political Philosophy of Michael Oakeshott* (New Haven: Yale University Press, 1990), p. 2.

8. See, for example, Richard Rorty, *Contingency, Irony and Solidarity* (Cambridge: Cambridge University Press, 1989) and Chantal Mouffe, "Democratic Citizenship and the Political Community," in *Dimensions of Radical Democracy: Pluralism, Citizenship and Democracy* ed. Chantal Mouffe (London: Verso, 1992), pp. 225-239.

9. Jeremy Rayner, "The Legend of Oakeshott's Conservatism: Sceptical Philosophy and Limited Politics," *Canadian Journal of Political Science* 18 (June, 1985), pp. 313-338.

10. Oakeshott, "The Voice of Poetry in the Conversation of Mankind," in *Rationalism in Politics,* pp. 488- 541.

11. Steven A. Gerencser, "Voices in Conversation: Philosophy and Politics in the

Work of Michael Oakeshott," *Journal of Politics* 57 (August 1995), pp. 724-742, see especially pp. 739-741.

12. Richard Rorty, *Philosophy and the Mirror of Nature,* (Princeton: Princeton University Press, 1979), p. 264.

13. Cornel West, "Afterword," in *Post-Analytic Philosophy,* eds, John Rajchman and Cornel West. (New York: Columbia University Press, 1985), p. 267. West further entertains "the sinister possibility that the antiepistemological radicalism of neo-pragmatism—much like the antimetaphysical radicalism of postmodernism—may be an emerging form of ideology in late capitalist societies which endorses the existing order while undergirding sophisticated antiepistemological and antimetaphysical tastes of postmodern avant-gardists." P. 269.

14. Mosher, "The Skeptic's Burke," p. 404.

15. Oakeshott, *Morality and Politics in Modern Europe,* ed. Shirley Robin Letwin (New Haven: Yale University Press, 1993); and "Political Philosophy" in *Religion, Politics and the Moral Life,* ed. Timothy Fuller (New Haven: Yale, 1993), pp. 138-155.

16. Oakeshott, *Experience and Its Modes* (Cambridge: Cambridge University Press, 1933; also in paperback by the same publisher, 1985).

17. Oakeshott, *On Human Conduct* (Oxford: Oxford University Press, Clarendon Press, 1991).

18. See for instance Franco, *The Political Philosophy of Michael Oakeshott,* and Tariq Modood and Dale Hall, "Oakeshott and the Impossibility of Philosophical Politics," *Political Studies* 30 (1982): 157-176.

19. Oakeshott, "The Authority of the State," in *Religion, Politics and the Moral Life,* (originally published in 1929), pp. 74-90.

20. Oakeshott, *Experience and Its Modes,* p. 341.

21. Oakeshott, "The Concept of a Philosophy of Politics" in *Religion, Politics and the Moral Life,* pp. 119-137.

22. Oakeshott, "Political Philosophy," in *Religion, Politics and the Moral Life,* pp. 138-155. Fuller dates this essay "1946-1950."

23. I focus in this chapter primarily upon Oakeshott's "Thomas Hobbes," *Scrutiny* 4 (1935-6), pp. 263- 277, "Introduction to *Leviathan,*" pp. 221-294, and "The Moral Life in the Writings of Thomas Hobbes," pp. 295-350, in *Rationalism in Politics.*

24. Oakeshott, "Thomas Hobbes," p. 277.

25. Oakeshott, *On Human Conduct,* p. 158.

Notes for Chapter One

1. Robert Grant, *Oakeshott* (London: The Claridge Press, 1990), p. 13.

2. Hannah Fenichel Pitkin, "The Roots of Conservatism," *Dissent* 20 (1973), p. 497, note.

3. W. H. Greenleaf, *Oakeshott's Philosophical Politics* (New York: Barnes and Noble, 1966), p. 2.

4. Ibid., pp. 2, 5.

5. Michael J. Oakeshott, *Experience and Its Modes* (Cambridge: Cambridge University Press, 1933; also in paperback by the same publisher, 1985), p. 6.

6. Rudolf Metz, *A Hundred Years in British Philosophy,* trans. J. W. Harvey, T. E. Jessop, and Henry Stuart, ed. J. H. Muirhead (London: Allen and Unwin, 1938), p. 258.

7. A. M. Quinton "Absolute Idealism," *Proceedings of The British Academy,* 57 (1971), p. 305.

8. Oakeshott, *Experience and Its Modes,* p. 6.

9. Paul Franco, *The Political Philosophy of Michael Oakeshott* (New Haven: Yale University Press, 1990), p. 15. Franco discusses the positivist and neo-Kantian heritage of these claims in the preceding pages.

10. Oakeshott, *Experience and Its Modes,* p. 7.

11. Greenleaf, *Oakeshott's Philosophical Politics,* p. 1 and Quinton, "Absolute Idealism," p. 302. Greenleaf reports that "Unkind commentators have said that Sterling, if he did posses this secret, kept it uncommonly well." P. 1.

12. Metz, *A Hundred Years in British Philosophy,* p. 239.

13. Ibid. A similar claim is made by Etienne Gilson, Thomas Langan and Armand Maurer: "The first diffusion of German idealism in England was largely the work of poets and essayists like Coleridge and Carlyle and not of academic professors"; but they also place the introduction of Hegel and "full metaphysical idealism" to England with Stirling. *Recent Philosophy: Hegel to the Present* (New York: Random House, 1962), pp. 455, 456.

14. Metz, *A Hundred Years in British Philosophy,* p. 249.

15. Ibid., p. 251.

16. Quinton, "Absolute Idealism," p. 305.

17. Greenleaf, *Oakeshott's Philosophical Politics,* p. 6.

18. Ibid.

19. Ibid., p. 7. Franco suggests that this was exclusively "what British idealism was directed against: namely, British empiricism. It was against the empiricist theory of knowledge." *The Political Philosophy of Michael Oakeshott,* p. 18.

20. Greenleaf, in discussing idealism's poor repute, claims, "We are told that, as philosophy, [idealism] is meaningless jargon or rhetoric, if not downright fraud." *Oakeshott's Philosophical Politics,* p. 1

21. Quinton, "Absolute Idealism," p. 327.

22. Ibid., p. 328.

23. F. H. Bradley, *Appearance and Reality,* 2nd ed., (London: Oxford University Press, 1897), p. 123. Later Bradley summarizes "There is but one Reality, and its being consists in experience. In this one whole all appearances come together. . . . Everything is experience and experience is one." Pp. 403, 405.

24. Quinton, "Absolute Idealism," p. 328.

25. Bradley, *Appearance and Reality,* p. 321.

26. Ibid., 322.

27. Quinton, "Absolute Idealism," p. 328.

28. Bradley, *Appearance and Reality,* p. 518.

29. Ibid., pp. 518-9.

30. Quinton, "Absolute Idealism," p. 328.

31. Bradley, *Appearance and Reality,* p. 127.

32. Ibid.

33. Ibid., pp. 128-9.

34. Quinton, "Absolute Idealism," p. 328.

35. Bradley, *Appearance and Reality,* p. 124.

36. Ibid.

37. Oakeshott, *Experience and Its Modes,* p. 10.

38. Ibid., p. 11.

39. Ibid., p. 48.

40. Ibid., p. 42.

41. Ibid.

42. Ibid., p. 45.

43. Ibid., p. 46.

44. Ibid.

45. Ibid., p. 33.

46. Ibid., p. 2.

47. This is an aspect of idealism that Quinton did not mention the thesis that within the Absolute there are divergences of one sort or another. Thus, for example, Bradley claims there are appearances distinct from, as well as part of, reality. He claims "The Absolute is each appearance, and is all, but it is not any one as such." *Appearance and Reality,* p. 431. Oakeshott's concept of "modifications" is his own variation upon this idealist thesis.

48. Oakeshott, *Experience and Its Modes,* p. 84.

49. Ibid., p. 71.

50. Ibid., p. 2. In an essay written a few years after *Experience and Its Modes,* "The Concept of a Philosophical Jurisprudence," Oakeshott, in a singular exception, does suggest that philosophy can order other experience. He states, "[philosophical jurisprudence] will be one explanation of the nature of law in a hierarchy of explanations. It has the authority to create this hierarchy by supplying a universal criterion by which the adequacy, the relative completeness of all explanations may be determined." "The Concept of a Philosophical Jurisprudence," *Politica* 3 (1938), p. 352. Again, however, while in *Experience and Its Modes* Oakeshott does see philosophical experience as a criterion, he dismisses the interest in ranking various modal explanations, because while

> It is, of course, true that modes of experience do not fall equally short; in the end the distinction between them is, simply, that they

represent different degrees of abstraction.... In order [then] to realize its purpose, in order to keep itself unencumbered by what is abstract and defective, it is not necessary for philosophy to determine the exact degree of defect belonging to any presented abstract world of ideas, it is necessary only to recognize abstract and overcome it. (p. 84)

51. *Experience and Its Modes,* p. 4.

52. Ibid., p. 5.

53. Ibid.

54. Ibid., p. 320.

55. Timothy Fuller, the editor of the volume that includes "The Concept of a Philosophy of Politics," which was "an undated hand-written original," chooses to date this piece "1946?" "Preface" and editor's notes to Michael Oakeshott, *Religion, Politics and the Moral Life,* ed. Timothy Fuller (New Haven: Yale University Press, 1993), pp. vii, 119. It seems much more likely, however, that the essay was written by Oakeshott in the thirties, especially since Oakeshott did publish almost a quarter of it in 1938 as part of "The Concept of a Philosophical Jurisprudence." For a full discussion of the dating of this essay, see Chapter Three: Section IV.

56. Oakeshott, "The Concept of a Philosophy of Politics," p. 137.

57. Oakeshott, *Experience and Its Modes,* p. 71.

58. Ibid., p. 35.

59. Ibid., p. 3.

60. Ibid., p. 46.

61. Ibid., p. 47.

62. Ibid., p. 356.

63. Skepticism is not a manner of thought that I have entirely imposed on Oakeshott. Oakeshott himself identifies this aspect of his philosophy as skepticism in "The Concept of a Philosophical Jurisprudence," where he argues that "Philosophical enquiry is peculiar mainly because in the pursuit of this process it is governed by a radical scepticism with regard to every stopping place that is suggested; it is suspicious of every attempt to limit the enquiry." P. 348.

64. Oakeshott, "Religion and the Moral Life," originally published 1927, and "The Importance of the Historical Element in Christianity," originally published in 1928, both in *Religion, Politics and the Moral Life.*

65. Oakeshott, "The Importance of the Historical Element," p. 64.

66. Oakeshott, *Experience and Its Modes,* p. 4.

67. Oakeshott, "The Concept of a Philosophical Jurisprudence," p. 351.

68. Ralph Ross, *Scepticism and Dogma,* (New York: n.p., 1940), p. 10.

69. Ibid.

70. Ibid., p. 147.

71. Bradley, *Appearance and Reality,* p. 459.

72. Ibid., p. 498.

73. An argument similar to mine but about Bradley is made by Charles A. Campbell in *Scepticism and Construction* (London: Allen and Unwin, 1931). Campbell argues there is not a tension at all between a skeptical philosophy and a constructive one, and points to how for Bradley these coalesce. He summarizes:

> Metaphysical scepticism is thus, in my view, the convergence of a variety of independent lines [of Bradley's] thought.... But what room does this leave for construction? None, it is obvious enough, for a constructive philosophy which aims at knowing the ultimate nature of things. But for a constructive philosophy that is less exalted, though still, as I believe, vitally important, there is room. (p. vi)

Notes for Chapter Two

1. Michael J. Oakeshott, *Experience and Its Modes* (Cambridge: Cambridge University Press, 1933; also in paperback edition by the same publisher, 1985), p. 7.

2. Oakeshott, "The Concept of a Philosophical Jurisprudence," *Politica* 3 (1938, December), p. 345.

3. During this time Oakeshott was lecturing in history as a Fellow at Gonville and Caius College, Cambridge, and he wrote a number of short articles and reviews, for example: an essay on Bentham, "The New Bentham," *Scrutiny,* (1931-32): 114-31; a review of *The Historical Element in Religion,* by C. Webb, *The Journal of Theological Studies* 37 (1936): 96-7; and an unexpected work on horse racing with G.T. Griffith (London: Faber, 1936), whose title has probably sent new students of Oakeshott scurrying for an insight to Greek and Roman philosophy, *A Guide to the Classics (or How to Pick the Derby Winner).* Oakeshott had even published two poems in the *Cambridge Review,* "Scutari," 53 (1931), p. 67 and "Cracow," 53 (1932) p. 266.

4. R. G. Collingwood, in a review in high praise of *Experience and Its Modes,* wrote of Oakeshott's chapter "Historical Experience," "Of this chapter, I can, in this brief notice, only say that it is the most penetrating analysis of historical thought that has ever been written." "Oakeshott and the Modes and Experience," in *The Cambridge Mind: Ninety Years of the Cambridge Review,* ed. Eric Homberger, William Janeway, and Simon Schama. (London: Jonathan Cape, 1970, review originally published in 1934), p. 132.

5. W. H. Greenleaf, *Oakeshott's Philosophical Politics* (New York: Barnes and Noble, 1966), pp. 2, 5.

6. Oakeshott, "The Voice of Poetry in The Conversation of Mankind," in *Rationalism in Politics and Other Essays* (Methuen and Company, 1962, reprinted with additions and edited by Timothy Fuller by Liberty Press, 1991): 488-541.

7. Oakeshott even considers *On Human Conduct* to be a "work . . . composed of three connected essays." *On Human Conduct* (Oxford: Oxford University Press, Clarendon Press, 1991), p. vii.

8. Oakeshott, "Political Education," p. 62 and "The Study of 'Politics' in a University," p. 187. Both essays can be found in *Rationalism in Politics.*

9. My interest here is not to examine Oakeshott's claims about the way in which learning and participating in the politics of a community is like learning and speaking a language. Rather my intention is to explore how his use of the metaphor of conversation indicates a change in his conception of philosophy.

10. Greenleaf, *Oakeshott's Philosophical Politics,* p. 5.

11. Ibid., p. 95. Greenleaf argues that "Oakeshott's political ideas are . . . very definitely the reflection of a philosophical standpoint," and that standpoint is "the idealist tradition of philosophy from which the rationale of Oakeshott's approach derives." Pp. 2, 4.

12. Paul Franco, *The Political Philosophy of Michael Oakeshott* (New Haven: Yale University Press, 1990), p. 13.

13. Tariq Modood has argued "that by 1959 the conversation of mankind has displaced philosophy as the unity of modes of experience [that Oakeshott argued for in *Experience and Its Modes*]. But this [change] has not been simply a *coup d'etat* by a new terminology; rather the nature of the union has been changed, some of the powers of the old regime seem to have been lost in the transfer." "Oakeshott's Conceptions of Philosophy," *History of Political Thought* 1 (1980), p. 318. However, he also suggested that "The Voice of Poetry was an idiosyncratic temporary alteration: "*On Human Conduct* also touches upon these issues, and once again in new terminology, but by now the scepticism and uncertainties of the middle period have disappeared and we are back to a view much closer to *Experience and Its Modes.*" The resulting view of the relationship of politics and philosophy is evident in another article Modood wrote a few years later with Dale Hall, wherein they deny the possibility on Oakeshott's terms of any relationship between philosophy and politics or any other endeavor of human existence. Modood and Hall state boldly "We should begin by being clear that the gulf between philosophy and practice, in Oakeshott's view, is total." Modood and Dale Hall, "Oakeshott and the Impossibility of Philosophical Politics," *Political Studies* 30 (1982), p. 162.

14. Franco, *The Political Philosophy of Michael Oakeshott,* p. 161.

15. Ibid.

16. Ibid., p. 64.

17. Jeremy Rayner in "The Legend of Oakeshott's Conservatism: Sceptical Philosophy and Limited Politics," *Canadian Journal of Political Science* 18 (1985), 313-338, claims while "the idealist idiom became less prominent Oakeshott's writing," as his title indicates, Oakeshott's position is one of

"sceptical philosophy." P. 324. I generally agree with the argument Rayner develops about Oakeshott's political philosophy, and with his position regarding Oakeshott's skepticism. Rayner, however, spends little time tracing out this development in Oakeshott's thought and ignores "The Voice of Poetry," focusing primarily upon *On Human Conduct.*

18. Oakeshott, "Voice of Poetry," p. 512.
19. Oakeshott, *Experience and Its Modes,* p. 82.
20. Oakeshott, "Voice of Poetry," p. 492.
21. Ibid., p. 491.
22. Oakeshott, *Experience and Its Modes,* p. 4.
23. Oakeshott, "Political Philosophy," in *Religion, Politics and the Moral Life,* ed. Timothy Fuller (New Haven: Yale University Press, 1993): 138-155. Fuller dates this essay "1946-1950."
24. Oakeshott, "The Concept of a Philosophy of Politics," in *Religion, Politics and the Moral Life,* pp. 134-5. For my argument that this essay was written contemporaneously with "The Concept of a Philosophical Jurisprudence" see Chapter Three, Section IV.
25. Oakeshott, "Political Philosophy," p. 141.
26. Ibid., p. 144.
27. Ibid., p. 155.
28. Oakeshott, "Voice of Poetry," p. 489.
29. Oakeshott, *Experience and Its Modes,* p. 5.
30. Ibid., p. 315.
31. Oakeshott, "Voice of Poetry," p. 489.
32. There is one place in *Experience and Its Modes* where Oakeshott does suggest a type of interaction of this contingent sort. When discussing the relationship between the worlds of scientific and practical experience Oakeshott states first the unsurprising claim that "scientific ideas are seen neither to work nor fail in the practical world; they are seen merely to be irrelevant." P. 314. This certainly agrees with everything else in *Experience and Its Modes,* with its characteristic concern with irrelevance and maintaining separation. Yet, he continues in a different vein, "Of course, it is possible to translate certain pseudo-scientific ideas to the worlds of practice, but the relation is itself a removal of them from the world of science to that of practical life, and with this they cease at once to be—or rather, even to seem to be—scientific ideas." P. 314. An example of this might be when engineers and architects adopt and adapt principles from physics to design physical structures and products in the practical world. They do so, however, not as physicists, nor as popularizers of physics, but as engineers and architects removing ideas "from the world of science to that of practical life" in order to build safer bridges, more efficient engines, et al. Oakeshott spends little time with this, and it is washed over by all the idealist warnings against any admixture.

33. Oakeshott, "Voice of Poetry," p. 492.
34. Ibid., p. 493.
35. Ibid., p. 492.
36. Ibid., 490.
37. Greenleaf, *Oakeshott's Philosophical Politics,* pp. 34–5. Thus, for Greenleaf, that Oakeshott uses "voice" instead of "mode" is of little importance.
38. It is important to recognize that Franco explicitly dismisses the notion that Oakeshott changed his conception of philosophy as I have suggested. He accomplishes this in some degree by all but neglecting "The Voice of Poetry." In examining Franco's more than six hundred endnotes one can find only three references to "The Voice of Poetry," two of which are merely parallel citations for a passage quoted from a different essay. Franco, *Political Philosophy of Michael Oakeshott,* p. 251, #49 and p. 252, #74. In the other endnote, Franco directly engages the questions raised about revisions in Oakeshott's conception of philosophy. He states:

    Of course, it may be contended that Oakeshott's conception of philosophy changes from *Experience and Its Modes* to "The Voice of Poetry in the Conversation of Mankind," and that it is [a] more "conversational" view of philosophy found in the latter. . . . I will take up and reject the view that Oakeshott's conception of philosophy changes substantially from *Experience and Its Modes* to "The Voice of Poetry in the Conversation of Mankind" in a later chapter. (p. 239, #9)

39. Oakeshott, *On Human Conduct,* p. 1.
40. Ibid., p. 2.
41. Oakeshott, *Experience and Its Modes,* p. 2.
42. Oakeshott, *On Human Conduct,* pp. 8-9.
43. Oakeshott, *Experience and Its Modes,* p. 2.
44. Oakeshott, "Philosophical Jurisprudence," p. 351.
45. Oakeshott, *On Human Conduct,* p. 11. Emphasis added.
46. Ibid.
47. Ibid.
48. Ibid., pp. 2, 3.
49. Ibid., p. 11.
50. Oakeshott, *Experience and Its Modes,* pp. 256-7.
51. A practice, Oakeshott explains, "emerges as a continuously invented and always unfinished by-product of performances related to the achievement of the imagined and wished for satisfactions. . . . It is a relationship between agents articulated in terms of specific conditional prescriptions." Oakeshott, *On Human Conduct,* p. 56. Oakeshott makes explicit this new use of practice in one of his seldom used footnotes, explaining "knowing how to participate in a 'practice' is not exclusive to conduct. It is present also, for example, in both 'historical' and in 'scientific' inquiry, both of which are engagements of theoretical understanding," p. 57, note.

176 Notes

52. Oakeshott in the essays in *Rationalism in Politics* had famously used the concept "tradition" for the type of knowledge that is generated and transferred in the practical activity of human endeavors. Oakeshott later acknowledges, however, "I have abandoned 'tradition' as inadequate to express what I wanted to express," and suggests that if the change of practice for tradition "is read back into what I had written earlier [it] make[s] it more exact." Oakeshott, "On Misunderstanding Human Conduct," *Political Theory* 4 (1976), p. 364.
53. Oakeshott, *On Human Conduct,* p. 26.
54. Franco, *Political Philosophy of Michael Oakeshott,* p. 165.
55. Oakeshott, *On Human Conduct,* p. 30.
56. Ibid.
57. Ibid., pp. 163–4.
58. Ibid., p. 164. Oakeshott here holds "The acquiescent ingredient is assent to its [*republica*] authority." I will spend considerable time with this claim in Chapters Five and Six.
59. Ibid., p. 174.
60. Ibid., p. 180.
61. Oakeshott is of course well known for his contributions to the conversation about education, many of which are included in *Michael Oakeshott on Education,* edited by Timothy Fuller, (New Haven: Yale University Press, 1989).
62. Oakeshott, *On Human Conduct,* p. 59.
63. Neal Wood, "A Guide to the Classics: The Skepticism of Professor Oakeshott," *Journal of Politics* 21 (1959), p. 649.
64. Ibid., pp. 648, 650.
65. Modood, "Oakeshott's Conceptions of Philosophy," p. 320. But recall that Modood that does not think Oakeshott retains this abandonment.
66. Wood, "A Guide to the Classics," p. 651. Bernard Crick considers Oakeshott to have gone beyond skepticism, and accuses him of journeying into the netherworld of "nihilism." "The World of Michael Oakeshott, or the Lonely Nihilist." *Encounter* 20 (June, 1963), p. 74.

Notes for Chapter Three

1. Michael Oakeshott, "The Authority of the State," in *Religion, Politics and the Moral Life,* ed. Timothy Fuller (New Haven: Yale University Press, 1993, originally published in 1929), p. 80.
2. Timothy Fuller, in the "Preface" to Michael Oakeshott, *Religion, Politics and the Moral Life* claims,
   > There is a typescript from the mid-1920s, about 190 pages in length, titled *A Discussion of Some Matters Preliminary to the Study of Political Philosophy. . . .* Numerous notebooks from the 1920s of his own extensive commentaries on Plato's dialogues, Aristotle's *Nico-*

machean Ethics and *Politics* and Spinoza's writings and those of others, include parallel quotations from commentators Oakeshott was reading at the time. (p. vii, note.)

3. Oakeshott, *Experience and Its Modes* (Cambridge: Cambridge University Press, 1933; also in paperback by the same publisher, 1985), p. 9.

4. Bernard Bosanquet, *The Philosophical Theory of the State* (London: Macmillan, 1925).

5. L. T. Hobhouse, *The Metaphysical Theory of the State: A Criticism* (London: Allen and Unwin, 1918). Stefan Collini, "Hobhouse, Bosanquet, and the State: Philosophical Idealism and Political Argument in England 1880-1918," *Past and Present* 72 (August, 1976), p. 86. See Collini passim for a detailed account of the general acceptance of Hobhouse's critique.

6. A. D. Lindsay and H. J. Laski, "Symposium: Bosanquet's Theory of the General Will." *Aristotelian Society,* Supplementary Volume 8 (1928). Laski had himself published in 1919 a book titled *Authority in the Modern State* (New Haven: Yale University Press, 1919) which had in fact been reprinted in 1927.

7. Oakeshott, "Authority of the State," p. 74.

8. Ibid., pp. 74-5.

9. Ibid., p. 75. While Oakeshott provides examples of what he means by this, he provides no reasons or examples for why we should accept these as the common aspects of authority, and if we do not accept this initial common understanding as he suggests, his piece fails completely. He may be simply setting up an argument of straw to knock it down. I will not challenge this initial starting point, but it is worth noting that he does nothing to justify it.

10. Ibid., p. 75.

11. Ibid.

12. Ibid., p. 76. Oakeshott provides another interesting example:

Or again, the ground of belief in an historical fact, is not that it is recorded by an historian, nor that it is asserted by a contemporary, nor that it is asserted by an eye-witness, it is an independent judgement we make about the credibility of the fact proposed, by which we test these other, secondary witnesses and beside which they are nothing other than the causes of belief.

13. Ibid., p. 78. Emphasis added.

14. Ibid.

15. Ibid., 76.

16. Richard Flathman, in *Toward a Liberalism* (Ithaca: Cornell University Press, 1989), discusses Oakeshott's understanding of authority as it is found in later works, but his analysis of how Oakeshott breaks down the distinction between "in authority" and "an authority" could easily attend to this essay, Oakeshott's first discussion of authority as well. "An authority" for Oakeshott is as dependent upon judgment and recognition as "in author-

ity," collapsing the former into the latter. See Flathman, Chapter Two, esp. pp. 53-55.

17. Oakeshott, "Authority of the State," p. 77.
18. Ibid.
19. Ibid., p. 78.
20. Ibid., p. 79.
21. See Peter P. Nicholson, *The Political Philosophy of the British Idealists* (Cambridge: Cambridge University Press, 1990) for the most recent sustained discussion of the concept of the state in the theories of main actors in that tradition: F. H. Bradley, T. H. Green, and Bernard Bosanquet. He also discusses, to some extent, lesser figures in the pantheon of British idealists who concentrated on political philosophy, with the noticeable exception of Oakeshott. Nicholson explains:

    It is not exactly agreed precisely who should be considered British Idealists, so I cite only writers whose credentials are strong and who discussed issues of political philosophy at some length: William Wallace, D. G. Ritchie, R. B. Haldane, John Watson, John MacCunn, J. S. MacKenzie, J. H. Muirhead, Henry Jones, and H. J. W. Hetherington.

    These writers are all generally of a generation immediately prior to Oakeshott's, giving some more credence to the claim that Oakeshott suffered from a form of philosophical necrophilia by his investment in the moribund tradition of idealism. Nicholson cites one passage from *Rationalism in Politics,* (from the essay "The Tower of Babel"), but he makes no mention of "The Authority of the State," *Experience and Its Modes,* or *On Human Conduct* even though it may be tempting to view Oakeshott's work as a continuation of the political philosophy of British idealism. The fact that Nicholson does not even suggest this step as a possibility may lend some support to my claim that Oakeshott in fact abandoned the absolute idealism that typified the British idealist tradition. The place of the concept of the state in this tradition is also examined by Stefan Collini in a broader context in his *Public Moralist, Political Thought and Intellectual Life in Britain, 1850-1930* (Oxford: Clarendon, 1991).
22. Oakeshott, "Authority of the State," p. 81.
23. Ibid., p. 84.
24. Ibid., p. 83.
25. Ibid., p. 80.
26. Bosanquet, *Philosophical Theory of the State,* p. 250. See all of Chapter X for his full discussion of Hegel and his conception of the modern state.
27. Ibid. See also "Part Three" generally of G. W. F. Hegel, *Philosophy of Right,* trans. T. M. Knox (Oxford: Clarendon, 1952), pp. 105-223. For an analysis of Hegel's theory of the state and these various components, see Charles Taylor, *Hegel* (Cambridge: Cambridge University Press, 1975), especially chap-

ters XV and XVI, and Z. A. Pelczynski, ed., *Hegel's Political Philosophy* (Cambridge: Cambridge University Press, 1971), especially Pelczynski, "The Hegelian Conception of the State," pp. 1-29.

28. Oakeshott, "Authority of the State," p. 83. Oakeshott had begun to work toward these ideas in an essay he wrote a few years earlier but did not publish. In "The Nature and Meaning of Sociality," (in Fuller, ed., *Religion, Morality and the Moral Life*), Oakeshott developed the idea of the "social whole" that he here associates with the state. In that earlier essay he claimed,

> The possibility of sociality, that is, the possibility of a society, rests upon the discovery that in the end moral obligation cannot be divided into exclusive areas, but is a single and self-sufficing whole. It rests upon a unity which is not merely a practical unity of action . . . but a unity of mind based on, and arising from a real wholeness and comprehensiveness of life. (p. 52)

29. Franco, *The Political Philosophy of Michael Oakeshott* (New Haven: Yale University Press, 1990), p. 77.

30. I do not disagree with Franco's characterization as far as it goes, but noticeably lacking from Oakeshott's conception of the state is the central Hegelian notion of the will. Hegel's concept of the will pervades *The Philosophy of Right,* but see especially paragraph 258 for the explicit link of the will to the state. Franco's attempt to draw out and emphasize the Hegelian elements in Oakeshott's thought, a strategy that I consider especially insightful in this early stage of Oakeshott's work, becomes more problematic later. The difficulty is clear in a footnote Franco writes during his discussion of *On Human Conduct.* After suggesting that Oakeshott takes "will or freedom as the starting point for his political philosophy," (p. 167) Franco has to explain:

> I am, of course, aware that Oakeshott does not generally speak of "will" [in *On Human Conduct*] *except in contrast to his own view of human agency.* His avoidance of the term, however, stems more from its identification as a faculty separate from the intellect than from a rejection of the notion of the will altogether. For Oakeshott, as we shall see, will is simply intelligence in doing; it is not something unconditional or separate from thinking. This view of the will he annunciated as early as [*Experience and Its Modes*] . . . and indeed it goes all the way back to Hegel. . . . Oakeshott's (and Hegel's) identification of thinking and willing is not to be understood as a rejection of the notion of the will; it is a theory of will itself. (Note 22, p. 256. Emphasis added)

Franco, I think, cannot dissolve the predicament he finds himself in by simply recognizing Oakeshott's rejection of the concept of will in *On Human Conduct,* while also maintaining he held the same view as in *Experience and Its Modes,* all without acknowledging the will is not even present in "The Authority of the State."

31. Bosanquet, *Metaphysical Theory of the State,* pp. 140-1.

32. Earlier Oakeshott had attempted to work out what gives unity to the social whole that he would come to define as the state. In "The Nature and Meaning of Sociality," Oakeshott already suggested that "Society is not a machine or organism, it is a spiritual whole, a unity of mind." P. 57. But when it came to providing an understanding of this unity he offered a disunified front of answers. First, he suggests that the "best name" of that which explains the unity is "the principle of the good"; then, however, he explains the unity of society as "the unity of life and the mind which we call love and friendship"; and then, finally, "Men are united, society is society, only so long as they live after the guidance of reason." Pp. 57, 58, 60. In the first and third of these there is a strong normative concept that may act as the unifying principle, but in that essay, Oakeshott neither links them nor weaves in the separate theme of friendship. However, while in the earlier essay, he does recognize the need to supply an answer to what allows us to think of the state as a unified social whole, in "The Authority of the State," the state remains for Oakeshott the undifferentiated and unmodified "social whole."

33. Oakeshott *On Human Conduct* (Oxford: Oxford University Press, 1975, Clarendon Press, 1991), p. 88. Oakeshott's attitude toward the concepts of society, social, etc. is complex and changes over time. On the one hand, he ridiculed any use of society to represent an unmodified, unqualified form of association, as in the passage just quoted. So also in an essay contemporary with *On Human Conduct,* he claims, "Human association is always in terms of beliefs and ascertainable conditions; . . . there can be no unconditional human association such as the current words 'social' and 'society' suggest"; at the same time he recognizes, and eventually advocates a conception of the state he labels with the latinate *societas,* holding, "A state might be recognized as what was known as a *societas;* that is, human beings associated solely in being related to one another in terms of their common acknowledgement of the authority of rules of conduct," Oakeshott, "The Vocabulary of the Modern European State, *Political Studies* 23 (2 and 3), p. 336. His disregard for the concept "society" is also seen in the following passage of ridicule from another essay contemporary with *On Human Conduct.* While discussing the difficulty of investigating the mode of association known as the state Oakeshott claims, "This inquiry has been obliterated by drivel about something called 'society,' a fanciful total of unspecified relationships which only a simpleton would think of identifying with a state." "Talking Politics," in *Rationalism in Politics and Other Essays* (Methuen and Company, 1962, reprinted with additions and edited by Timothy Fuller by Liberty Press, 1991), p. 450.

34. Hobhouse, *Metaphysical Theory of the State,* pp. 72, 75-6. Hobhouse's rather nasty allusion to the Germanic acceptance of such a doctrine comes in the context of his association of the idealist view of the state with German

aggression in the Great War. See for example his "Dedication" to his son who was serving in the R.A.F. during 1917, when Hobhouse was giving the lectures out of which his book was drawn. In that dedication he describes how he was reading Hegel when an air attack on London began. He writes in the aftermath:

> As I went back to my Hegel my first mood was one of self-satire. Was this a time for theorizing or destroying theories? My second thoughts ran otherwise. To each man the tools and weapons he can best use. In the bombing of London I had just witnessed the visible and tangible outcome of a false and wicked doctrine, the foundations of which lay in the book before me. (p. 6)

35. Oakeshott, "Authority of the State," p. 84. Surprising, at least, to those mostly familiar with *Rationalism in Politics.*
36. Hegel, for instance, provides just such a discussion in *Philosophy of Right* in paragraphs 189–195, especially par. 194, where he describes "social needs, as the conjunction of immediate or natural needs with mental needs arising from ideas." *Hegel's Philosophy of Right,* trans. T. M. Knox (Oxford: Oxford University Press, 1952, also in paperback by same publisher, 1967).
37. Oakeshott, "Authority of the State," p. 83.
38. Ibid., p. 86.
39. Ibid.
40. Ibid. Again, Oakeshott seems to be following Hegel here in the rejection of contract or consent as a basis of authority. For comparisons, see especially par. 75 and par. 258 in *The Philosophy of Right.*
41. Oakeshott, "Authority of the State," p. 87.
42. Ibid., p. 87.
43. Taylor, *Hegel,* p. 387.
44. Ibid., p. 389.
45. Oakeshott, "Authority of the State," p. 87.
46. Oakeshott, *Experience and Its Modes,* p. 332.
47. Oakeshott is quick to point out that such are not "floating ideas," since they do have a world of ideas to which they belong, the concrete word of ideas, p. 333.
48. Ibid., p. 334.
49. Ibid., p. 325. Earlier Oakeshott had maintained, "Error and defect is not excluded from this world [of concrete experience] anymore than it is excluded from the worlds of history, science, or practice; it merely becomes error of a certain kind, philosophical error," p. 324.
50. Ibid., p. 335, note.
51. Ibid.
52. Ibid., p. 341.
53. Ibid., p. 344. Emphasis added.
54. Ibid., p. 345.

55. Timothy Fuller, "Preface" to *Religion, Politics and the Moral Life,* p. vii.
56. Oakeshott, "The Concept of a Philosophy of Politics," in *Religion, Politics and the Moral Life,* p. 119.
57. Oakeshott's "Introduction" was originally published in an edition of *Leviathan* that he edited and that was published by Basil Blackwell in 1946. The "Introduction" was not included in the original edition of *Rationalism in Politics,* but was included in an amended form in Oakeshott's collection of essays on Hobbes, *Hobbes on Civil Association,* (Berkeley: University of California Press, 1975). In its amended form, it has now been collected in the new edition of *Rationalism and Politics.*
58. Oakeshott, "Thomas Hobbes," *Scrutiny* 4 (1935-6): 263-277 and "Dr Leo Strauss on Hobbes," in *Hobbes on Civil Association,* pp. 132-149 (originally published in 1936-7).
59. Oakeshott, "Concept of Philosophical Jurisprudence," *Politica* III (September and December 1938), pp. 203-222 and pp. 345-360.
60. Oakeshott, "Concept of Philosophical Jurisprudence," p. 348, and "Concept of a Philosophy of Politics," p. 129. Those attributes—that a philosophical concept "is (i) New, (ii) Categorical, (iii) Affirmative, and (iv) Indicative"— Oakeshott explains using the same words in both essays, with the minor changes being that in one essay he uses the examples law and in the other the study of politics.
61. Oakeshott, "Political Philosophy," in *Religion, Politics and the Moral Life.* In dating these two pieces, Fuller simply places "1946 (?)" below the title of "A Concept of a Philosophy of Politics," while he places "1946-50" below "Political Philosophy," leading me to believe he has more confidence in the dating of the latter than the former. Also, because Fuller makes no claim to have titled these pieces, I am assuming that Oakeshott had himself titled the unpublished works.
62. Both the essays "The Concept of a Philosophy of Politics" and "Political Philosophy" were, according to Fuller, "undated, hand-written originals," p. vii.
63. Oakeshott, "Concept of a Philosophy of Politics," p. 120.
64. Ibid., p. 121.
65. Ibid., p. 122.
66. Ibid., p. 123.
67. There is an important distinction here between Oakeshott and Bosanquet, with whom Oakeshott's earlier "The Authority of State" shared so much. Recall that in *Experience and Its Modes* Oakeshott maintains an absolute separation of the modes from each other and philosophy from the modes. This attitude is reflected here in "The Concept of a Philosophical Politics." Yet Bosanquet advocated a strong connection of the philosophy and practice. For instance, in the long "Introduction to Second Edition" of *The Philosophical Theory of the State,* Bosanquet maintains, "I believe that it could be

shown that the views of the type here advocated not only give the truest interpretation of social forces and processes, but have in the recent past proved the most fruitful guide and inspiration of social improvement," p. xliv.

Similarly, Bosanquet also advocates a relationship between philosophy and sociology, another boundary crossing that Oakeshott would not allow. After comparing a philosophical understanding of society with that achieved by sociology, Bosanquet suggests, "But, at any rate, the points of view of sociology, and of social philosophy as described above, will continue to supplement each other. Philosophy gives a significance to sociology; sociology vitalizes philosophy," p. 48.

68. Oakeshott, "Concept of a Philosophy of Politics," p. 126-7.
69. Ibid.
70. Ibid., p. 131.
71. Ibid., pp. 132-3.
72. Ibid.
73. Ibid., p. 134.
74. Ibid., pp. 134-5. Notice also a similarity here to "The Concept of a Philosophical Jurisprudence," where Oakeshott claims that a philosophical explanation involves expanding the context of an explanation to a "context which criticism cannot itself turn into a text requiring a greater context," p. 355.
75. Oakeshott, "Concept of a Philosophy of Politics," p. 137.
76. Ibid., p. 136.
77. Oakeshott, "Political Philosophy," p. 141.
78. Ibid., p. 143.
79. Ibid., p. 150.
80. Oakeshott, "Concept of a Philosophy of Politics," p. 127.
81. Oakeshott, "Political Philosophy," p. 144.
82. Ibid., p. 155. Even in this essay, however, while Oakeshott maintains this separation he recognizes other forms of reflection about politics that do at least share certain qualities with what he calls political philosophy. Oakeshott discusses two such forms of political reflection that he calls "reflection *in the service of politics*" and a "reflective enterprise turned towards the construction of what I shall call a political *doctrine.*" (pp. 146, 147) Each of these is subversive and reflective, but only in a limited way. In the metaphor of ascent of the tower, each has a desire to stop at a certain level in order to adopt its prospect. The danger in this, as Oakeshott makes clear in the more famous essays of *Rationalism in Politics,* is to assume that any of these levels is the final or most complete level. Also notable here is that while he is careful to delineate these from political philosophy and to outline the result of confusing them, he is much less critical of the desire to formulate a "policy or "doctrine" here than he is in an essay such as "Rationalism in Politics."

83. Oakeshott, review of *Bernard Bosanquet's Philosophy of the State,* by Berti Pfannenstill, in *Philosophy* 11 (1936), p. 482.

84. Oakeshott, "Concept of a Philosophy of Politics," p. 137. In "Political Philosophy" he suggests that as examples of the attitude of radical subversiveness, "it is precisely this which seems to me to distinguish Plato's *Republic,* Hobbes's *Leviathan,* Spinoza's *Ethics,* and Hegel's *Grundlinien der Philosophie des Rechts,*" p. 150.

Notes for Chapter Four

1. Franco, *The Political Philosophy of Michael Oakeshott* (New Haven: Yale University Press, 1990), p. 88.

2. Patrick Riley, "Michael Oakeshott, Philosopher of Individuality," *The Review of Politics* 54 (Fall 1992), p. 655.

3. Ian Tragenza pursues a similar argument from a somewhat different perspective. Like my argument, he observes different stages in Oakeshott's philosophy by identifying "a shift of interpretive frameworks" in his analysis of Hobbes, one more idealist and critical of Hobbes, in the thirties, and one more sympathetic in the later work. "The Life of Hobbes in the Writing of Michael Oakeshott," *History of Political Thought* 18 (Autumn 1997), p. 446. One of the few others to pay such close attention to the relation of Oakeshott's interpretation of Hobbes to his own thought is Bruce Frohnen in "Oakeshott's Hobbesian Myth: Pride, Character and the Limits of Reason," *The Western Political Quarterly* 43 (December 1990), pp. 789-809.

4. Oakeshott, "Thomas Hobbes," *Scrutiny* 4 (1935-6), p. 263.

5. Ibid. Notice that this is still three years before A. E. Taylor published "The Ethical Doctrine of Hobbes," in 1938, initiating another round of "new" interest in Hobbes. A. E. Taylor, "The Ethical Doctrine of Hobbes," in *Hobbes Studies,* ed. K. C. Brown, (Oxford: Basil Blackwell, 1965, originally published in 1938).

6. Oakeshott, "Thomas Hobbes," p. 263.

7. Ibid., p. 264. Oakeshott gives no citation to the original author.

8. Ibid., p. 265.

9. Ibid., p. 273.

10. W. H. Greenleaf, "Hobbes: The Problem of Interpretation," in *Hobbes and Rousseau,* Maurice Cranston and Richard S. Peters, eds. (New York: Anchor Books, 1972), p. 6. Greenleaf suggests that not only was this view "something like the view of Hobbes put on him by his contemporaries," but also that it was still being defended as he wrote in 1972, p. 6.

11. Frithiof Brandt, *Thomas Hobbes' Mechanical Conception of Nature* (London: Librairie Hachette, 1928), would be an example of such an interpretation.

12. Oakeshott, "Introduction to *Leviathan,*" in *Rationalism in Politics and Other Essays* (Methuen and Company, 1962, reprinted with addition and edited

by Timothy Fuller by Liberty Press, 1991), p. 235. Oakeshott's "Introduction" was originally published in an edition of *Leviathan* that he edited and that was published by Basil Blackwell in 1946. The "Introduction" was not included in the original edition of *Rationalism in Politics,* but was included in an amended form in Oakeshott's collection of essays on Hobbes, *Hobbes on Civil Association* (Berkeley: University of California Press, 1975). In its amended form, it has now been collected in the new edition of *Rationalism and Politics,* and because it is the most readily available, I will refer to this version, although below I will also refer to the earlier edition.

13. Ibid., p. 235. An example of this might be John Laird who had argued:

    Clearly Hobbes possessed a flair for philosophical architecture, . . . His designs, however, were in parts very incomplete. A ground-plan of bodies in motion; . . . the plans for an entire storey devoted to sensation; very sketchy designs regarding the anatomy and physiology that should have connected the sensory storey with the materialist foundations . . . very full plans for a higher storey of introspective psychology . . . ; at the top an elaborate political philosophy with a character all its own and planed in terms of a psychology of self-interest that could hardly be reconciled with the monistic determinism of the ground-plan of the edifice. *Hobbes* (New York: Russel & Russel, 1934, reissued in 1968), pp. 244-5.

14. Oakeshott, "Introduction," p. 236.
15. Ibid., pp. 236-7.
16. Ibid., p. 238. Greenleaf interprets Oakeshott's claims in this way: "[Hobbes] see things on the analogy of a machine not because he is a scientific mechanist but because his conception of causal reasoning unavoidably turns whatever he looks at (including man and society) into a mechanism." Greenleaf, "The Problem of Interpretation," p. 22.
17. Oakeshott, "Thomas Hobbes," p. 273.
18. Oakeshott, "Introduction," p. 236. Oakeshott uses one of his rare footnotes here, calling on the following aphorism to explain this notion of system. "Confucius said 'T'zu, you probably think that I have learned many things and hold them in my mind.' 'Yes,' he replies, 'is that not true?' 'No,' said Confucius: 'I have learned one thing that permeates everything.' Confucius, *Analects,* XV, 2," cited in "Introduction," p. 236.
19. Ibid.
20. Ibid.
21. Sheldon Wolin, "Hobbes and the Culture of Despotism," in Mary G. Dietz, ed., *Hobbes and Political Theory* (Lawrence, KA: University of Kansas Press, 1990), p. 18.
22. Oakeshott, "Thomas Hobbes," p. 268.
23. Ibid.
24. Ibid.

25. Oakeshott, "Introduction," p. 238.
26. Ibid., p. 239.
27. Ibid. In making this case for Hobbes, Oakeshott seems to be criticizing the, by this time classic, *Hobbes* by George Croom Robertson (Edinburgh, 1886, AMS reprint: New York, 1971) and the more contemporary *Thomas Hobbes* by A. E. Taylor. Robertson, like Oakeshott, had asserted,

> The difference [is] now well understood, between Science and Philosophy. . . . The modern way of knowledge, which supplements that manifold lines of phenomenal inquiry by an express consideration of things in their relation to mind, was prepared rather than trodden throughout the greater part of the 17th century. *It is first distinctly traceable in Locke.* (p. 77, emphasis added.)

Seemingly following Robertson, Taylor, a generation later claimed "*With [Hobbes's] immediate successor,* Locke, begins that distinction between science and philosophy by which the scope of the latter is closely restricted to epistemological inquiries into the conditions and nature of knowledge in general." P. 28, emphasis added.
28. Oakeshott, "Introduction," p. 239.
29. Oakeshott, "Dr. Leo Strauss on Hobbes," in *Hobbes on Civil Association* (originally published in 1936), p. 142. Oakeshott's interpretation may seem similar to that of Strauss, who claims that for Hobbes "political philosophy is independent of natural science." *The Political Philosophy of Hobbes* (Chicago: The University of Chicago Press, 1952, originally published by The Clarendon Press, 1936), p. 6. While Oakeshott may agree with this, Strauss goes on to argue that Hobbes by "turning to Euclid and naturalism . . . [adopted] the mathematical method and materialist metaphysics [which] each in its own way contributed to disguise the original motivation-nexus and thus to undermine Hobbes's political philosophy." P. 170. For Oakeshott this trend does not mean Hobbes was abandoning philosophy for science, but that he was becoming more philosophical. Hobbes's philosophy, he holds, "is 'naturalistic' not in contrast to 'moral,' but in an attempt to find a firmer basis than merely a moral opinion." "Dr. Leo Strauss on Hobbes," p. 143.
30. Oakeshott, "Introduction," p. 239.
31. Ibid., p. 240. J. W. N. Watkins agrees with Oakeshott that Hobbes rejected Baconian experimental science; however, Watkins does suggest that Hobbes's philosophy was one strongly influenced by what he calls the "Paduan Methodology" of Galileo (pp. 32–42 and passim), *Hobbes System of Ideas* (London: Hutchinson and Co, 1965), pp. 17–22 and pp. 32–42. Richard Tuck, while he dismisses Watkins's claim that Hobbes adopted Galileo's methodology, does suggest "there are good grounds for supposing that Hobbes began his philosophical enquiries because he was intrigued by the problems raised by modern natural science, and particularly with the possibility of replacing late Renaissance scepticism with a philosophy accom-

modated to the ideas (above all) of Galileo." *Hobbes* (New York: Oxford University Press, 1989), pp. 105-6, 40.

32. Oakeshott, "Introduction," p. 240.
33. Oakeshott, "Introduction," p. 238.
34. Oakeshott, "Thomas Hobbes," p. 268.
35. Ibid.
36. Ibid.
37. Ibid., pp. 268-9.
38. Ibid., p. 268.
39. Richard Tuck, in commenting on Oakeshott's interpretive strategy, suggests, "The problem with Oakeshott's interpretation [of Hobbes] was partly, as a number of early critics observed, that it is hard to find clear textual evidence for it." *Hobbes,* p. 111.
40. Oakeshott, "Introduction," p. 230.
41. Ibid.
42. Ibid., p. 231.
43. Tuck also emphasized Hobbes's skepticism, but as I implied in note 31 he modifies it by suggesting Hobbes and others of his generation were attempting to replace "late Renaissance scepticism with a philosophy accommodated to the ideas (above all) of Galileo." Tuck develops this not only in *Hobbes,* but in his "Grotius, Carneades, and Hobbes" *Grotiana* N.S. 4, pp. 43-62 and his "Optics and Skeptics: The Philosophical Foundations of Hobbes's Political Thought," in Edmund Leites, ed., *Conscience and Casuistry in Early Modern Europe* (Cambridge: Cambridge University Press, 1987).

For his main thesis, Tuck seems to be following the outline of Richard Popkin's *The History of Scepticism from Erasmus to Spinoza* (Berkeley: University of California Press, 1979). While Tuck may be correct in characterizing the generation of philosophers in the first half of the seventeenth century, with Hobbes this is less clear. Tuck is unable to produce a passage in which Hobbes disavows the claims of the earlier skepticism or announces an intention to provide an alternative. Instead, Tuck follows Oakeshott in showing the philosophical underpinnings of Hobbes's skepticism, arguing that his skepticism was not just an attitude about the world, but a philosophical position. Thus although Tuck suggests that, "Instead of scepticism, [Hobbes] offered science," he also has to admit, "but when one looks closer, one finds that his science is of an extremely exiguous kind." *Hobbes,* p. 114. Oakeshott would probably suggest this is because it is not an offering against skepticism, but a limited, hypothetical science developed in accord with skepticism.

44. Oakeshott, "Introduction," p. 233.
45. Ibid.
46. Ibid., p. 280.
47. Ibid., p. 237.
48. Ibid., p. 242.

49. Ibid.
50. Ibid.
51. Ibid., p. 240.
52. Ibid.
53. Ibid. While he does not refer to it here Oakeshott seems also to have in mind a passage from the next page in Hobbes's text where he claimed, "But seeing names ordered in speech are signs of our conceptions, it is manifest they are not signs of the things themselves." Thomas Hobbes, *De Corpore,* in Sir Thomas Molesworth ed., The English Works of Thomas Hobbes, Volume I (London: John Bohn, 1839), p. 17.
54. Oakeshott, "Introduction," p. 242.
55. Hobbes also claims "For . . . these, a *man,* a *tree,* a *stone,* are the names of the things themselves." Hobbes, *De Corpore,* p. 17. Oakeshott, however, does not mention this passage from the same context as the passage he cites.
56. Aloysius Martinich, "Translator's Commentary" to Thomas Hobbes, *Computatio Sive Logica: Logic,* Isabel C. Hungarland and George R. Vick, eds. (New York: Abaris Books, 1981), p. 353. Martinich suggests this error results from a confusion of two of Hobbes's terms. He argues

    In order to understand Hobbes's theory we must carefully distinguish between what a name *signifies* (in the context of speech) and what a name *names,* if anything. . . . The Latin for 'signifies' and 'stands for' are 'significare' and 'denotare' respectively. Aside from one apparent exception Hobbes never conflates the meaning of these terms. (p. 353-4)

57. Oakeshott, "Introduction," p. 242.
58. It is curious to note that Oakeshott focuses almost exclusively upon the nature of language and its potential for reason within an individual, all but neglecting the conventional or communal character and function of language. Hobbes himself claims,

    Again, though some one man, of how excellent a wit soever, should spend all his time, partly in reasoning and partly in the inventing marks for the help of his memory, and advancing himself in learning; who sees not that the benefit he reaps to himself will not be much, and to others none at all. . . . It is therefore necessary, for the acquiring of philosophy, that there be signs, by which what one man finds out may be manifested and known to others. (*De Corpore,* p. 14)

    This would seem only to amplify Oakeshott's interpretation. For instance, Hobbes recognizes natural signs, but he claims "others are arbitrary, namely those we make a choice of at our own pleasure, as a bush hung up, signifies that wine is sold there; a stone in ground signifies the bound of a field; and words so and so connected, signify the cogitations and motions of our mind." *De Corpore,* pp. 14-5. Each of these forms of "arbitrary" signification are in fact a set of equally arbitrary conventions held with others. Both the

arbitrary and conventional nature of these signs are most clear to this twen-
tieth-century American reader in the first of the examples. A bush hung up
outside an establishment would signify nothing to me, or if anything, perhaps
a nursery; but to the seventeenth-century English seeker of a hostelry it
meant "wine is sold there." But the point is not only that the sign is arbitrary,
but that to act as sign for Hobbes it is dependent upon others being able to
recognize it as such. So, while there is no *a priori* reason to use the word
"arbor" rather than "tree" for what I recognize as the leafy affair out my window, there is a strong *a posteriori* reason for it: I am primarily a speaker of
English, but only an occasional reader of Latin. Using "tree" may be arbitrary
but it is not wholly idiosyncratic. The conventions of my expression make
my written speech in this case more meaningful by participating in this convention. This of course does not preclude me from using the Latinate "*a priori*" or "*a posteriori*" precisely because I also am expressing myself in a
scholarly convention in which these terms are meaningful. Mysteriously,
Oakeshott neglects this aspect of Hobbes's understanding of language.

59. Watkins, *Hobbes's System of Ideas,* p. 104.

60. Ibid.

61. Watkins suggests, however, "Hobbes did not consistently abide by his radical nominalism: he sometimes allowed that a common name may stand for
something that is *not* individual and singular—for some characteristic theory or property or (as he called it) *accident* which may be shared by many
individual things," Ibid. Thus for Watkins, Hobbes admitted that there were
in fact common and observable properties in the world outside of the
human mind (he had already argued that for Hobbes there was such a
world). For Oakeshott, Hobbes simply held that there were sensations that
leave images in our minds, and language is the human assignment of names
to the "fleeting images" in an arbitrary fashion. There may be consistencies
among images that we use to group them under certain names, but these
are consistencies that our minds impose, not that nature provides.

62. Richard Tuck, in a manner that would align with Oakeshott, suggests, "Man
is effectively a prisoner within the cell of his own mind, and has no idea
what in reality lies outside his prison wall"; and this, Tuck proposes, "Hobbes
had come to believe . . . by 1637." (*Hobbes,* p. 4.) Tuck cites the following
passage from Hobbes's *Elements of Law* (which he calls "often the most
accessible statement of [Hobbes's] general philosophy") to substantiate his
claim: "whatsoever accidents or qualities our senses makes us think there be
in the world, they are not there, but are seemings and apparitions only. The
things that are really in the world without us, are those motions by which
these seemings are caused." Pp. 40–41. Hobbes quoted from *Elements* I.2.10.
This passage also gives support to Oakeshott's interpretation above by dismissing accidents as also only "seemings and apparitions" within the mind,
not reliable or accessible properties in the "world without us."

63. Oakeshott, "Introduction," p. 243.

64. Ibid.

65. Ibid.

66. Richard Popkin, *The History of Scepticism from Erasmus to Spinoza* (Berkeley: University of California Press, 1979), pp. 129-150.

67. Ibid., p. xv.

68. Ibid., pp. 147-8.

69. Ibid. I suggested in note 43 above that Tuck seemed to be following Popkin when arguing that Hobbes and his generation were responding against skepticism, and here it is clear why: Popkin does seem to be suggesting that Gassendi and Mersenne were responding to skepticism. Popkin, however, makes it clear it was to pyrrhonism as a form of skepticism—not all skepticism—that they were responding with their own constructive or mitigated skepticism.

70. J. M. Brown, "A Note on Professor Oakeshott's Introduction to *Leviathan*," *Political Studies* 1 (1953), p. 53. The pages to which Brown refers comprise section "Six: The Argument of *Leviathan*," in the "Introduction"; they are pp. 248-274 in the LibertyPress edition. It is, I believe, to Brown, perhaps among others, that Tuck alluded when he referred to "a number of early critics" who claimed "that it is hard to find clear textual evidence" for Oakeshott's interpretation of Hobbes. Brown actually goes further, suggesting that Oakeshott displays "a singular lack of interest in what Hobbes actually said," p. 55.

71. W. H. Greenleaf, *Oakeshott's Philosophical Politics* (New York: Barnes and Noble, 1966), p. 6.

72. Ibid., p. 7

73. Ibid.

74. Michael J. Oakeshott, *Experience and Its Modes* (Cambridge: Cambridge University Press, 1933; also in paperback by the same publisher, 1985), p. 10.

75. Ibid., p. 42.

76. Flathman, *Thomas Hobbes: Skepticism, Individuality and Chastened Politics* (Newberry Park, CA: Sage Press, 1993), p. 1.

77. Oakeshott, *Experience and Its Modes*, p. 48.

78. Oakeshott, "Introduction," p. 237. Oakeshott has claimed that for Hobbes, philosophy is reasoning; here he assumes that theology is faith.

79. Ibid.

80. Ibid.

81. Oakeshott also places this aspects of Hobbes's thought in a form of the tradition of skepticism. He claims

> This method of circumscribing the concerns of philosophy is not, of course, original to Hobbes. It has roots that go back to Augustine, if not further, and it was inherited by the seventeenth century (where one side of it was distinguished as the heresy of Fideism:

both Montaigne and Pascal were Fideists) directly from its formulation in the Averroism of Scotus and Occam. Indeed, this doctrine
is one of the seeds in scholasticism from which modern philosophy
sprang. ("Introduction," p. 273.)

For a discussion of the relationship of Fideism and skepticism see espe-
cially the first chapter of Popkin's *The History of Scepticism from Erasmus to
Spinoza,* Chapter 8, and Terence Penelham, "Skepticism and Fideism," in *The
Skeptical Tradition,* ed. Miles Burnyeat (Berkeley: University of California
Press, 1983), pp. 287-318, although neither mentions Hobbes in this context.

82. Oakeshott, *Experience and Its Modes,* p. 2.
83. Ibid., p. 356.
84. Oakeshott, "Thomas Hobbes," p. 274. In the intervening passage Oakeshott
drily observes: "As a nation we are more easily alarmed at the creations of
our intellectual than our practical activity; and we do not require to be per-
suaded that the truth and moderation live on the same street, we believe it
on instinct."
85. Oakeshott, "Introduction," p. 231.
86. Ibid., p. 243.
87. Ibid., p. 245.
88. Ibid., p. 244.
89. Oakeshott, "John Locke," *The Cambridge Review* 54 (1932) p. 72.
90. Ibid.
91. Ibid.
92. Oakeshott, "Introduction," p. 232.
93. Ibid.
94. Oakeshott, "John Locke," p. 72.
95. Flathman, *Thomas Hobbes,* p. 22, note 9.

Notes for Chapter Five

1. Michael J. Oakeshott, "Introduction to *Leviathan,*" in *Rationalism in Politics
and Other Essays* (London: Methuen and Company, 1962, reprinted with
additions and edited by Timothy Fuller by Liberty Press, 1991), pp. 282-3.
2. Paul Ricouer, "Hermeneutics and the Critique of Ideology" in *Hermeneutics and Modern Philosophy,* ed. Brice W. Wachterhauser (Albany, NY: State
University of New York Press, 1986), p. 332.
3. Oakeshott, "Thomas Hobbes," *Scrutiny* 4 (1935-6), p. 277.
4. Oakeshott, "Introduction," p. 248.
5. Thomas Hobbes, *Leviathan,* ed. C. B. MacPhearson (London: Penguin,
1968), p. 217. Hobbes continues this passage, "But yet if we consider these
same theorems, as delivered in the word of God, that by right commandeth
all things; then they are properly called Lawes." Oakeshott does consider this
condition, and I will discuss it below.

6. Oakeshott, "Introduction," p. 245.

7. Ibid., p. 243.

8. Oakeshott, "The Moral Life in the Writings of Thomas Hobbes," in *Rationalism in Politics,* p. 315.

9. Ibid., p. 324.

10. Ibid.

11. Oakeshott interprets Hobbes's attitude toward scripture like this:

    Scripture is an artifact. It is, in the first place an arbitrary selection of writings called canonical by the authority that recognizes them. And secondly, it is nothing apart from interpretation. . . . And interpretation is a matter of authority: for, whatever part of reasoning may play in the part of interpretation, what determines everything is the decision, *whose* reasoning shall interpret. ("Introduction," p. 269.)

12. Oakeshott, "Introduction," p. 245.

13. Oakeshott's criticisms of Warrender's thesis may be fundamental, but he still gave a generous review of Warrender's *The Political Philosophy of Thomas Hobbes* (Oxford University Press, 1957) in *The Spectator* (August 9, 1957, p. 198). Oakeshott claims "It is a brilliant performance which even those who remain at some points unconvinced must recognize to be head and shoulders above anything else of its kind."

14. Oakeshott, "Moral Life," p. 317.

15. Oakeshott does draw back somewhat from this extreme formulation that disregards completely the substance of the law and focuses solely on its form. He states, "The terms of the covenant exclude, and are designed to exclude, any undertaking to surrender rights which cannot be given up without a man risking all that he designed to protect in making the covenant: that is, his pursuit of felicity and even his life." "Introduction," p. 265. Oakeshott implies that the individual retains a right to interpret and judge this situation as well, thus leaving open the possibility of at least private questioning of the sovereign authority in matters concerning the "pursuit of felicity."

16. Oakeshott, "Moral Life," p. 315.

17. Ibid. Quote from Hobbes, *Leviathan,* p. 268.

18. Oakeshott, "Introduction," p. 260. Oakeshott continues: "Thus the condition of peace and security is said to be the effect of "a covenant of every man, in such a manner, as if every man should say to every man, *I authorize and give up my right of governing myself, to this man, or to this assembly of men, on this condition, that thou give up thy right to him, and authorize all his actions in like manner.*"

19. Oakeshott, "Introduction," p. 257.

20. In 1946 Oakeshott edited *Leviathan* for a Basil Blackwell Political Texts series. It was for this edition that Oakeshott wrote his "Introduction." His edition of *Leviathan* was later available in the Collier Classics in the History

of Political Thought series, although abridged and lacking Oakeshott's "Introduction," instead having one by Richard S. Peters.

Until this point, because the passages and sections to which I have referred are not those that reveal important changes from the earlier version, I have consistently referred to the easily available version of the "Introduction to *Leviathan*" that Oakeshott published in the recent edition of *Rationalism in Politics*, a reproduction of the version in *Hobbes on Civil Association*. From this point on, however, in both footnotes and in the text, I will refer to the original Basil Blackwell introduction as "Introduction, 1946" and to the later Hobbes on Civil Association version as "Introduction, 1975."

21. Oakeshott, *Hobbes on Civil Association*, "Preface," p. vi. In an odd note of perhaps disingenuous modesty Oakeshott claims that while perhaps it has been overtaken, "It has a certain meretricious buoyancy." P. vi.

22. Reviewers of *Hobbes on Civil Association* either ignored the alterations to the "Introduction," e.g. Kenneth Minogue, *Political Studies* 24 (June 1976), p. 213, or accepted Oakeshott's word that they were insignificant, e.g. Thomas Spragens, who claims that the "Introduction" in the new edition is "slightly revised" American Political Science Review 72 (1978), p. 652. Even as careful a reader of Oakeshott as Paul Franco merely claims that Oakeshott's introduction was "reprinted with some modification in *Hobbes on Civil Association*," and he makes no comment on those modifications. Franco, *The Political Philosophy of Michael Oakeshott* (New Haven: Yale University Press, 1990), pp. 246-7. A notable exception to this trend is Ian Tragenza in his essay "The Life of Hobbes in the Writings of Michael Oakeshott," *History of Political Thought* 28 (Autumn 1997): 531-557, see especially 547-552.

23. Oakeshott, "Moral Life," p. 314.

24. Oakeshott, "Introduction, 1946," p. lix.

25. Ibid.

26. It may be possible to see these changes as a response to the harsh criticisms made by J. M. Brown in 1953 in "A Note on Professor Oakeshott's Introduction to *Leviathan*," *Political Studies* I (1953), pp. 53–64. Brown leveled a series of broadsides against Oakeshott, claiming that "by positive distortion here and by silence there, [Oakeshott] misrepresents throughout" p. 63; since Brown give no direct object for his "misrepresents" we can only assume it is everything Oakeshott presents. One of Brown's harshest criticisms is focused on Oakeshott's account of obligation in Hobbes. As I mentioned above, Oakeshott responds directly to Brown's preferred interpretation in "The Moral Life." However, while he does alter the language of his discussion of Hobbes's theory of obligation as I have noted, the central feature that Brown objects to, that prior to the covenant humans have no obligations, remains in Oakeshott's later versions. Tragenza suggests that beyond Brown, "Oakeshott's revised discussion of Obligation in Hobbes seems to be at least

partly a response to Warrender." "The Life of Hobbes in the Writings of Michael Oakeshott," p. 550, note 75. This addition makes perfect sense, and his argument only adds to my contention that these are substantive changes Oakeshott makes to the "Introduction." See also Oakeshott's comment on Warrender in note 13 above.

27. Oakeshott also drops the category of "physical obligation" from his analysis ("Introduction, 1946," p. lix), but this seems less important given the specific argument against "rational obligation" in "Moral Life."

28. Among the most recent is Noberto Bobbio's *Thomas Hobbes and the Natural Law Tradition* (Chicago: University of Chicago Press, 1993). As indicated in the title, Bobbio discusses Hobbes's relationship to natural law theory throughout. See especially pp. 44-46 for a specific discussion of the "Dictates of Right Reason."

29. Oakeshott, "Introduction, 1946," p. xl.

30. Ibid., p. lxiv.

31. Ibid., p. xxxix.

32. Oakeshott, "Introduction, 1975," p. 261.

33. Ibid., p. 267.

34. A few sections are completely rewritten. For example, compare pp. xxxvi-xxxix of "Introduction, 1946" to pp. 256-261 in "Introduction, 1975," and pp. lix-lxii in "Introduction, 1946" to pp. 284 289 in "Introduction, 1975."

35. Oakeshott, "Introduction, 1946," p. xxvii.

36. Oakeshott, "Introduction, 1975," p. 246.

37. Oakeshott, "Introduction, 1946," p. x and "Introduction, 1975," p. 225.

38. Oakeshott, "Introduction, 1946," p. lxiv.

39. Oakeshott, "Introduction, 1975," p. 291. Emphasis added.

40. Hobbes, *Leviathan*, p. 81, see also pages 227 and 311.

41. Oakeshott, "Introduction, 1946," p. xxxviii.

42. Oakeshott, "Introduction, 1975," pp. 260-1.

43. Hobbes, *Leviathan*, p. 376.

44. Ibid., p. 599.

45. Richard Flathman, *Thomas Hobbes: Skepticism, Individuality, and Chastened Politics* (Newberry Park, CA: Sage Press, 1993), p. 72.

46. Oakeshott, "Introduction, 1975," p. 283.

47. Oakeshott, "Introduction, 1946," p. lx.

48. Flathman, *Hobbes: Skepticism, Individuality, and Chastened Politics*, p. 73.

49. Oakeshott, "Moral Life," p. 318. Emphasis added.

50. Ibid., p. 318.

51. Ibid., p. 322, see also pp. 328, 329, 331, and 345.

52. Hobbes, *Leviathan*, p. 211.

53. Ibid., p. 227.

54. Oakeshott, "Introduction, 1975," p. 287.

55. Ibid.

56. Oakeshott, "The Rule of Law," in *On History and other Essays* (Totowa, NJ: Barnes and Noble, 1983), p. 157.

57. Helpful etymologies of "acknowledge" and "recognize" can be found in the *Oxford English Dictionary*. The *OED* shows that by the end of the sixteenth century, recognition could mean "a formal acknowledgement by subjects of (the title of) a sovereign or other ruler." However, Oakeshott neither makes reference to the fact that Hobbes chooses not to use it in this fashion, nor does he explain his choice in reference to this past usage. An especially interesting word history of "acknowledge" is provided in The *American Heritage Dictionary of the English Language*, 3rd edition (Boston: Houghton Mifflin, 1992).

58. Hobbes describes God's relationship to the Jews as his "peculiar people" by putting into God's mouth the words "*All the Nations of the world are mine*; but it is not so that you are mine, but in a speciall manner: For they are all mine, by reason of my Power, but you shall be mine by your own Consent, and Covenant; which is in addition to his ordinary title to all lands." *Leviathan*, pp. 444–445.

59. Again, see Oakeshott, "Moral Life," p. 337. This may, in fact, be construed as the argument of the last two parts of *Leviathan*. Oakeshott suggests these parts act to give the particular setting of the general argument of the first two parts. He claims, "The second half of the argument of *Leviathan* is . . . to show more clearly the local and transitory mischief in which the universal predicament of mankind appeared in the seventeenth century." "Introduction, 1975," p. 267.

60. Oakeshott, "Moral Life," p. 339.

61. Ibid., p. 340. Bruce Frohnen draws special attention to this feature of Oakeshott's interpretation of Hobbes, suggesting that it reveals the unique character of "the moral basis of Oakeshott's vision of civil association." "Oakeshott's Hobbesian Myth: Pride, Character and the Limits of Reason," *The Western Political Quarterly* 43 (December 1990), p. 793.

62. *Oxford Latin Dictionary* (New York: Oxford University Press, 1982), p. 412.

63. Oakeshott, "Introduction, 1975," p. 281.

64. Tragenza argues that a distinctive shift occurs in Oakeshott's reading of Hobbes when he changes his placement of him from a tradition of "Will and Artifice," during the idealist period to the tradition of "the morality of individuality," in the later period. "Hobbes in the Writings of Michael Oakeshott" pp. 533–4, and passim.

65. Oakeshott, "Introduction, 1975," pp. 281–2. It is interesting to note here that Oakeshott is not speaking for Hobbes, but making this claim for himself. That is, he is defending Hobbes by defending the point about authorizing a representative.

66. Ibid., p. 283.

67. Oakeshott, "Thomas Hobbes," p. 276.

68. Oakeshott, "Introduction, 1975," p. 282.
69. Hobbes, *Leviathan*, p. 233.
70. Oakeshott, "Introduction, 1975," p. 282.
71. Ibid., pp. 266-7.
72. Ibid., p. 273.
73. Ibid., p. 274. Oakeshott here may be able to maneuver around the rights of the sovereign to control subjects' opinions, and the regulation of doctrines, by discussing only the public cultus. Oakeshott, however, still would have to deal with the close association Hobbes makes between opinion and action.
74. Oakeshott makes a case for "A More Tolerant Hobbes" almost forty years before Alan Ryan wrote in defense of such in his chapter with that name in *Justifying Toleration: Conceptual and Historical Perspectives*, ed. Susan Mendes (Cambridge: Cambridge University Press, 1988). See also his "Hobbes, Toleration and the Inner Life," in *The Nature of Political Theory*, eds. David Miller and Larry Seidentrop (Oxford: Oxford University Press, 1982), pp. 197-218. A rigorous exploration of Hobbes's understanding of tolerance can also be found in Richard Tuck, "Hobbes and Locke on Toleration," in *Thomas Hobbes and Political Theory*, ed. Mary G. Dietz (Lawrence, KA: University Press of Kansas, 1990), pp. 153-171.
75. Oakeshott, "Introduction, 1975," p. 260.
76. Hobbes, *Leviathan*, p. 223. Another good example from Hobbes's primary discussion of justice and the third law of nature reads, "Therefore, before the names of Just and Unjust can have place, there must be some coercive Power to compel men equally to the performance of their Covenants, by the terror of some punishment," p. 202.
77. Franco, *The Political Philosophy of Michael Oakeshott*, p. 182. Franco discusses Oakeshott's focused interpretation of Hegel in *On Human Conduct*, attending to the understanding of *Sittlichkeit* and *Moralität* especially in pages 207-209.
78. Ibid.
79. Oakeshott, "Introduction, 1975," p. 230.
80. Ibid.

Notes for Chapter Six

1. Sheldon Wolin, "The Politics of Self-Disclosure," *Political Theory* 4 (August 1976), p. 324.
2. Paul Franco, *The Political Philosophy of Michael Oakeshott* (New Haven: Yale University Press, 1990), p. 90.
3. Ibid. Oakeshott would say simply "authority"; if it is not legitimate it is not authority.
4. Michael Oakeshott, *On Human Conduct* (Oxford: Oxford University Press, Clarendon Press, 1991), p. 108.

5. David Spitz criticizes Oakeshott's practice, disclaiming, "Here almost as if he were parroting Bertrand de Jouvenel's Sovreignty, is a recourse to Latin terms as if there could be no sensible English equivalents." "Rationalist *Malgre Lui:* The Perplexities of Being Michael Oakeshott," *Political Theory* 4 (August 1976), p. 343. Spitz seems not to note the irony of his own use of French terms in his title "as if there were no sensible English equivalents."

6. Oakeshott, *On Human Conduct*, p. 242.

7. Ibid., p. 195.

8. Ibid., p. 194.

9. David Mapel, "Civil Association and the Idea of Contingency," *Political Theory* 18 (August 1990), p. 404.

10. Oakeshott, *On Human Conduct*, pp. 194–5.

11. John Liddington's essay "Oakeshott: Freedom in a Modern European State," in *Conceptions of Liberty in Political Philosophy*, eds. Zbigniew Pelczynski and John Gray (New York: St. Martins Press, 1984) provides a thorough discussion of Oakeshott's conception of human agency and freedom.

12. Oakeshott, *On Human Conduct*, p. 40.

13. Ibid., p. 41.

14. Ibid., p. 158.

15. Ibid., p. 114.

16. Ibid.

17. Oakeshott's choice to include "believers in a religious faith" alongside the joint-stock company of the bassoon factory may appear crude. However, it appears that he wants to point to the fact that those who share a religious faith also share a common, substantive conception of the highest good and beliefs about the rightness and wrongness of particular, substantive human actions; perhaps reflecting a particular form of Christianity, Oakeshott also seems to assume that making a choice to establish (or reject) a relationship with God is central to religious experience.

18. Oakeshott, *On Human Conduct*, p. 158.

19. Hannah Fenichel Pitkin criticizes Oakeshott for conceptual slippage in his usage of enterprise association. She notes that he begins by defining "it as an association with one and one purpose only, known and shared collectively by all members; this last proviso is reinforced with the requirement that members be required to withdraw at will." And yet she observes that "as his argument progresses, Oakeshott comes to use enterprise association as a model of totalitarianism, in which the managerial few dictate to the oppressed and unengaged majority." "Inhuman Conduct and Unpolitical Theory: Michael Oakeshott's *On Human Conduct*," *Political Theory* 4 (August 1976), p. 308. Pitkin, however, misses the distinction between Oakeshott's understanding of enterprise association as the ideal character of certain human relationships and his negative judgment of it as a model for the state, as one that cannot maintain the "proviso" Pitkin mentions.

20. Oakeshott, *On Human Conduct*, p. 158. Recall that Oakeshott emphasized in his interpretation the claim that for Hobbes an associate in a state "cannot himself retract the authorization he has given." Oakeshott, "Introduction to *Leviathan*," in *Rationalism in Politics and Other Essays* (Methuen and Company, 1962, reprinted with additions and edited by Timothy Fuller by Liberty Press, 1991), p. 265.

21. Oakeshott, *The Politics of Faith and the Politics of Skepticism*, ed. Timothy Fuller (New Haven: Yale University Press, 1996).

22. See, for example, Oakeshott "The Masses in Representative Democracy," in *Rationalism in Politics*.

23. Oakeshott, *On Human Conduct*, p. 128.

24. Ibid., p. 57. Emphasis added.

25. Ibid., p. 126.

26. Ibid., p. 58. Oakeshott also uses the adverb idea, claiming that a practice is indicated when a performance of a human agent is qualified by "words such as punctually, considerately, civilly, scientifically, candidly, judicially, poetically, morally, etc." Pp. 55–6.

27. Ibid., pp. 79–80.

28. Ibid., p. 128. Oakeshott explains his choice of *lex*: "Such rules I shall call 'law'; and, so that they not be confused with the heterogeneous collection of rules and rule-like instructions, instruments, provisions, etc. which constitute the conditions of those ambiguous associations we call states, I will call them *lex*." P. 128.

29. Also, it would seem that an enterprise model can pose as a civil association if its rules are cast as adverbial modifiers. If the rule to "act virtuously in public affairs" can be defined to mean "act with the common good in mind," what has been protected?

30. Liddington, "Freedom in a Modern European State," p. 313.

31. Richard Flathman, *Reflections of a Would-Be Anarchist: Ideals and Institutions of Liberalism* (Minneapolis: University of Minnesota Press, 1998), p. 72.

32. Oakeshott, *On Human Conduct*, p. 170.

33. Flathman, *Would-Be Anarchist*, p. 75.

34. Ibid., p. 76.

35. Oakeshott, *On Human Conduct*, p. 158.

36. Ibid., p. 121.

37. Oakeshott offers the following rather odd footnote to illustrate the advantage of this view over that offered by enterprise association. "On a mountain track in the Epirus a Greek peasant was furiously beating his laden donkey. When asked why he did so, for the animal seemed to be going well enough, he answered, 'Yes, but he does not want to.'" *On Human Conduct*, p. 168.

38. Mapel, "Civil Association and the Idea of Contingency," p. 405.

39. Oakeshott, "The Authority of the State," in *Religion, Politics and the Moral*

Life, ed. Timothy Fuller (New Haven: Yale University Press, 1993, originally
published in 1929), p. 78.

40. Oakeshott, *On Human Conduct*, p. 128.

41. Ibid., p. 149. One might criticize Oakeshott for adopting *respublica*, questioning whether he paradoxically adopts the language of classical republi-
canism, with its focus on civic virtue and the public good, that Hobbes and
he dismiss. However, it is not Romans as republicans that Oakeshott cites,
but Romans as practitioners and theorists of law and authority to whom he
alludes. Wolin observes "it is characteristic that Oakeshott should resurrect
an archaic Roman vocabulary of *civis, civitas, lex, respublica*, and so on that was
originally employed by the most legalistic and bureaucratic of Western societies." Wolin, "The Politics of Self-Disclosure," p. 331. This vocabulary may
also reflect a medieval tradition of legal theorizing that of course Hobbes
claimed to reject. But recall from Chapter Four that Oakeshott took with a
grain of salt Hobbes's declamations against the "schoolmen."

42. Oakeshott, *On Human Conduct*, p. 148. There may appear a similarity here
between Oakeshott and H. L. A. Hart's concept of the "rule of recognition."
The Concept of Law (Oxford: Oxford University Press, 1961), p. 92, see especially Chapter 6. Indeed, Oakeshott, like Hart, claims that "it is a virtue of
respublica that it contains rules in terms of which the authority of other rules
may be recognized." Oakeshott, *On Human Conduct*, p. 150. However, Hart
suggests that in a system of law there is an "ultimate rule of recognition"
that "provides criteria for the assessment of the validity of other rules; but it
is . . . unlike them in that there is no rule providing criteria for the assessment of its own legal validity." *The Concept of Law*, p. 104. Oakeshott, however, claims, pace Hart, "Nor can there be a single ultimate rule of
recognition, an unconditional and unquestionable norm from which all
others derive authority." *On Human Conduct*, p. 151.

43. Oakeshott, *On Human Conduct*, pp. 152-3. Oakeshott does accept that some
of these, particularly the desirability of the conditions, can be allowed into
the discussion of which rules are to be adopted and which revoked—an
activity he calls politics—but this does not affect the authority of these
rules. I discuss this more fully below.

44. Ibid., p. 154. Oakeshott had earlier maintained that "the authority of *respublica* is, then, a postulate of the civil condition." P. 150.

45. Ibid., p. 124.

46. Ibid., p. 150.

47. Richard Flathman has also observed that theorists of a formal conception
of authority like Oakeshott, while disavowing a need for consensus, still
rely upon it. Flathman emphasizes that even in rejecting the idea of shared
purposes and values, formal theories like that of civil association still
require their own set beliefs and values: those about authority. "In order for
there to be rules that carry and bestow *authority*, . . . there must be values

and beliefs that have *authoritative* standing among the preponderance of those persons who subscribe to the authority of the rules." *The Practice of Political Authority* (Chicago: University of Chicago Press, 1980), p. 6. Flathman emphasizes not only that there must be such beliefs and values, but that they must be shared to understand authority as associational, not simply subjective.

48. Oakeshott, *On Human Conduct*, p. 163.

49. Ibid., pp. 165–6.

50. Ibid., p. 164.

51. Glenn Worthington captures Oakeshott's meaning in this way: "In questioning the desirability of a civil rule, politics must forego questioning the desirability of the whole of civil association. The act of questioning the whole of civil association, which is the authority of the civil rules rather than the desirability of particular rules, is not an act of politics but an act of either (self) exile or subversion." "Oakeshott's Claims of Politics," *Political Studies* 45 (1997), p. 733. This accurately catches the bifurcated character of Oakeshott's thoughts here, although it places discussion of authority only in terms of desirability as opposed to any other belief on which it might be based.

52. Oakeshott, commenting on the relationship of "practice" to "tradition," remarks that Josiah Lee Auspitz "notices I have become much more strict with the word 'practice' and that I have 'abandoned' tradition as inadequate to express what I want to express. And he appreciates that if such changes are read back into what I had written earlier they make it more exact." Oakeshott, "On Misunderstanding Human Conduct." *Political Theory* 4 (August 1976), p. 364.

53. Oakeshott, "Political Education," in *Rationalism in Politics*, p. 56.

54. Ibid., pp. 56–7.

55. Ibid., p. 60.

56. Ibid.

57. Oakeshott, *Morality and Politics in Modern Europe*, ed. Shirley Robin Letwin (New Haven: Yale University Press, 1993), p. 8.

58. Ibid., p. 9.

59. Ibid.

60. Oakeshott, *On Human Conduct*, p. 192.

61. Ibid., p. 180.

62. Ibid., p. 172.

63. Oakeshott, "The Rule of Law," in *On History and Other Essays* (Totowa, NJ: Barnes and Noble, 1983).

64. In "Rule of Law" Oakeshott favors the usage of authenticity over authority, although he employs them as synonyms; for instance he claims the validity of a command ought to be understood "solely in its authenticity or authority." "Rule of Law," p. 129.

65. Oakeshott, "Rule of Law," p. 136.

66. Ibid., p. 137.

67. Ibid., p. 143.

68. Ibid.

69. Flathman, *Practice of Political Authority*, p. 40.

70. Oakeshott does have one curious note about the identification of jus with "the provisions of a 'higher' or 'fundamental' law, a Law of Nature or of God." It would seem that the skeptic Oakeshott would dismiss such claims out of hand, but as is usual he complicates the issue. He claims, "And for the convenience of having a more readily available norm of justice, the *jus* of *lex* has often been identified with its reflection of . . . a 'basic law,' not fetched from Sinai but the product of human deliberation, which itself incorporates the 'higher' law. Here there may be a variety of beliefs in respect of the authority of this 'higher' law, but there is no confusion: it is law." "Rule of Law," p. 142. Oakeshott leaves the reader to guess what makes this so certain. Is it simply that it is recognized that 'higher' law is unmistakably law? Is it that it is actually the creation of human deliberation, "not fetched from Sinai?"

71. "Rule of Law," p. 160.

72. Ibid.

73. Oakeshott, *On Human Conduct*, p. 69.

74. Oakeshott, "Rule of Law," p. 140.

75. Ibid.

76. Oakeshott, *On Human Conduct*, pp. 192–3.

77. Ibid., p. 191.

78. Ibid.

79. For example, in the historical essay of *On Human Conduct*, Oakeshott describes how, in early modern Europe, "The first business of a new ruler in a new state was to acquire authority by getting his new title (and himself as holder) acknowledged by his subjects," p. 190.

80. Pitkin similarly has criticized Oakeshott's conception of politics and authority, claiming, "political association concerns not an achieved body of authoritative rules but the continual recreation of authority out of conflict, out of needs and interests and ideas in various power relationships." "Inhuman Conduct," p. 316. I agree with the main point of Pitkin's claim regarding conflict. However, Pitkin's inclusion of "needs and interests" in discussions of authority is not necessary to criticize Oakeshott. That is, one can retain his exclusion of those, and still criticize his neglect of conflict in belief about authority.

Notes for Chapter Seven

1. Michael Oakeshott, "Political Education," in *Rationalism in Politics and Other Essays* (Methuen and Company, 1962, reprinted with additions and edited by Timothy Fuller by Liberty Press, 1991), p. 56.

2. Ibid., p. 57.

3. Ibid.

4. Glenn Worthington, "Oakeshott's Claims of Politics," *Political Studies* 45 (1997), pp. 737-8. I am thankful to Worthington for reminding me of the significance of this passage and its relationship to issues of politics and authority.

5. Oakeshott, *On Human Conduct* (Oxford: Oxford University Press, Clarendon Press, 1991), p. 164.

6. Ibid., p. 158.

7. Oakeshott, "Political Education," p. 69.

8. Colin Falck, "Romanticism in Politics," *New Left Review* 18 (January–February 1963), p. 68.

9. Ibid., p. 69.

10. Chantal Mouffe, "Democratic Citizenship and the Political Community" in *Dimensions of Radical Democracy: Pluralism, Citizenship, and Democracy*, ed. Chantal Mouffe (London: Verso, 1992), p. 225. David Mapel, "Civil Association and the Idea of Contingency," *Political Theory* 21 (August 199), p. 405. Interesting democratic interpretations and appropriations include some of Richard Rorty's works, especially *Contingency, Irony and Solidarity* (Cambridge: Cambridge University Press, 1989), Fred Dallmayr's *Politics and Praxis: Exercises in Contemporary Political Theory* (Cambridge: The MIT Press, 1984), John Wallach's "Liberals, Communitarians, and the Task of Political Theory," *Political Theory* 12 (December 1987), pp. 581-611, and most recently Richard E. Flathman's *Reflections of a Would-Be Anarchist* (Minneapolis, MN: University of Minnesota Press, 1998).

11. Anthony Quinton, *The Politics of Imperfection* (London: Faber and Faber, 1978), p. 292. Perry Anderson, "The Intransigent Right at the End of the Century," *London Review of Books* 14 (September 1994) p. 8.

12. Mouffe, "Democratic Citizenship," p. 231.

13. Ibid., p. 234. Recall *societas* and *universitas* are variant terms for civil and enterprise association respectively.

14. Ibid., p. 239n.

15. Recall from Chapter Six, Oakeshott does claim at one point that the proscription against pursuing substantive wants in politics does not mean they still cannot find their way in an appropriate fashion into politics. "What it means is that a proposal that has to do with a want, a wish for a benefit, a plea for the removal of a disadvantage must lose this character and acquire another (a political character) in being understood, advanced and considered as a proposal for the amendment of the *respublica* of civil association." Oakeshott, *On Human Conduct*, p. 170. Mouffe, however, does not refer to this passage.

16. Mouffe, "Democratic Citizenship," p. 234.

17. Ibid., p. 235.

18. Ibid., p. 234.
19. Mapel, "Civil Association and the Idea of Contingency," p. 405.
20. Martin Luther King, Jr., "Letter from Birmingham Jail," in *Why We Can't Wait* (New York: Harper and Row, 1964), pp. 84–85.
21. Oakeshott's example of women's suffrage seems to involve both the pursuit of legal means for altering the prevailing law and the activities of civil disobedience. It is interesting to recall as well that he regarded "Arguments drawn from abstract natural right, from 'justice,' . . . as either irrelevant or as unfortunately disguised versions of the one valid argument; namely that there was incoherence in the arrangements of society which pressed convincingly for remedy." King's letter clearly incorporates this "one valid argument."
22. A democracy can even make place for those who do not recognize the authority of all of its offices; thus in some states the conscientious objector to war can find an official status alternative to conscription.
23. Stephen L. Carter, *The Dissent of the Governed*, (Cambridge: Harvard University Press,1998), p. 8.
24. Ibid., p. 10 & 11.
25. Oakeshott, "Political Education," pp. 56–7.

Bibliography

Anderson, Perry. "The Intransigent Right at the End of the Century." *London Review of Books* 14 (September 24, 1992): 7-11.

Bobbio, Noberto. *Thomas Hobbes and the Natural Law Tradition*. Chicago: University of Chicago Press, 1993.

Bosanquent, Bernard. *The Philosophical Theory of the State*. London: Macmillan, 1925.

Boucher, David. "The Creation of the Past: British Idealism and Michael Oakeshott's Philosophy of History." *History and Theory* 23 (1984): 193-214.

Bradley, F. H. *Appearance and Reality*. 2nd ed. London: Oxford University Press, 1897.

Brandt, Frithiof. *Thomas Hobbes' Mechanical Conception of Nature*. London: Librairie Hachette, 1928.

Brown, J. M. "A Note on Professor Oakeshott's Introduction to *Leviathan*." *Political Studies* 1 (1953): 53-64.

Campbell, Charles, A. *Scepticism and Construction*. London: Allen and Unwin, 1931.

Carter, Stephen L. *The Dissent of the Governed: A Meditation on Law, Religion, and Morality*. Cambridge: Harvard University Press. 1998.

Collingwood, R. G. "Oakeshott and the Modes and Experience." Review of *Experience and Its Modes* by Michael Oakeshott, in *The Cambridge Mind: Ninety Years of the Cambridge Review*, pp. 132-4. Edited by Eric Homberger, William Janeway, and Simon Schama. London: Jonathan Cape, 1970, originally published in 1934.

Collini, Stefan. "Hobhouse, Bosanquet, and the State: Philosophical Idealism and Political Argument in England 1880-1918." *Past and Present* 72 (August, 1976): 86-111.

—————. *Public Moralist, Political Thought and Intellectual Life in Britain, 1850-1930*. Oxford: Clarendon, 1991.

Crick, Bernard. "The World of Michael Oakeshott, or the Lonely Nihilist." *Encounter* 20 (June, 1963): 65-74.

Dallmayr, Fred R. *Politics and Praxis: Exercises in Contemporary Political Theory.* Cambridge: The MIT Press, 1984

Devigne, Robert. *Recasting Conservatism: Oakeshott, Strauss, and the Response to Postmodernism.* New Haven: Yale University Press, 1994.

Falck, Colin. "Romanticism in Politics." *New Left Review,* 18 (January–February 1963): 60–72.

Flathman, Richard. *The Practice of Political Authority.* Chicago: University of Chicago Press, 1980.

—————. *Toward a Liberalism.* Ithaca: Cornell University Press, 1989.

—————. *Thomas Hobbes, Skepticism, Individuality, and Chastened Politics.* Newberry Park: Sage, 1993.

—————. *Reflections of a Would-Be Anarchist.* Minneapolis, MN: University of Minnesota Press, 1998.

Frohnen, Bruce P. "Oakeshott's Hobbesian Myth: Pride, Character, and the Limits of Reason." *The Western Political Quarterly,* 43 (December 1990): 789–809.

Franco, Paul. *The Political Philosophy of Michael Oakeshott.* New Haven: Yale University Press, 1990.

Fuller, Timothy. "Preface" and editor's notes to Michael Oakeshott, *Religion, Politics and the Moral Life.* Edited by Timothy Fuller. New Haven: Yale University Press, 1993.

Gerencser, Steven A. "Voices in Conversation: Philosophy and Politics in the Work of Michael Oakeshott," *Journal of Politics,* 57 (August 1995): 724–742.

Grant, Robert. *Oakeshott.* London: The Claridge Press, 1990.

Greenleaf, W. H. *Oakeshott's Philosophical Politics.* New York: Barnes and Noble, 1966.

—————. "Hobbes: The Problem of Interpretation." In *Hobbes and Rousseau,* pp. 5–36. Edited by Maurice Cranston and Richard S. Peters. New York: Anchor Books, 1972.

Hall, Dale, and Modood, Tariq. "Oakeshott and the Impossibility of Philosophical Politics." *Political Studies* 30 (1982): 157–176.

Hart, H. L. A. *The Concept of Law.* Oxford: Oxford University Press, 1961.

Hegel, G. W. F. *Hegel's Philosophy of Right.* Translated by T. M. Knox. Oxford: Oxford University Press, 1952, also in paperback by same publisher, 1967.

Hobbes, Thomas. *The English Works of Thomas Hobbes.* Edited by Sir Thomas Molesworth. Volume I: *De Corpore.* London: John Bohn, 1839.

—————. *Leviathan.* Edited by C.B. MacPhearson. London: Penguin, 1968.

Hobhouse, L. T. *The Metaphysical Theory of the State: A Criticism.* London: Allen and Unwin, 1918.

King, Martin Luther, Jr. "Letter from Birmingham Jail." In *Why We Can't Wait.* New York: Harper and Row, 1964.

Laird, John. *Hobbes.* New York: Russel & Russel, 1934

Laski, H. J. *Authority in the Modern State.* New Haven: Yale University Press, 1919.

Liddington, John. "Oakeshott: Freedom in the Modern European State." In *Conceptions of Liberty in Political Philosophy.* Edited by Z. Pelczynski and J. Gray. New York: St. Martins Press, 1984.

Lindsay, A. D., and Laski, H. J. "Symposium: Bosanquet's Theory of the General Will." *Aristotelian Society,* Supplementary Volume 8, 1928.

Mapel, David R. "Civil Association and the Idea of Contingency." *Political Theory* 18 (August 1990): 392-410.

————. "Purpose and Politics: Can There Be a Non-Instrumental Civil Association?" *Political Science Reviewer* 21 (Spring 1992): 63-80.

Martinich, Aloysius. "Translator's Commentary" to *Computatio Sive Logica: Logic,* by Thomas Hobbes. Edited by Isabel C. Hungarland and George R. Vick. New York: Abaris Books, 1981.

Metz, Rudolf. *A Hundred Years in British Philosophy.* Translated by J. W. Harvey, T. E. Jessop, and Henry Stuart. Edited by J. H. Muirhead. London: Allen and Unwin, 1938.

Modood, Tariq. "Oakeshott's Conceptions of Philosophy." *History of Political Thought* 1 (1980): 315- 322.

Mosher, Michael A. "The Skeptic's Burke: *Reflections on the Revolution in France, 1790-1990.*" *Political Theory* 19 (August): 391-418.

Minogue, Kenneth. Review of *On Human Conduct,* by Michael Oakeshott. *Political Studies* 24 (June 1976): 213.

Mouffe, Chantal. "Democratic Citizenship and the Political Community." In *Dimensions of Radical Democracy: Pluralism, Citizenship and Democracy,* pp. 225-39. Edited by Chantal Mouffe. London: Verso, 1992.

Nicholson, Peter P. *The Political Philosophy of the British Idealists.* Cambridge: Cambridge University Press, 1990.

Pelczynski, Z. A., ed. *Hegel's Political Philosophy.* Cambridge: Cambridge University Press, 1971.

Penelham, Terence. "Skepticism and Fideism." In *The Skeptical Tradition,* pp. 287-318. Edited by Miles Burnyeat. Berkeley: University of California Press, 1983.

Pitkin, Hanna Fenichel. "The Roots of Conservatism." *Dissent* 20 (1973): 496-525.

————. "Inhuman Conduct and Unpolitical Theory: Michael Oakeshott's *On Human Conduct.*" *Political Theory* 4 (August 1976): 301-320.

Popkin, Richard. *The History of Scepticism from Erasmus to Spinoza.* Berkeley: University of California Press, 1979.

Quinton, A. M. "Absolute Idealism." *Proceedings of The British Academy,* 57 (1971): 303-329.

————. *The Politics of Imperfection.* London: Faber and Faber, 1978.

Rayner, Jeremy. "The Legend of Oakeshott's Conservatism: Sceptical Philosophy and Limited Politics." *Canadian Journal of Political Science* 18 (June 1985): 313-338.

Ricouer, Paul. "Hermeneutics and the Critique of Ideology." In *Hermeneutics and Modern Philosophy,* pp. 300-339. Edited by Brice W. Wachterhauser. Albany, NY: State University of New York Press, 1986.

Riley, Patrick. "Michael Oakeshott, Philosopher of Individuality." *Review of Politics* 54 (Fall 1992): 649- 674.

Robertson, George Croom. *Hobbes.* Edinburgh, 1886, AMS reprint: New York, 1971.

Rorty, Richard. *Philosophy and the Mirror of Nature.* Princeton: Princeton University Press, 1979.

—————. *Contingency, Irony and Solidarity.* Cambridge: Cambridge University Press, 1989.

—————. *Philosophical Papers.* Volume 1: *Objectivity, Relativism, and Truth* and Volume 2: *Essays on Heidegger and Others.* Cambridge: Cambridge University Press, 1991.

Ross, Ralph. *Scepticism and Dogma.* New York: By Author, 1940.

Ryan, Alan. "Hobbes, Toleration and the Inner Life." In *The Nature of Political Theory,* pp. 197-218. Edited by David Miller and Larry Seidentrop. Oxford: Oxford University Press, 1982.

—————. "A More Tolerant Hobbes." In *Justifying Toleration: Conceptual and Historical Perspectives,* pp. 37-59. Edited by Susan Mendes. Cambridge: Cambridge University Press, 1988.

Spitz, David. "A Rationalist *Malgre Lui:* The Perplexities of Being Michael Oakeshott." *Political Theory* 4 (August 1976): 335-352.

Strauss, Leo. *The Political Philosophy of Hobbes: Its Basis and Genesis.* Chicago: The University of Chicago Press, 1952. Originally published by The Clarendon Press, 1936.

Taylor, A. E. "The Ethical Doctrine of Hobbes." In *Hobbes Studies,* pp. 35-56. Edited by K. C. Brown. Oxford: Basil Blackwell, 1965. Essay originally published in 1938.

Taylor, Charles. *Hegel.* Cambridge: Cambridge University Press, 1975

Tragenza, Ian. "The Life of Hobbes in the Writings of Michael Oakeshott." *History of Political Thought,* 18 (Autumn 1997): 531-557.

Tuck, Richard. "Grotius, Carneades, and Hobbes." *Grotiana* N.S. 4 (1983): 43-62.

—————. "Optics and Skeptics: The Philosophical Foundations of Hobbes's Political Thought." *Conscience and Casuistry in Early Modern Europe,* pp. 235-263. Edited by Edmund Leites. Cambridge: Cambridge University Press, 1987.

—————. *Hobbes.* New York: Oxford University Press, 1989.

—————. "Hobbes and Locke on Toleration." In *Thomas Hobbes and Political Theory,* pp. 153-171. Edited by Mary G. Dietz. Lawrence, KA: University Press of Kansas, 1990.

Wallach, John. "Liberals, Communitarians and the Tasks of Political Theory." *Political Theory* 12 (December 1987): 581-611.

Watkins, J. W. N. *Hobbes System of Ideas.* London: Hutchinson and Co, 1965.

West, Cornel. "Afterword." In *Post-Analytic Philosophy,* pp. 259-275. Edited by John Rajchman and Cornel West. New York: Columbia University Press, 1985.

Wolin, Sheldon. "The Politics of Self-Disclosure." *Political Theory* 4 (August 1976): 321- 334.

—————. "Hobbes and the Culture of Despotism," In *Thomas Hobbes and Political Theory,* pp. 9-36. Edited by Mary G. Dietz. Lawrence, KA: University Press of Kansas, 1990.

Wood, Neal. "A Guide to the Classics: The Skepticism of Professor Oakeshott." *Journal of Politics* 21 (1959): 645-62.

Worthington, Glenn. "Oakeshott's Claims of Politics," *Political Studies* 45 (1997): 727-738.

Works by Michael J. Oakeshott arranged chronologically by first publication date

"Religion and the Moral Life." In *Religion, Politics and the Moral Life,* pp. 119-137. Edited by Timothy Fuller. New Haven: Yale University Press, 1993. Originally published in 1927.

"The Concept of a Philosophy of Politics." In *Religion, Politics and the Moral Life,* pp. 39-45. Edited by Timothy Fuller. New Haven: Yale University Press, 1993.

"The Importance of the Historical Element in Christianity." In *Religion, Politics and the Moral Life,* pp. 63-73. Originally published in 1928.

"The Authority of the State." In *Religion, Politics and the Moral Life,* pp. 74-90. Originally published in 1929.

"The New Bentham." In *Rationalism in Politics and Other Essays,* pp. 132-150. Edited by Timothy Fuller. Methuen and Company, 1962, reprinted with additions by Liberty Press, 1991. Originally published 1932.

"John Locke." *The Cambridge Review* 54 (1932): 72-73.

Experience and Its Modes. Cambridge: Cambridge University Press, 1933. Also in paperback by the same publisher, 1985.

"Thomas Hobbes." *Scrutiny* 4 (1935-6): 263-277.

Review of *Bernard Bosanquet's Philosophy of the State,* by Berti Pfannenstill. *Philosophy* 11 (1936): 482.

with Griffith, G. T. *A Guide to the Classics (or How to Pick the Derby Winner).* London: Faber, 1936.

"Dr. Leo Strauss on Hobbes." In *Hobbes on Civil Association,* pp. 132-49. Berkeley: University of California Press, 1975. Originally published in 1937.

"The Concept of a Philosophical Jurisprudence." *Politica* 3 (September and December 1938): 203-22 & 345-60.

"The Claims of Politics." In *Religion, Politics and the Moral Life,* pp. 91-96. Originally published 1939.

"Introduction" to *Leviathan* by Thomas Hobbes. Oxford: Basil Blackwell, 1946.

"Rationalism in Politics." In *Rationalism in Politics,* pp. 6-42. Originally published 1947.

"*Leviathan*: A Myth." In *Hobbes on Civil Association,* pp. 150-4. Originally given as a radio talk in 1947.

"Political Education." In *Rationalism in Politics,* pp. 43-69. Originally published 1951.

Review of *The Political Philosophy of Thomas Hobbes* by Howard Warrender. *The Spectator* (August 1957): 198.

"The Voice of Poetry in the Conversation of Mankind." In *Rationalism in Politics,* pp. 488–451. Originally published 1959.

"The Moral Life in the Writings of Thomas Hobbes." In *Rationalism in Politics,* pp. 295–350. Originally published 1962.

"On Being Conservative." In *Rationalism in Politics,* pp. 407–37. Originally published 1962.

"The Study of Politics in the University." In *Rationalism in Politics,* pp. 184–218. Originally published 1962.

"The Vocabulary of the Modern European State, *Political Studies* 23 (1975): 319–347 & 409–414.

"Talking Politics." In *Rationalism in Politics,* pp. 488–461. Originally published 1975.

Hobbes on Civil Association. Berkeley: University of California Press, 1975.

"Introduction to *Leviathan.*" In *Hobbes on Civil Association,* pp. 1–74, also in *Rationalism in Politics,* pp. 221–294.

On Human Conduct. Oxford: Oxford University Press, 1975, Clarendon Press, 1991.

"On Misunderstanding Human Conduct." *Political Theory* 4 (August 1976): 353–67.

"The Rule of Law." In *On History and Other Essays,* pp 119–64. Totowa, NJ: Barnes and Noble, 1983.

Michael Oakeshott on Education. Edited by Timothy Fuller. New Haven: Yale University Press, 1989.

Rationalism in Politics and Other Essays. Edited by Timothy Fuller. Indianapolis: Liberty Press, 1991. Originally published in 1962.

"The Concept of a Philosophy of Politics." In *Religion, Politics and the Moral Life,* pp. 119–137.

"Some Remarks on the Nature and Meaning of Sociality." In *Religion, Politics and the Moral Life,* pp. 46– 62.

"Political Philosophy." In *Religion, Politics and The Moral Life,* pp. 138–55.

Religion, Politics and the Moral Life. Edited by Timothy Fuller. New Haven: Yale University Press, 1993.

Morality and Politics in Modern Europe. Edited by Shirley Robin Letwin. New Haven: Yale University Press, 1993.

The Politics of Skepticism and the Politics of Faith. Edited by Timothy Fuller. New Haven: Yale University Press, 1996.

Index